Ascent to Being

Vincent P. Miceli, s. j.

Ascent to Being

Gabriel Marcel's
Philosophy of communion

Foreword by Gabriel Marcel

Desclee Company

NEW YORK - TOURNAI - PARIS - ROME

IMPRIMI POTEST

John J. McGinty, S.J.

Praep. Prov. Neo Eboracensis

NIHIL OBSTAT

John A. Goodwine, J.C.D.

Censor Librorum

IMPRIMATUR

✠ Terence J. Cooke, V.G.

July 6, 1965

/ /

The nihil obstat and imprimatur are official declarations that a book or pamphlet is free of doctrinal or moral error. No implication is contained therein that those who have granted the nihil obstat and imprimatur agree with the contents, opinions or statements expressed.

Library of Congress Catalog Card Number: 65-20316

Printed and bound in Belgium

In Memory of My

Mother and Father

Contents

FOREWORD

Dear Father,

Upon my visit to New Orleans last March, you were kind enough to ask me to write a foreword to the book which you have written on the philosophy of communion in my work. I agreed without hesitation, though perhaps not without rashness, for I could not content myself with merely sending you a few lines of thanks for your magnificent work; but on the other hand, I find it quite unnecessary to take up again the themes which your yourself have discussed with so much insight, and summarize once again the meaning of my work. I am all the less disposed to take on this latter task, since a large number of articles, particularly in magazines, concerning my work—to be sure, there is no book such as yours—are, as far as I am concerned, a little like handfuls of earth thrown on the living; or in another metaphor, the image which these studies give me of myself is somewhat that of a cadaver.

I should therefore prefer to try to state very briefly how I myself tend to react today when confronted with this work which—it must be admitted—has so little the aspect of a monument such as is characteristic of the great philosophical systems. And that this may be a lack or deficiency, I will not deny; on the other hand, I would say that this work surely reveals me more directly or more personally than it would have, had it a more formal structure. I believe that it resembles me and that therefore one can also find in it the signs of my shortcomings, and in particular the one which undoubtedly prevented me from reaping with sufficient care and perseverance the consequences of what had been given me at the beginning in a sort of central apperception.

In answering a rather prying questionnaire recently, in order to satisfy my publisher, I said that one of my main defects, insofar as I can judge, is undoubtedly impatience in all its forms. This, to be sure, is what has led me so frequently not only to take shortcuts, but also to leave to others—perhaps inconsiderately—the task of developing a given thought still in embryonic stage. I am thinking here above all of certain statements which appear in the second part of the JOURNAL METAPHYSIQUE. If this constituted a discovery, as I tend to believe without taking undue glory in it, I do not believe that I went far enough, deep enough. It seems to me that those who would like one day to extend my own work must begin their research at this point. I refer to everything concerning what is improperly called the " union of soul and body " and which I have named the " non-mediatizable immediate. "

Reflecting on the impatience of which I accuse myself, I realize that it certainly contributed to making me give up at an early age the idea of teaching. Was I wrong? This is a question which, in all sincerity, it is difficult for me to answer. I am convinced, to be sure, that teaching in lycees, with the tedious correction of themes which it entails, would soon have become unbearable for me; but should I not have had to comply with the formalities which would have permitted me to teach in the universities, that is to say, write theses in accordance with the rules of the art? I do not know. It is obvious that by freeing myself of this, I condemned myself, so to say, to a marginal sort of activity which may appear little in keeping with what one ordinarily expects of a philosopher. But here the other aspect of my vocation intervenes; I mean the theatrical aspect. What Martin Buber said about himself when he called himself an " Atypischer Mensch," I can apply to myself without the shadow of a doubt. Without subscribing entirely to the severe judgments made by Schopenhauer and Nietzsche of teachers of philosophy, I must admit that my spontaneous reaction is rather close to theirs; although I have felt much admiration, and even some envy, with regard to certain teachers of philosophy whom I have personally known and who have dedicated themselves with indefatigable fervor to their teaching. A Louis Lavelle or a René Le Senne, an Amédée Ponceau, a Jean Nabert. This is certainly not the only field in which I feel irreducible contradictions within me.

I submit, however, that this singularity of my destiny, I might almost say of my condition, has been such as to sustain in me a perhaps healthy dissatisfaction guarding me constantly against the temptation of being complacent with what I have been able to do.

If I should now be asked to which of the various aspects of my activity I would give priority, I would reply without hesitation *that my preference goes to my plays, rather than to my philosophical writings; this despite the fact that the latter have obtained more widespread acceptance than my plays. These have undeniably suffered from the fact that without having been understood or even simply read, they have been judged by the axiom that, being the work of a philosopher, they could not be " good theatre. " There is much that could be said on this, but I shall not dwell on it. What I only wish to point out is that here, more than elsewhere, I have the conviction of having realized what I wanted to do; and it is much more important for me, I believe, that in plays such as* Le Chemin de Crete *or* Le Dard, Les Cœurs Avides *or* Le Signe de la Croix, *I have reached what is essential for me, namely, I have encountered human beings, I have recognized them and loved them in their individuality and in such a manner that they can be loved and encountered by others.*

I return here of course, Father, to the central theme of your excellent work, that of communion. If there is any thought which I abhor, which appears to me a scandalous defiance of creation or I would say of universal polyphony, it is monadism. I do not believe that I ever wrote anything which does not dispute the validity of this aberration—and I have had the opportunity, I may say by way of confirmation, during the course of my life and my extensive travels, to meet countless persons whom I hailed with a sort of amazement as true companions in the adventure on earth in which it was given to me to partake. On earth, I have said, but we know well, do we not, that its goal is elsewhere—and it is surely towards this " elsewhere " that our hopes and our prayers are directed.

Please accept, my dear Father, the expression of my gratitude and respectful friendship.

G. Marcel

September 1965

G. Marcel
de l'Institut

Author's Preface

The present study is based on the life and major works of Gabriel Marcel and on the outstanding themes and insights that have naturally developed and matured from his philosophy of communion. Its purposes may be classified under two headings: (1) to effect a certain unity and order in Marcel's thought in terms of what would appear to be the key to that unity: the principle in all being of the need for transcendence; (2) to reflect more deeply on the service that this living principle could render a "broken" society. The analogy employed in this dual exposition is based on the process of life, growth, and dissolution that is common to all organisms.

It is pointed out that the metaphysical root of Marcel's thought is the *besoin d'être*, the need that every being has for self-achievement. This hunger for transcendence leads Marcel to stress the mystery of the Full and the Empty in all being, rather than the superficial dichotomy of the One and the Many. In man the need for transcendence is fulfilled through communication, communion and community: three horizontally and vertically spiralling degrees of union that express the basic principle of all reality: *Esse est co-esse*.

The advance towards the fulness of communion ascends through various stages: (1) *incarnation*, which expresses the fundamental rise of man from non-being to existence as being in a body; (2) *sensation*, a second degree of incarnation within the sensible world; (3) *presence*, which is more comprehensive than sensation in that it represents an advance to a meeting with the other in the world of the spirit; (4) *primary reflection*, or the transsubjective analysis of objects; (5) *secondary reflection*, or the recovery of original experience, as a cognitive act that is superior to the previous stages of transcendence both in intensity and finality.

Closely related to the above—as a sort of metaphysical temptation—is the principal obstacle to communion: the tendency to "objectify." It introduces a divisive and diminishing force into being which is made clearer in Marcel's treatment of the distinction between problem and mystery. *Problems* are handled by an inquiry into an object that is exterior to me and unconcerned about me. *Mystery*, on the other hand, involves an encounter with being which includes the seeking subject. To problematize all being is to foster the spirit of abstraction which only succeeds in dissolving the concrete and in dismissing mystery. In practice, this is accompanied by techniques that enable one to dominate matter (and even men) by subjecting them to the mechanics of a depersonalized plan.

By way of contrast, the quest for communion is achieved by respect for mystery. The man of engagement, the creative witness, the man of fidelity, hope, love, engages in activities that intensify the continued presence of the "I" to the "thou," especially under the most tragic circumstances. Availability and personal permeability heighten the influx and overflow of persons into one another when they are uncluttered with themselves.

For Marcel, then, today's dilemma may be expressed as follows: either to fulfill oneself or to escape. Yet the nostalgia for communion in community has grown to a pathological pitch. Men are adhering to two major forces that promise to sate this homesickness. To confuse these forces would lead to social suicide. The forces engaged in a struggle to the death over the family of mankind are identified by Marcel as "the termite colony and the Mystical Body."

Marcel's philosophy is "open" in the sense that, while it moves upward towards its natural maturation in community through genuine communion, it expects and receives further completion from a dialectic of love from above, from a new and

gratuitous influx of the Absolute into the human being and
milieu. Marcel moves from the phenomenological and psychological thrusts towards fulfilment in communion and community
to their metaphysical and theological plenitude. His philosophy
stresses availability to whatever comes from above—new mysteries,
a new Incarnation, new communions, a new community.
Preoccupied with the salvation of society from both atomization
and collectivization, Marcel invites the modern philosopher to
examine the implications of the Christian idea of the Mystical
Body.

V. P. M.

New Orleans

Key to Abbreviations

BH   *Being and Having*, trans. Katherine Farrer (Westminster, England: Dacre Press, 1949).

DS   *Le déclin de la sagesse* (Paris: Plon, 1954).

HP   *L'homme problématique* (Paris: Editions Montaigne, 1955).

HV   *Homo Viator, Introduction to a Metaphysics of Hope*, trans. Emma Craufurd (Chicago: Regnery, 1951).

MMS   *Man Against Mass Society*, trans. G. S. Fraser (Chicago: Regnery, 1952).

MJ   *Metaphysical Journal*, trans. Bernard Wall (Chicago: Regnery, 1952).

MB   *The Mystery of Being*, 2 Vols. (Chicago: Regnery, Gateway Edition, 1960).
      MB (I)—Vol. I, *Reflection and Mystery*, trans. G. S. Fraser.
      MB (II)—Vol. II, *Faith and Reality*, trans. Rene Hague.

PE   *The Philosophy of Existence*, trans. Manya Harari (New York: Philosophical Library, 1949).

PI   *Présence et Immortalité* (Paris: Flammarion, 1959).

PAC   *Position et approches concrètes du mystère ontologique* (Paris: Vrin, 1949).

RI   *Du refus à l'invocation* (Paris: Gallimard, 1940).

Acknowledgements

I am especially glad to render thanks here for the guidance and inspiration of an internationally outstanding philosopher, Dr. Dietrich Von Hildebrand, professor emeritus of Fordham University, who introduced me to the thought of Gabriel Marcel. The great lead others to the great. And thus, when I was academically orphaned upon the retirement of Dr. Hildebrand, Dr. Balduin V. Schwarz of the same university, patiently and generously directed my researches into the depths of Marcel's philosophical and dramatic work. I am most grateful to Dr. Schwarz, himself a Christian philosopher of extraordinary merit. Rev. James M. Somerville, S.J., Chairman of the Graduate Department of Philosophy at Fordham, Rev. John Flynn, S.J., Rev. Herbert A. Musurillo, S.J. and Dr. Kenneth T. Gallagher of the same university, all read the manuscript and, by their illuminating criticisms, helped shape and reshape it into its present form. For their generous assistance I thank them cordially. To my very good friend and mentor, Rev. Joseph F. Costanzo, S.J., Professor of Historical Jurisprudence, I owe a special debt of gratitude. He has the rare gift of spurring his friends on to exercise their powers perseveringly for the attainment of excellence. Whatever is profitable in this work is due more to the assistance of such consummate scholars than to my efforts; whatever is unprofitable is due to my shortcomings.

My deepest gratitude is expressed to Gabriel Marcel for his kindness in visiting Loyola University of New Orleans where he lectured not only to the public but to the students engaged in a seminar on his thought. He encouraged and aided this work by his conversations, suggestions, and willingness to write its foreword. His presence among us for three days revealed M. Marcel to be a man of warm charm, one who in his personal life transcends by far the excellence of his many writings.

N Y. 29 — 2

Finally, I thank the editors of Thought, *a quarterly of idea and culture, for their gracious permission to republish material which initially appeared in that journal's pages.   Chapter VII, "Transcendence Through Tragedy" appeared in* Thought, *Summer 1965, under the title: "Marcel: The Drama of Transcendence."*

V.P.M.

CHAPTER I

Marcel and His Work

Gabriel Marcel is an original thinker. He has developed into an outstanding Christian philosopher of creative insight and fresh inspiration the hard way—through long years of patient suffering. He was born in Paris on December 7, 1889. As an only child, rather puny and possessed with extreme sensibility, he endured the bitterness of loneliness in an areligious, but culturally advanced, family milieu. To break through the barrier of isolation and to fulfill his desire to communicate with others in a world beyond his own, Marcel developed a great love for the theatre, communicating with imaginary companions of his own creation, in the absence of live age-mates.

As a youth he attained his secondary education at the Lycée Carnot. From there he pursued university courses at the Sorbonne and, at the age of twenty, won a fellowship in philosophy on the staff of the university by brilliantly passing the competitive examination.

While yet a young student, Marcel was subjected to the rigors and tensions of the fiercely competitive learning-process on the Continent. This took its toll of his health and caused much bodily suffering.

A. Jourdain relates that, even from his earliest years, Marcel suffered "the *insolubilia* of human existence, the difficulties in ourselves and in others which impede the bilateral movement toward our communion." [1] Gifted with a spirit that could respond

---

[1] Alice JOURDAIN, "Von Hildebrand and Marcel: A Parallel," *The Human Person and the World of Values*, ed. Balduin V. SCHWARZ (New York: Fordham University Press, 1960), p. 13.

joyously to the beauty of the classics, Marcel encountered in
class a wall of pedantic aridity and the inhuman pressures of
prolonged, cold-blooded competition. These barred his ascent
to self-realization in communion with the great men of the past.
Never very robust, his health slipped dangerously under these
hostile pressures. Yet such early afflictions produced good as
well as evil effects. They formed a man deeply sensitive to the
sufferings in his fellowmen.

They oriented him, even then, towards a philosophy of
communion by leading him down the byways of sorrow—the way
of isolation, estrangement and physical debilitation. In the
future, because of these desolate experiences, Marcel will be
incapable of extending superficial sympathy. He will, instead,
become, in his own words, "a witness to the spiritual," and never
more so than when he freely involves and identifies himself with
those who suffer.

At first an enthusiastic Hegelian, Marcel, in 1909 at the
Sorbonne, held that "the most truly real could not by any means
be what is most immediate, but on the contrary, the most truly
real is the fruit of a dialectic, the crowning completion of an
edifice of thought." [2]   German constructed philosophic systems
exercised an extraordinary ascendency over him and filled him
with "the intrepidity of an idealist."   But he soon became irritated
with and incredulous of these systems because of the impossibility
of passing in them from the Absolute I to the concrete I, the
latter being regarded by Marcel as the only true I. Thus the
young philosopher was enveloped in a desert universe, furrowed
with moral imperatives and darkened with the clouds of invincible
despair.   Marcel lived in a state of hypertension and in interior
worry, reaching at certain times an unbearable paroxysm. Could
the end of all philosophic endeavor be the immersion of reality
and of all individual destinies into an Absolute where all are
actually absorbed and lost?   Marcel resented and finally refused

---

[2] R. TROISFONTAINES, S. J., *De l'existence à l'être* (Paris: Vrin, 1953),
I, p. 41. "Le plus véritablement réel pourrait fort bien n'être pas ce qui
est le plus immédiat, mais au contraire, le fruit d'une dialectique, le
couronnement d'un édifice de pensée."

this philosophic doctrine. He abandoned his attempt to write a systematic synthesis on the whole of philosophy *à la post-Kantian*, stating that "he decidedly would not be conformed to the rules of the philosophic game such as these have been observed up to contemporary times. [3]

With that declaration of philosophic independence, Marcel was at last free of his idealistic strait-jacket and plunged directly into that current of personal and passionate research into lived experience—which is the very heart of his thought in its original impulse. Etienne Gilson writes of this fresh Marcellian approach:

> Through an initial procedure, which he has never since betrayed, this philosopher has written nothing which has not been reaped from the depths of his being or directly tested by his own experience. There is scarcely anyone, even among the greatest to whom we can attribute that praise. And the most constant historical experience seems to assure works sprung from that source a perpetual freshness, which so many philosophical systems, ambitiously erected by dint of artificial contrivances, have lacked from their birth. In philosophy as elsewhere, only the authentic endures, and that is why, like Montaigne, like Pascal, like Maine de Biran, Gabriel Marcel is assured of always having readers. In his work man speaks directly to man; he will always have readers because he will never cease to make new friends. [4]

From the moment Marcel rejected Idealism in search of created presence, his philosophy took on freshness and directness. He now saw things with a mind uncluttered with the prepossessions of immature system-builders. He saw things in wonderment, with precision, in their plenitude. Once he had willed to encounter the created thou, he was drawn as by a magnet, all unknowingly at first, to the tri-personal presence of the Absolute Thou. When he opted to concentrate on concrete reality, he ceased being an observer, a ratifier, and became a witness for the spiritual. As witness he contributed to the enrichment of the

[3] *Ibid.*, p. 41.
[4] Etienne GILSON, "Un exemple," *Existentialisme chrétien*, ed. Gilson (Paris: Plon, 1947), p. 2.

revelation of natural mysteries, to the renewed advent and
the growth of the truth that is in need of being brought to
articulate awareness under the circumstances of the contemporary
crisis. Through the years he was to become fully conscious of
the significance of his concrete philosophy:

> A concrete philosophy is drawn as by a magnet by the
> Christian data. For the Christian, there is an essential
> conformity between Christian revelation and human nature.
> Thus, the more one penetrates into man's nature, the more
> one places oneself within the axis of the great Christian
> truths. [5]

But what are the actual concrete circumstances of the
human condition that Marcel has been encountering ever since
he descended from his Hegelian empyrean? He has worked in
an era of catastrophic social unrest in a world broken by two
major wars and still plagued by cold ones. Fear, repression,
insecurity are still characteristic of modern man. Marcel sees
that even today, after so much suffering and disillusionment,
modern man, in his effort to escape from subjective loneliness,
is still desperately fleeing from and clinging to heartless
collectivities.

Marcel is quick to accept and utilize what underlies this
mass flight of individuals to collectivized society, namely that
the peace, happiness and prosperity of man depend upon his
life within community. It is not by insertion into the colony
of the masses, but by a conversion to the communion of loving
intersubjective living, that the displaced man of our era will
attain his spiritual and social maturity.

In World War I Marcel worked with the Red Cross,
devoting himself to its investigations concerning persons who
had disappeared in the war. Each day the broken human spirit
sought his services as parents and friends groped to find, in and
through him, their missing loved ones. Contact with so many
sorrows revealed to Marcel the drama of human existence. He

[5] *RI*, p. 109.

rebelled against the depersonalized questionnaires, the arbitrary simplifications, the superficial arrangements to which these suffering souls were submitted. In World War II the odious experience of the German occupation frequently precipitated him into melancholic moods. Yet, all through these experiences, he continued to grasp the pulse of existence and, because of his spontaneous interest in others and his sympathy, he renounced even more emphatically the facile intellectualism and the way of abstraction that contributed so much to the dehumanization of persons. He gave himself to moving meditation on the fate of man. This sensitive vibration to the least aspiration of his fellowman kept him, as a philosopher, open and accessible to every inspiration of God and men. Few men have opened themselves with greater graciousness to so many aspects of the spiritual world and responded to them with more dedication. With such affective richness and depth, it is not surprising that he continued to advance along the great lines of his personalist philosophy.

How may we explain this advancement more fully? A look into Marcel's conversion will give us an appreciation of what was taking place in his soul. Marcel tells us that "he has always been partial to religion even when he belonged to no determined confession." [6] In the winter of 1916-1917 he gave himself up to the experiences of spiritualism. These he quickly abandoned, but not before they definitely convinced him of the reality of the metapsychical world of being.

His next step was to try to justify in his own mind the act of faith. Gradually and more clearly, he disentangled the conditions, the internal structure of authentic faith whose act he saw was possible, legitimate and even necessary, if man wished to ascend to a spiritual personality, to his being. Despite his inquiry into faith, Marcel came to no immediate conclusion. He still lacked any experience of God. All the while his hunger for concrete being increased intensely. At any rate, he felt no

[6] Gabriel MARCEL, "Interview sur l'Influence des Lectures Spiri-tuelles," *Témoignage, Cahiers de la Pierre-qui-vire*, XIX, 1948.

need as yet to serve God in a definite Church. Thus the quest for God seemed ended and when Marcel, from 1924 to 1929, even abandoned his philosophical endeavors, the very hunger for transcendence seemed to have died out in him. He lost himself during these years in his work as critic and dramatist. Then the Transcendent found him.

He had just reviewed Mauriac's *Dieu et Mammon* and was reading the author's appreciative letter, when his eyes caught these words: "But, after all, why are you not one of us?" [7] It was February 25, 1929 in the afternoon. Marcel alone can relate his experience: "With the brilliance that comes from a lightning flash I knew immediately that through and beyond this letter of my correspondent, God was extending me a direct and personal invitation." [8]

In the prayer Marcel then gave himself up to and during the following days he grasped clearly the role of the free will in the commitment of faith. He could steal away and refuse its appeal. He could correspond with grace. Which would he do? Calmly he decided to say "yes" and to remain faithful forever after. At this moment he understood that faith "is essentially a fidelity, the sublimest there is."

But the great illumination of his whole being took place a few days later, when he made his response: On March 5, 1929, Marcel entered these ardent words into his journal:

> I have no more doubts. This morning's happiness is miraculous. For the first time I have clearly experienced *grace*. A terrible thing to say, but it is so. I am hemmed in at last by Christianity—in, fathoms deep. Happy to be so! But I will write no more. And yet, I feel a kind of need to write. Feel I am stammering childishly ...this is indeed a birth. Everything is different. Now, too, I can see my way through my improvisations. A new metaphor, the inverse of the other—a world which was there, entirely present, and at last I can touch it. [9]

[7] R. TROISFONTAINES, *op. cit.*, p. 23.
[8] *Ibid.*, pp. 23-24.
[9] *BH*, p. 15.

Up to this time Marcel had been more attracted by Protestantism than by Catholicism. He felt that Catholics were not free. Whenever he conversed with his Protestant brother-in-law, a pastor in the village of Ardèche, he felt himself closer to him than to his Catholic friends. Thus, he could not explain why he chose Catholicism in answer to Mauriac's appeal. Reflecting on the matter, he told himself: "Yes, I am a Christian. It would be cowardice to run away from this truth any longer. But I was conscious, at that time, of an appeal coming from much further back than Mauriac and I felt obligated to choose Catholicism." [10]

Having encountered God within the Catholic Church at the age of thirty-nine, Marcel irrevocably dedicated himself to Him and asked for baptism. This he received on March 23, 1929, with a disposition which "was more than he dared to hope for: no transports, but peaceful, balanced, and full of hope and faith." [11]

The results of his conversion were very normal. His spiritual experiences aroused new reflections on so many rich and concrete themes. Contact with the Faith made him realize himself and manifest himself in his work and within the purity of a philosophy of communion. He began to explore both the foundations of human communion and the appeal that characterizes man's union with God. He became a Christian philosopher in quest of presence.

How, then, does Marcel understand the role of the Christian philosopher in this age of crisis? Despite the attack on Christianity, Marcel has developed no defense mechanism, no inferiority complex in the face of the enemy. Without any diminution of Christian courage, nor any abdication of his liberty of spirit, nor of his frankness, Marcel stands forth as the philosopher of faithfulness and is frequently referred to as the greatest living Christian Existentialist. His popularity as a thinker and lecturer in the non-Catholic academic world has been remarkable.

[10] R. TROISFONTAINES, *op. cit.*, p. 24.
[11] *BH*, p. 24.

It has been noticed by Christian philosophers that non-Christian and even, at times, non-sectarian thinkers are fascinated by a forthright philosophy that explores the data of Christian theology and harmoniously incorporates its findings into the discipline of philosophy. The realistic freshness and creativity of this unintimidated approach to being avoids the pitfalls of a stifling abstractionism which paralyzes Christian philosophy by isolating it from any intercourse with theology. As if the phenomena of Revelation and sanctity are not realities *given* independently of any subjective acceptance or rejection of them. Marcel has no inferiority complex over using theological phenomena in his philosophical deliberations; he rejects the sterile criticisms of the rationalists and secularists. For him "... *la sainteté est* ... *une donnée*." [12]

The role of the Christian philosopher for Marcel, then, is, negatively, to defend man against the withering effects of his own narrow and abstractive systems of thought that drain reality of all mystery, of all transcendent values; positively, it is to extend the horizons of being, of presence, of participation by witnessing to the need for a world of communion.

> Today, the first and perhaps the only duty of the philosopher is to defend man against himself: to defend man against the extraordinary temptation towards inhumanity to which—almost always without being aware of it—so many human beings today have yielded. [13]

To live with is for Marcel a need of nature that calls for fulfilment in a spirituality of communion within a fraternity of community. Because he is capable of receiving, because he chooses to give himself, Marcel makes the powers of his temperament reach their highest perfection in his free choice for a philosophy of communion. The gift of self and of receptivity expand and fulfill themselves in the works of life only through mutual exchanges.

[12] *RI*, p. 190.
[13] *MMS*, p. 193.

There can be no authentic depth where there can be no real communion; but there will never be any real communion between individuals centered on themselves, and in consequence morbidly hardened, nor in the heart of the mass, within the mass state. The very notion of intersubjectivity, on which all my own recent work has been based, presupposes a reciprocal openness between individuals without which no kind of spirituality is conceivable. [14]

"A reciprocal openness between individuals" is the clue to the foundation of Marcel's philosophy, a philosophy which, because it is founded on the datum of the exigence for intersubjective communion, is willing to enter into the defense and the love of created and Absolute Thou's. It is when he is discovering new philosophic frontiers in the universe of communion that Marcel's genius is at its best. Marcel has explored and developed this region perhaps with greater insight and thoroughness than any other philosopher of our times. He has made innumerable reflective investigations into this sphere of the spiritual. His unexpected discoveries have been enlightening. And Marcel never tires of extending the frontiers of "ontological communion," for the simple reason that he knows that this area of the mystery of being is inexhaustible and can never be fully mapped.

In what spirit does he proceed as a philosopher to explore this area of the mystery of being? First he seeks and presents a desirable clarity on the most personal and universal characteristics of human existence. Secondly, he humbly and gladly yields to whatever light is granted him on this subject, admitting that man is grounded in his deepest being in a community of limitless Love and Truth. The philosopher of concrete experience, in drawing his fellowmen to the spiritual and to the Christian data, is making men see that at bottom all his social problems and their solutions are rooted in theology. The philosopher of the concrete approach to lived experience knows that man's social viewpoints on the fundamental relations

---

[14] *Ibid.*, p. 200.

of community life, of his just claims and moral obligations, are influenced and almost inevitably determined by his care or carelessness about God, his fellowmen and the human predicament. This means for the Christian philosopher that, while remaining distinct, his philosophy will be assumed into his Christian theology; the two will be fused to constitute a total wisdom which alone can reassemble the broken world of our day. Marcel would certainly agree with the expression of this truth that is given by Donoso Cortes:

> Proudhon has written in his *Confessions of a Revolutionary* these famous words: "It is a cause of wonderment to see how in all our political problems we invariably stumble up against theology." There is nothing here that should cause surprise, except the surprise of Proudhon. For theology, by the very fact that it is the science of God, is the Ocean that contains and embraces all the sciences, just as God is the Ocean that contains and embraces all things. [15]

This investigation into Marcel's concrete philosophy is an attempt to examine, evaluate and order, to some extent, the genuine insights concerning a philosophy of community which Marcel is ever advancing in his efforts to save the community of men from insertion into collectivized communes, and to lead them rather into the City of Light. The reader will not find here an elaborated system of Social Philosophy. Marcel purposely eschews total systems of philosophy which claim to be able, if not today then sometime in the future, to explain the *totum* of truth. Such claims betray the arrogance of total systems. Marcel who is impressed with the limitless plenitude of all being and truth holds the position expressed by B. V. Schwarz toward every authentic philosophy:

---

[15] Donoso CORTES, *Ensayo Sobre el Catolicismo, el Liberalismo y el Socialismo* (Buenos Aires: Editorial Americales, 1943), p. 23. "Mr. Proudhon ha escrito, en sus *Confesiones de un revolucionario*, estas notables palabras: 'Es cosa que admira el ver de que manera en todas nuestras cuestiones politicas tropezamos siempre con la teología.' Nada hay aqui que pueda causar sorpresa, sino la sorpresa de Mr. Proudhon. La teología por lo mismo que es la ciencia de Dios, es el Océano que contiene y abarca todas las ciencias, asi como Dios es el Océano que contiene y abarca todas las cosas."

There is a paradox inherent in the very undertaking of philosophy, and it results in a dilemma seemingly insurmountable. Philosophical truth cannot possibly be isolated truth. The *totum* of truth must in some way make its presence felt, but philosophy itself cannot give the total truth. The history of its systems bears empirical witness to this fact. As Kierkegaard puts it, "the world is a system but only God knows the system." [16]

By "concrete philosophy" Marcel conceives the purpose of philosophy to be not the erection of abstract systems of thought by depersonalized thinkers who, as mere spectators of being and existence, sit back detached and assign each thing its place and function in a tight and tidy world. His philosophy plunges into the infinite complexities of lived experience in all its concreteness and encounters the "sting of the real." Participation is the key to his philosophizing. Man has no isolated experiences of existence. For man to be is to be-in-a-situation. Man becomes conscious of the only self he really knows by participating actively and freely within a dynamically inter-acting world and within inter-subjective communion with other persons. Concrete philosophy must discover and delineate the thrust and sublimity that growth in transcending participation produces in the human person.

We do not wish to say that Marcel has not written much on the subject of the human community. He has, but his philosophical method of inquiry and dialectic, though rigorous, is also sinuous. His is the winding way of researches and he tells us himself that "I will only reach my goal through roundabout ways." [17] His vision of the City of Light is what initiates his pilgrimage toward the truth; there lies at the beginning of all philosophy what he calls a "blinded intuition," which gives us the primitive assurance of the indubitable presence of being. Marcel freely attests to it.

    [6] Balduin V. SCHWARZ, "Introduction," *The Human Person and the World of Values*, ed. Balduin V. Schwarz (New York: Fordham University Press, 1960), p. xiii.
    [17] *MJ*, p. 316.

> For my method of advance does invariably consist. . .
> in working my way up from life to thought and then down
> from thought to life again, so that I may try to throw more
> light upon life. But it would be a hopeless undertaking,
> I think, to attempt to ensconce oneself, once and for all,
> in the realm of pure thought. [18]

Ever since he broke out of his social isolation, ever since
he escaped from philosophic narrowness, Marcel has found his
excursions into life hopeful and fruitful undertakings. He has
deeply realized the ontological hierarchy of being; he has hungered
to arrive at the summit of this hierarchy. But he has appreciated
also that there is no direct route to that summit open to man in
his present position as pilgrim. So quite humbly and realistically
he has employed a method which Marcel de Corte has called
the "ascending spiral," a method which moves ceaselessly up the
ladder of participation from spirit to spirit until it arrives at the
peak of communion. The stages of that journey will be the
concern of this book, especially as they effect the growth of
communion in community. These stages are: incarnation,
sensation, primary reflection, secondary reflection, communication,
community, intersubjective communion, the divine and human
community of love.

Just as a living thing assimilates all sorts of foods, so
Marcel's procedure will synthesize all methods of approaching
and arriving at the achievement of communion. Lived experience
demands this dynamic approach for the experience of being
arises for each man in communion, and the experience of
communion can never be handed down in abstract concepts
of the deductive type. Marcel's philosophic critique of being
will be seen to be not one of dissolution but of purification. His
very negativism towards pernicious abstractions is already a
concrete approach to the constitutive mystery of man in
communion. His despair of the ghosts of being is already a
springboard to a higher affirmation of being. His is a philosophy

[18] *MB* (I), p. 51.

of conversion, the negation of negation, from which being arises in all its freshness and takes its honored and established place in the field of communion.

But Marcel's drive for communion is by no means restricted to the field of philosophy. He is also an original and prolific playwright, a professional drama and music critic and an accomplished pianist. All of these activities are integral to his concrete philosophy. He claims that music has been the single most important influence on his philosophy.

Troisfontaines tells us that music is never a passing diversion for Marcel. It is an interior discipline and an essential nourishment, indeed, a superior life where he finds recoupment from the forces of dispersion and dilution to which the human spirit is exposed. Marcel himself tells us that as a child of unbelieving parents his early religious life was "nutured by the music of Bach." Music was his true vocation because, in music above all, he found he did his most creative work. Bach had greater influence on his work than Pascal, than Augustine, than any author. Marcel found the authentically spiritual incarnated in the highest forms of musical expression. Music, in its negative influence on his philosophy, preserved him from speculative conformism. Now music would reveal to Marcel a tragic wisdom entirely in harmony with his hunger for being. Then again it would inundate his soul with a clear, piteous, tragic illumination resembling the light of metaphysics which he hoped to explore and focus within himself.

In Beethoven's last works he clearly caught an appreciation of the superior finality of thought. He found in musical works concrete aspects of categories over which he would labor for metaphysical precision—humility in the *Boris* of Moussorgski, unity between pure thought and essential sensibility in Faure. The sonatas of Beethoven will always be associated with his conversion, "with those unforgettable moments." Marcel's involvement in music indicates strikingly his conviction that philosophy is a total, indivisible activity. Even his musical critiques reveal his preoccupation with metaphysics:

Because Mozart is so far from us, from our actual existence, is the very reason he is so near to our hearts, somewhat like our childhood to which we become more attached the moment we realize it is finished. Nothing more transcends our unstable, feverish, cinematographic present than this spirit who controls himself miraculously even in his light music and in his most flighty fantasies. There is an eternity in Mozart which is not, as in Bach, the perpetuity of a faith or of a spiritual substance, but of a delightful melody, of an unexpected illumination in which the universe is obliterated. [19]

Speaking of the influence of his plays on his thought, Marcel writes: "It is in and through drama that metaphysical thought grasps and defines itself *in concreto*." [20] Music sates Marcel's drive for the interior recoupment of his spiritual forces; drama satisfies his urge for exterior self-expression in the company of others. When we recall that he deplored the absence of any brothers and sisters in his life, we understand why drama became another form of creative participation for him. His plays are not philosophical theses; no preconceived doctrines are demonstrated in the words and actions of his characters. His plays are metaphysical experimentations. His characters are living persons, expressing their own mysterious sentiments. Now clear, now obscure in their hopes and fears, they face a double threat to their existences: the inability to grasp their own intentions and the refusal to open themselves to others. They are free to choose the drama of communion or the tragedy of estrangement.

Marcel calls his theatre the "drama of the soul in exile." All men are ambiguous and a sense of this ambivalence pervades all his plays. The characters are all in communication and in conflict; their tragedy is that they are not in communion. Each person is a subject, situated in a metaphysical dimension of being and endowed with the usual faults and virtues of real persons. The drama always disquiets us, forces us to engage in secondary reflection on the interior lies that break the bond of communion

---

[19] R. TROISFONTAINES, *op. cit.*, p. 29.
[20] Gabriel MARCEL, *La Soif* (Paris: Desclée de Brouwer, 1938), quoted by Fessard, p. 7.

in a soul with itself and with others. Alienated souls become strangers to themselves, lost in an utter incomprehension of their selves. Infinitely varied, the theme is the same in all the plays, excellently expressed by Claude Lemoyne at the end of *Un homme de Dieu*: "To be known as one is...." [21]

Understandably, Marcel presents the main obstacles to communion: lying, stubborness, pride, banality, treason, false fidelity and a thousand forms of egoism, rejections of love, tragic misunderstandings.

These hardly light up the road to resurrection. Death plays a leading role; it is the supreme test for faithful communion. Yet the most desperate experiences of isolation—"there is only one suffering, that is, to be alone"[22]—serve as stepping-stones for an affirmation of the highest hope. For the very injuries that lead to the brink of despair may become the gateway to the spirit of humility and charity which will penetrate and renew persons to their profoundest depths. Thus, Marcel's plays end up instilling hope and gratitude in their viewers. From the side of alienation from being, they paradoxically beget a sense of the need to love life and to find its transcendent meaning in total self-donation in communion. The plays orchestrate the theme of the need for intersubjectivity by displaying the tragic disintegration of souls in exile. Marcel's drama is a dialectic of self-discovery in which the need for communion, for living *with*, in the presence of others is grasped as the *sine qua non* for metaphysical self-consciousness and self-maturity.

Man of communion, musician, dramatist, critic and philosopher, Marcel is a living demonstration of man's hunger to ascend to being through the concrete complexities of lived experience and not through abstractions that are mere facsimiles of being. We shall see that his philosophy is animated by the conviction that the human person and milieu will attain the plenitude of fulfilment only in communion with the Transcendent Being.

[21] Gabriel MARCEL, *Three Plays*, trans. Rosalind Heywood and Marjorie Gabain (New York: Hill and Wang, 1958), p. 114.
[22] Gabriel MARCEL, *Le Cœur des Autres* (Paris: Grasset, 1921), p. 111.

N Y. 29 — 3

CHAPTER II

Marcel's Philosophic Point of Departure

The disease at the spiritual center and heart of modern society is the topic of much philosophical inquiry. The many analyses of what is wrong with the West, with the East, with the whole world reveal the general concern over the health and survival of civil, political and even familial society itself. That social upheaval is a widespread phenomenon is testified to by the forces of revolution that are in the field and acting as catalysts toward community chaos in many nations throughout the world. Anxiety and fear are a very common and prolonged experience in our times.

The philosopher of depth sees that certain realities are involved in these physical and psychological experiences, realities that have ontological priority over the experiences themselves and must be presupposed as authentic, if these experiences are to be meaningful at all.

What are some of these analyses about the community-crisis and what are the presupposed realities upon which they are based? What of the validity of these analyses and of their presupposed realities? How does Marcel explore this problem and upon what metaphysical foundation does he base his own analyses? These are some of the areas of reality we hope to touch on in this chapter.

Some social philosophers, rather superficially it seems, explain the present isolation-community tension as nothing more than an extreme condition of the ageless antinomy between the One and the Many, the natural opposition of the law of unity to the law of multiplicity having to evolve necessarily into this concrete and hardened confrontation of the individual *vis à vis* society at large.

Presupposed in this theory is the fact, not only that all reality is simultaneously one and many, but also the assumption that this multiplicity is essentially explained by a principle of opposition and of natural intersubjective hostility that lies, itself unexplained, at the source of being. A sort of metaphysical Darwinism will alone decide whether the individual or the group will gain the final ascendency. Marxism, of course, has made a blind act of faith in the final evolutionary absorption of the individual into the classless community.

Both Hegel and Marx posit the principle of contradiction at the heart of all reality, thus taking it for granted that the normal state of all being is one of raw hostility. Marx chooses the dialectic of the drawn dagger to attack and form reality. Marcel chooses the dialectic of the wedding ring to participate in its mysteries. No one denies that violent competition does exist. Sartre is a consummate master at delineating the nauseous aspects of such competition. But must we conclude, with Marx, that violent revolution is essential to existence and, with Sartre, that "hell is other people"?[1] Is the only method of receiving that of destructive and violent appropriation? Is the only method of giving that of brutal imposition? Has Camus accurately described the metaphysical situation of man as the being found in the *Myth of Sisyphus?*

The tendency among many social philosophers is to decide the dilemma of the individual or the community according to their individualistic or communal prejudices. "They equate their preferences with the truth."[2]

The view that concentrates on the individual holds that the individual is to be regarded as the principal, the all-important value in society. The individual is an autonomous being; he is the source of his own spiritual reality. The individual freely

---

[1] Jean-Paul SARTRE, *No Exit*, adapted from French by Paul Bowles (New York: Samuel French, 1945), p. 52.
[2] SCHWARZ, *op. cit.*, p. 169.

constitutes the community and can freely recede from it. The community is and exercises all its being from the collectivity of its members. Society, as a matter of fact, is nothing more than the sum total of autonomous individuals. The terminal point of this thought-route is exaggerated individualism. Is there a crisis in society? Then refashion individuals and these renewed units of society will inevitably be sanative of society itself. Obviously in such a social milieu man has only purely external relations with all other individuals. This is Social Atomism.

For others, the community is considered as the primordial, the rudimentary reality. Society is a whole whose parts are its individuals. O. Spann [3] sees all relations under the conformity and harmony of part to whole. Hence the individual draws his spiritual being from the social totality. Contacts among men are nothing more than connections of the parts in the whole. The part has its being only in the whole as the hand has its being only in the body or the rhyme in a poem. From this point of departure one arrives at Universalism.

Which position is the truth of the matter? The philosopher, in order to seek and find that truth, will have to steer a course that escapes the Scylla of individualism and the Charybdis of collectivism, a course that replaces the alternatives of Atomism or Universalism with concrete Realism. He will have to restrict himself to an analysis of the given data, to submit to the light of lived experience which is a field that is made fertile by the social philosopher.

Spann studies the essential features of social facts, but he gives them a special interpretation. The great social fact is the relationship of reciprocation, of interchange, the mutual relation existing between man and man. Thus, friendship creates a reciprocity, a harmony between two friends. This reciprocation is a totality, a wholeness in which the two friends participate. This friendly interchange constitutes the spiritual life of the friends, constitutes their individual spirits. Family life is also

[3] Othmar SPANN, *The History of Economics*, trans. Eden and Cedar Paul (New York: Norton, 1930), p. 61.

a totality and wholeness. The members of the family are parts of this totality. There is a mutual influence between parents and children. The mother forms the child, but the child acts upon the mother, thus developing within her the qualities which make her a mother. Society is a whole mass of reciprocal relations. Its members are what they are because they are parts of society.

What of Spann's position? If we restrict ourselves to follow the leads of the given data, leads that come to us through an existential analysis of lived experience, we find that Spann's explanations have many valid truths. Certainly, they are opposed to the individualism of the nineteenth century. They are right in emphasizing that society is "not only the sum total of its individuals." One ought not to exaggerate the individual aspect of man, for his spiritual formation is largely due to his social relations. So much *contra* individualism and *pro* Spann.

Yet the mistake Spann makes is to set up only *one* alternative as his point of departure—the individual or society. Is this exhaustive of the total context and complexity of human existence? Is there not another point of departure? Marcel, Von Hildebrand and Scheler certainly think so. They take their point of departure from the individual. They find that in fact man is autonomous but also social. Both these characteristics are primordial. When they analyze this fundamental ambivalence of the essence of man, they uncover the amazing richness and the deep importance of his relationship to other men. By comparison with the levels of being below him, man is in a totally new and unique way, both as a being *in se* and as a being in, of and for community. [4]

The trouble with Spann's theory on community, and with that of many other philosophers who are partial to the social aspects of man, is that they hold a *univocal* conception of the relation of the whole to the part and vice versa and they apply

---

[4] Thomas J. OWENS, S. J., *The Problem of Interpersonal Relationships as Posed in Contemporary Thought* (New York: Fordham University Doctoral Dissertation, 1952), p. 163. We have in this work a treatment of some contemporary philosophers' thought on community. The spokesman for the case against community is Sartre; Scheler presents the case for; Von Hildebrand profoundly surpasses their inadequate theories. The whole makes for rewarding reading.

this conception univocally to whatever is in any way unified; to machines, animals, men, families, communities. But an existential analysis of the data of experience reveals that there exists a rich and actually mysterious hierarchy in the participation of the whole-part relationship and that, consequently, there must be an analogous application of this reciprocal relation to different spheres of being. Thus, for example, the unity of man's nature is substantial; the unity among the parts of a clock is only accidental; the unity in a community is such that men remain individuals even after they have united themselves into societies and they do not form from these unions any new substance; the unity among the members of the Christian Community is neither substantial nor accidental, yet it is real, physical and mystical—a transcendental unity.

Plato and Aristotle, quite understandably, failed to grasp the transcendence of the human person. Although their desire to attain moral perfection for every citizen and their insistence that in the exercise of power justice should be substituted for force were genuine insights into the dignity of man, yet in their efforts to define justice they always left the person wholly subordinate to the City-State. The inadequacy of their metaphysics is its failure to arrive at adequate knowledge of the personality of the individual and the specific equality of human beings. To be sure, this failure also led them to miss what is correlative to the truth of the essential equality of man, namely the inherent duty of each person to pursue a goal that transcends the State and even defines the State's rights and duties. [5]

---

[5] A penetrating and accurate analysis of the causes for the Greek organism-error about man in the State is presented by Joseph F. COSTANZO, S. J., "The Graeco-Roman Politeia—The City of Men," *Fordham Law Review*, XX, No. 2 (New York: Fordham University Press, June 1951), pp. 139-40: "The failure of the Greeks to attain to the adequate conception of the specific equality of men (as the Schoolmen say in Latin, *constitutive*, *exegetive*, and *consecutive*) was due to historical, sociological and metaphysical reasons. The popular (and Aristotelian) concept of manual labor and menial services as an impediment to the freedom and leisure necessarily requisite for the development of virtue, the experience of factual inequality, the pride of the cultured Greek freeman, who considered the barbarian as inferior by nature—only added to the inadequate metaphysics of the Greeks which did not attain to the knowledge of an Eternal

Plato found the principle of integration and harmony for his "ideal" political community in its hierarchical organization according to the visionary planning of the philosopher-king who would rule by the intellectual insight. Yet Plato was not adverse to establishing his political, economic, educational and cultural utopia through a deliberate and cold-blooded "noble lie." Aristotle saw the weakness inherent in Plato's Republic; that

Divine Personality in whose image man was created. The Christian reve-lation of the universal salvific will of God and of the equality of men in the adopted sonship of God and the example and teaching of Christ on labor were morally necessary to remove the deeply rooted prejudices of society and to enlighten the thought of the philosopher. Inequality in nature is implied in Plato's concept of virtue. The *arete* of a thing is its proper function or that quality "in virtue of which" it does its particular work well, and each individual has a specific function that constitutes his distinct perfection. Though it is to Aristotle's credit to have conceived of human nature in a normative way, his immanent teleology unwittingly devolves into a crude externalism. A large class of non-citizens are sub-sidiary to the citizens and as a means to an end external to themselves. The end or function of the State is moral life but only those who have leisure and economic freedom are capable of it. Labor and suffering as means of sanctification or virtue was inconceivable to Aristotle. While Plato's inequality of men was intellectual, Aristotle's was moral. Aristotle's teleology introduces a hierarchy of values which discriminates between the moral capacity of the individuals. Though his teleology preserved the household (against Plato), it justified at the same time a fixed class of slaves. What misled Aristotle was an excessively close comparison of the State with the organism of the human body. The contributory parts of the body (v.g., blood, bones, sinews) are really the same as the integral (v.g., hands and feet) of which they are the conditions. The contributory parts of the State (v.g., traders, artisans, laborers) are not the same as the integral (v.g., for Aristotle, the citizens and governmental agencies). The sound organic theory of the State is based on an analogy which properly harmonizes the paramountcy of the common good with the transcen-dental significance of each and every individual, whether he be a citizen or not. The attempt to erect a valid ethical system on the basis of pure functionalism must logically conduce to a differentiation of a scale of values according to the various functions of the members of society, and end by making one set of functions instrumental to another. A moral act inferior in virtue as compared to another does not entitle the agent of the higher moral act to a superior right over the agent of the lesser virtue. Nor does the more significant Aristotelian citizen fare better than the non-citizen in his organic theory of the State. The individual citizen is dependent upon the State not only for his *fulness* of life but, further, for his *very* life. Because the individual citizen cannot realize his moral per-fection apart from the Constitution of the State which defines the moral life of State and citizen as one, he too is dependent upon the State as absolutely as a hand or foot is dependent upon the body, equally and in the same degree. The equality and identity of dependencies is simply assumed."

Republic was an ideocracy, that is, the government therein depicted represented the despotism of an idea. [6]

Attempting to escape the pitfalls of Platonic transcendentalism, Aristotle envisaged the principle of order as immanent, that is, essential and inherent in the individual who required life in the State for the realization of his intrinsic finality. The perfection of the State for Aristotle, in marked disagreement with Plato, is embodied in the Constitution, which becomes the norm of the legal, moral and intellectual perfection of its citizens. [7] Both the Platonic impress of the Perfect Idea from above that should lead to the "ideal State," and the Aristotelian growth of the potential capacity of man, through immanent forms, that should arrive at the "best State"—both these metaphysical constructions produced a framework of life in antiquity in which the individual was subjected to a comprehensive scheme of social planning, and where "function" was adjusted to capacity within the "constitutional" or "heavenly" pattern; in neither social milieu was the individual truly free to pursue a destiny that transcends the State.

Cochrane has clearly seen that Classicism committed the radical error of treating the history of mankind as if it were another "object" in a world of objects, something that could be analyzed into its parts, metaphysical and physical. It applied the conventional concepts of matter and form to reveal the nature of this thing called history. This procedure reduced individual human beings to "specimens" embodying a "type," who became fully intelligible only in terms of structure and function, somewhat

---

[6] PLATO, *The Republic*, trans. B. Jowett (New York: Random, Modern Library paperback, 1960), p. 124.

[7] ARISTOTLE, *Politics*, trans. B. Jowett (New York: Viking, 1959), p. 6: "A social instinct is implanted in all men by nature, and yet he who first founded the state was the greatest of all benefactors. For man, when perfected, is the best of animals, but when separated from law and justice, he is the worst of all; since armed injustice is the more dangerous, and he is equipped at birth with arms, meant to be used by intelligence and virtue, which he may use for the worst ends. Wherefore, if he have not virtue, he is the most unholy and the most savage of animals, and the most full of lust and gluttony. But justice is the bond of men in states, for the administration of justice, which is the determination of what is just, is the principle of order in political society."

like machines. Now types qua types are static and cannot change;
they are really universal abstractions. Only individuals achieve
self-fulfilment, dynamic self-realization. In a formalized and
schematized frame of life the individual is essentially related to
the "type" to which he naturally belongs. But, through this
restrictive and static relationship, the individual is severed from
the rich, vital relationships he experiences with other concrete
individuals. Taken in by this philosophical explanation, the
Sophists went on to call relationships among concrete individuals
artificial conventions, relationships, therefore, that are unnatural.
Other philosophers, misled by this same explanation, founded
these relationships on mere animal gregariousness or on a
community of interests in physical satisfactions, arising from the
association of male and female or master and slave. Idealists,
who hoped to avoid these inadequate explanations, came up with
a distinctive principle for harmonious integration among living
individuals—the ideal of justice which, Aristotle claimed, is the
common property of all intelligible beings. But the ideal of
justice as ideal is wholly formal and exists only in the logical
order. Aristotle undertook to give it vital content by identifying
the ideal of justice with the justice of the *polis*.

But what had Classicism actually done through this
procedure? It utilized abstract knowledge as a source and
means to power and not as an instrument to wisdom. It
substituted its own logical order of being for the only concrete
order of being which exists independently of the human thought-
processes in the universe. It supplanted the real, actual order
with its own fictitious order. It substituted dead concepts in
place of living realities. Classical antiquity proceeded to impose
its abstract order of justice on its subjects by initiating a politics
of power to persuade and compel men to accept as genuine its
own counterfeit of cosmic order and community. [8]

Just as the history of "politics" and of the community in
classical antiquity was due to the existential attempt to
implement, concretize and universalize the abstract absolutisms

    [8] Charles N. COCHRANE, *Christianity and Classical Culture* (New
York: Oxford, A Galaxy Book, 1957), pp. 97-98.

of the philosophers—the visionary idealism of Plato leading to the "ideal State" with its philosopher-king and the formal immanentism of Aristotle leading to the "best State" with the finest Constitution and legal system—so too the history of "politics" and of community in contemporary times continues to be subjected to the philosophers' attempts "to substitute their own notions of order for the order which exists in the universe." [9] Marcel calls these new schemes to substitute "the dead concept for the living reality," [10] pernicious products of the spirit of abstraction. The reason for Marcel's particular aversion for these new types of ideological absolutisms is that they not only do not embody the saving, humanistic features of classical intellectualism, but they displace metaphysics in favor of scientific positivism and actually glory in identifying *jus* with *potentia* in the management of man's affairs.

Out of such modern abstractions about man, there have necessarily emerged deformed solutions concerning the history, development, organization and problems of people living together as social groups. Comte's philosophic positivism begot social Darwinism; his religious positivism developed into a form of "sociolatry" and a "sociocracy." De Lubac reveals how Comte's positivism, both religious and philosophic, was constructed from his philosopher's lust for plenipotentiary spiritual power. A sociologist who meditated and planned social reconstructions, Comte decreed the absolute absence of all mysteries and demanded of men an unreserved belief in his system of thought and perfect fidelity to his political policies. His "social physics" terminated in a social mysticism which identified politics with the Religion of Humanity. His positivism aimed to organize the kingdom of earth under a hierarchy of scientists, Comte himself being the supreme Pontiff. Here again we have humanity and the universe subjected to the despotism of a thought-system spun out of the head of a self-appointed demigod. [11]

[9] *Ibid.*, p. 98.
[10] *Ibid.*, p. 99.
[11] Henri DE LUBAC, S. J., *The Drama of Atheist Humanism*, trans. Edith M. Riley (New York: Sheed, 1950), pp. 147-148.

Nietzsche's totally free man, to whom nothing was forbidden, once he had assassinated God, was intended to produce a society of ruthless supermen which, as a matter of history in the form of Nazism, attempted to impose upon the world an historically cataclysmic nihilism. In the dialectical materialism of Marx, a new man, *homo œconomicus*, is supposed to reach his peak of progress through the mechanisms of alienation known as "the techniques of economics and the tactics of class war." [12]

Marx attempted to replace "the cult of the abstract man" with the science of real men in historical, evolutionary and revolutionary advancement. The mystic halo surrounding religious man was ripped off. Real men are men within the world, the State, Society. But the State and Society, in order to subjugate men, produce religion as a false attitude toward the eternal, dynamic, materialistic universe. Religion constitutes a general, systematic view of the world. It produces for man an all-embracing compendium of reality. It attracts men with its popular logic, its inspiring points of honor and reverence, its moral rewards and censures, its comforting and salvific instruments. "Religion is but the imaginative realization" of a human nature that has no reality and no stability. Both a protest against misery and the expression of real misery, religion is an aspiration of desperate creatures, a spirit of a spiritless universe, a mentality of a mindless world; it is "opium" to people. [13]

In rejecting objective rationalistic systems that lead to the oppressive State-Family by badly dichotomizing reality into inimical groups through impersonal logic and ruthless planning, Marcel makes a penetrating observation. It is that, paradoxical as it may seem, the more collectivized the world becomes the less it becomes possible to construct any real community within it. He seconds Thibon's insight that, at bottom, both the process of atomization and collectivization, far from being mutually exclusive, actually work together to devitalize society. These processes are in reality complementary techniques producing

---

[12] *Ibid.*, p. 14.
[13] *Ibid.*, p. 16.

the disintegration and decomposition of *bona fide* communities. [14]

It would seem, then, that there is something inadequate with the One-Many approach to philosophizing about reality. As for himself, Marcel's point of departure in philosophizing about the modern cosmic and social crisis embodies a most refreshing and illuminating attitude to the whole of concrete experience. His insight consists, negatively, in refusing to concentrate on the numerically accidental character of being—the One and the Many—and, positively, in exploring with patient intensity the metaphysical and spiritual ambivalence of being as the Full and the Empty. The former view of reality is superficial and sterile; the latter, as infinitely more essential, is profound and eminently fruitful.

As we have seen, "a reciprocal openness between individuals" is the clue to the foundation of all Marcel's philosophy and especially to his philosophy of intersubjectivity or what might be called his social philosophy.

To begin with, for Marcel philosophy is a total act of vital concern; subjectivity is not divorced from reality but is a most important constituent of true philosophy. In the mind of Marcel philosophy is the reciprocal clarification of two unknowns—the object and the subject. In his concrete philosophy, therefore, the distinction between the Full and the Empty is much more important than perhaps any other distinction.

> I have written on another occasion that, provided it is taken in its metaphysical and not its physical sense, the distinction between the *full* and the *empty* seems to be more fundamental than that between the *one* and the *many*. [15]

Metaphysics is to be carried on, therefore, only in the function of the exigence and the radical need for being. But this openness to and fundamental need for being is not to be thought of as a mere passive condition of emptiness; it is rather a dynamic

[14] *MB*, p. 34.
[15] *PE*, p. 3.

principle within being which drives toward richer participation in Being itself.

Marcel tells philosophers to "get rid" of that false interpretation which identifies metaphysical hunger for being with some sort of extraordinary curiosity about being. For Marcel the metaphysical need for being is a radical, constitutive appetite of man's nature; it is the dynamic orientation and thrust of man's whole being toward higher, toward the plenitude of being. [16] For being is expectation fulfilled. And the activity of man's being must be exercised to the full in ascendence toward the transcendent, if he is to mature in a world of fulness. [17]

Thus whoever affirms or denies being does so in relation to this dynamic need for fulness. There must be being, and I desire to participate in it; to experience a thing as being is to experience it as plenitude; being is fulfilment; it is a principle of inexhaustibility.

This need for fulness which is seated in the person, in me, implies more than something which is *wanted;* it signifies something which is *demanded.* When Marcel says that being is fulfilment, he is not considering fulfilment on its own or as something in itself, but as what "is involved in the life of a consciousness which finds fulfilment something to satisfy a profound requirement." [18] For fulfilment is experienced as being seated in the spiritual core of man's being whenever man lives in the domain of personal and interpersonal intersubjectivity. This radical experience explains why ontology demands, if it is to investigate the whole richness of human reality, the inclusion of the subjective, of the intersubjective, dimension of being and its complementary addition to that of objective knowledge. Do we not have here a mysterious articulation and dovetailing of being and value? [19]

Moreover, the yearning for fuller being is not experienced as a downward movement, nor merely as a horizontal surge; it

[16] *MJ*, p. 288.
[17] *Ibid.*, p. 206.
[18] *MB* (II), p. 51.
[19] *Ibid.*, p. 52.

is, above all, a soaring above and beyond toward the principle of plenitude. In other words, the exigence for being coincides with the demand for a vertically-upward transcendence. To be is to participate in what is eternal. Marcel clings to the traditional antithesis between immanent and transcendent of the scholastic philosophers and theologians. He distinguishes, however, between a horizontal and a vertical "going beyond," and stresses the point that the latter is more truly the essence of transcendence. [20]

Although all reality has a certain characteristic aspect of transcendence, the idea of transcendence is fundamental to the general human condition. And paradoxical as it may seem, transcendence is grasped in and through intimately-lived experience, which experience, Marcel is forever insisting, is not an object, not something flung in my way, not something placed before me or in my path. [21]

For I am in my experience and much of my experience testifies to my need for transcendence. Certain dissatisfactions, restlessness of heart, yearnings for sanctity and for truly creative work, callings to fulfill high vocations constantly proclaim that I am, by my very existence, "caught up within the poles of transcendence." [22]

Further reflection on this intimately-lived experience brings Marcel to the following conclusions. Transcendence can never mean "transcending experience." Quite the contrary. If there were no experience of the need for transcendence, then this need could never be described, discussed or even mentioned. The very word would have no meaning. That it does have meaning brings out clearly that we do experience this exigence. Therefore, our need for transcendence can never be interpreted as a need to go above and beyond experience. For above and beyond experience, there is simply nothing in and for man. [23]

[20] *MB* (I), p. 49.
[21] *Ibid.*, p. 57.
[22] *Ibid.*, p. 55.
[23] *Ibid.*, pp. 57, 59.

Marcel's social philosophy can thus be seen to be founded on his own agonizing experience of the limitations of the isolated individual, of the spiritual starvation that even tempts such a lonely individual to suicide, but, above all, on the basic hunger and drive that every man has for self-transcendence toward fuller being, toward communion, toward the Absolute Thou. Marcel has also witnessed this tortuous groping for peaceful communion and reunion in the feelings, emotions, tragic aspirations and volitions of two generations of men who have been caught up in the social maelstrom of modern times. This intensely felt intuition that has permeated his whole being and that arises from the heart of human experience he has made the living center of his concrete thought.

He looked for "the elements of pure mysticism in an examination of the universal conditions of thought." Idealism failed him because it isolated him and locked him up within himself. The way of logic begot a dull, static world in a silent, logical universe. Rationalism begot deracinated, heartless men. Subjective feeling, spiritual experiences, subnormal psychology made "mincemeat" of his idealistic dialectic. "Ontological communion" then became the living center of his thought; existence, participation emerged superior to disintegrating objectivity, for existence sustained immediacy in all its dynamic and variegated fulness. [24]

This intuition states that all created being is simultaneously both participation in being and appetitive drive toward deeper enrichment in transcendent degrees of being. All being is oriented toward ontological communion. All being is insufficient and frustrated if isolated and self-enclosed from communion with other being. This is especially true of man the self-conscious being, who eminently embodies within himself the ontological demands for fulfilment, for transcendence, for communal plenitude, yet who is free and thus dangerously capable of shutting

---

[24] Roger TROISFONTAINES, S. J., *Existentialism and Christian Thought*, trans. Martin Jarrett-Kerr, C. R. (London: Adam & Charles Black, 1949), p. 17.

himself off from any inspirations and hopes for intersubjective participation in transcendent being through communion with the universe, with his fellowmen and with God.

The experience of individual beings only mollifies but does not sate man's yearning for participation in the plenitude of being. Yet the more man descends into intersubjective communion, the more he ascends into transcendence. By reading the transcendent aspects of lived experience and plunging into the depths of all that is actual, Marcel succeeds in mining and refining something of the precious mystery of being that is hidden in the complexity of being. His philosophical refinements assure us of much that is meaningful in being and yet insist that, despite perennial excursions into the profundities of being, being will always remain full of mystery. The principle of transcendence reveals its inexhaustibility, but it also reveals the dynamic openness, the outward and upward surge, the intersubjective sociality of being.

From these revelations certain truths about the whole of reality can be formulated. Nothing exists in ontological isolation or solitude, but rather everything exists in a family of intersubjective relationships. No created being is totally autonomous; no created being is its own, but is actively related to the Plenitude of Being. This is especially true of man, of whom St. Paul says: "You are not your own." [25] And this same Apostle, in his "philosophy of salvation," corroborates with superior light from Revelation, the priority of participation in which all beings stand and hold together. His mystical and poetical vision reveals that the ontological communion in which the universe was founded and which was disrupted by the fall of man will be regained, nay more, will be assumed into a theological communion of divine glorification in the "new heaven and the new earth."

> For the eager longing of creation awaits the revelation of the sons of God.... Because creation itself will be delivered from its slavery to corruption into the freedom of the glory of the sons of God.

[25] Rom. 8:19,21,23.

...but we ourselves also...groan within ourselves, waiting for the adoption as sons, the redemption of our body. [26]

Marcel thus sees man not as narrowly autonomous but as open to communion with every being. Man is oriented by nature not toward the chaos of social atomism nor toward the depersonalized universalism of Marxist communism. For Marcel too, the human person is simultaneously both autonomous and social. Both these characteristics indicate the primordial and rudimentary metaphysical bonds that bind man to his own being and to the community of all beings.

Man's autonomous dimension of being reveals the depths of his sacred dignity as an *imago Dei* who is called to a responsible participation in freedom that is exercised in an openness and disposability with respect to his fellowmen and God. His social dimension is realized in the attainment of a universality wherein he freely enters and embraces with love every member of the human and divine communities without exception.

The whole of reality for Marcel will be seen to consist not in the mechanized unity of the additive and integral parts of a meaningless universe. Wholeness consists rather in spiritual and polyphonic fulness. It is harmoniously orchestrated by each being's intersubjective participation and advancement in the transcendent symphony of Being and Love. The feeling, thinking, willing man in his existential situation, with all his contingency and anxious ambiguity—this human person called I and expectantly open to the other— is the point of departure, *par excellence*, for Marcel's philosophy of communion.

---

[26] I Cor. 6:19.

CHAPTER III

Metaphysical Roots of Communion

The ontological theme that lies at the heart of all lived experience and that fascinates Marcel is: To be means to participate. *Esse est co-esse.* And the clearest captivating expression of this metaphysical melody is sounded in the family of human persons. A man of communion himself and a champion of the human person, Marcel protests and fights against the "reification" of the human person. Man is not a machine and it is a pitiless sacrilege to treat the *imago Dei* merely as a *factum*.

For man is definitely above a *factum;* to be sure he is a *creatum*, but his unique substantial character locates his metaphysical center of gravity in a *genitum* whose *causa exemplaris* is the One, True, Personal God. The ontological taproot of man's being consists in his status of being a subject, that is, a free, conscious being, a being who is, unlike the dormant things around him, sensitively and intellectually awake. [1]

But to be a subject, to be a person is to be "with."

Perhaps the essential property and quality of man is, in a very real sense, to bear witness. Yet so many people, particularly in overcrowded cities, suffer from a fearful seclusion. Cut off from the divine, thrown back upon themselves, they experience the agony of metaphysical emptiness. Their lives are characterized by a spirit of continual boredom which Marcel calls the antithesis of Love. The very awareness of this bitter isolation, acting as a negative symptom, points up Marcel's

[1] Alice JOURDAIN, *op. cit.*, p. 28.

magnificent insight on the authentic nature of man: men are made
for communion.

From the moment man enters the field of the existential—
the realm of communication and participation as opposed to
the objective realm of being which is unconcerned about his
aspirations and purposes—from that moment man grows through
a dialogue of love and commitment, through self-donations
that transcend himself. Crowds are not needed for participation.
Far from it. Some of the most lonely souls in the world are
the celebrities who are mobbed wherever they go. Enthusiastic
contact with ephemeral masses is not authentically human.
Moreover, Marcel's plays keep revealing the startling lone-
someness of married people who, it would seem, should be
safely guarded at the family hearth against the sorrow of solitude. [2]
" It is terrifying how alone I can feel" [3] . . . . "One is alone." [4]

To be sure, man is born a person, but he may not
comfortably remain forever in the fetal stages of being a person.
To be "with" is an exalted dimension of being; it is inextricably
bound up with the dynamic drive for transcendence. It aims
not merely at enrichment in being, but far more at enrichment
in the superabundance of personal being. To be "with" involves
the human person in a self-commitment to a dialogue with the
animate and inanimate universe in the search for truth and
to a mutual self-donation with his fellowmen for the attainment
of the community of love.

But in order to actualize this self-commitment and to rejoice
in this self-donation, man must cease reducing himself, as subject,
to an abstract universal, and his world, as object, to a collection
of generalizations. He must cease merely conceptualizing.
To be "with" is a conquest and calls for retracing one's steps
through the logical mediation of abstract thought back to the

[2] *Ibid.*, p. 27.
[3] Gabriel MARCEL, "L'Emissaire," *Vers un autre royaume* (Paris:
Plon, 1949), p. 16.
[4] Gabriel MARCEL, "La Chapelle Ardente," *Trois pièces* (Paris: Plon,
1931), p. 223.

ontological plenitude and unity of concrete being. To be a subject, a person, is not a fact or a point of departure, but an achievement and a final goal.

Être sujet n'est pas un fait, ou un point de départ, mais une conquête et un but. [5]

The movement of being is not one of withdrawal nor of isolation, but one of participation and intersubjective communion. The movement of philosophic thought, if it is to reflect reality faithfully, must revolve upon the poles of incarnation and invocation that constitute the central axis for the metaphysical fulfilment and the spiritual maturation of the entire universe of being.

It belongs to the very essence of the self to be founded and constituted by participation. Man is embedded in his integral, experienced, human milieu. His first conscious discovery of himself is the awareness of his body, not as a disparate object known and possessed, but as that which is experienced as setting him down within existence and which makes of this first moment of existence the infallible exclamation: "Here I am! What luck!" [6]

Thus the only self I am aware of is the self that is participating in lived experience. The existential roots of my being are grounded in my experience of incarnation in my body which is a central given.

What Marcel means by "self" is brought out by Roberts in his treatment of the bond that exists between Existentialism and religion. He sees that the category of incarnation alone does justice to the meaning in which my body is not an object but a subject. The category of incarnation applies solely to a being possessing its subject-hood as fundamentaly rooted in a body. To think of my body on the analogy of subhuman physical events is to think not of my body as it is but of some body, any body as a thing, object, instrument. Whereas this body is a person, not just any person. It is I. [7]

---

[5] *RI*, p. 236.
[6] *MB* (I), p. 111.
[7] David E. ROBERTS, *Existentialism and Religious Belief* (New York: Oxford, A Galaxy Book, 1959), p. 301.

But this I who am my body—not in a materialistic identity of spirit and matter, but as one existential subject that enjoys in its unity of self and body a direct linkage not only with objective reality, but, above all, with "Being which is ulterior to any gap between subject and object" [8]—this I is non-detachable from the world of beings. To induce duality and disparateness between the self and its universe of lived experience is to isolate the self, to conceptualize the self, to introduce the rupture of discontinuity between the self and all other objects in the world. My experiences and even my existence can then be considered as detached realities looking around for a subject. Whereas in reality Marcel tells us that: "Existence and the thing that exists obviously cannot be dissociated." [9]

For there is an indissoluble bond between my existence and me, the existent subject. And my "I"— body-soul unity as subject—is so bound up and interrelated with the whole of the universe that Marcel can say that "I exist" tends to merge with "the universe exists." [10] In fact there is a sense in which the more exclusively I exist, the less I really exist. The more I escape the prison of ego-centricism, the more I actually participate in the plenitude of being, that is, the more I actually exist. [11] For the more my existence expands to welcome and admit others, the narrower becomes the gap that separates my existence from being; the more, in other words, I am. [12]

The "I" is thus engaged in a context greater than itself. When Marcel sets himself to philosophize *sub specie aeterni* and devotes himself to understanding his life's experiences, he comes upon a strange and wonderful experience—namely the greater the perception he attains of his concrete experience, the more effective is his understanding of others. A metaphysics of intersubjectivity becomes the ground upon which he bases all his philosophic inquiries. His position in philosophizing is radically anti-

[8] *Ibid.*, p. 301.
[9] *MJ*, p. 321.
[10] *Ibid.*, p. 323.
[11] *MB* (II), p. 38.
[12] *Ibid.*, p. 37.

Cartesian. True, we can say that Marcel addresses himself to a metaphysic of being. But his approach is more than just this. It is, in his own words, "a metaphysic of *we are* as opposed to a metaphysic of *I think*." [13]

But Marcel then asks himself: "Can we admit that we have reached a point where we can identify being with intersubjectivity? Can we say that being is intersubjectivity?" [14] The full answer seems to be lost in the mysterious depths of being, although Marcel asserts that it seems to him impossible to agree to this proposition, if it is taken literally. Yet he can assert with confidence that the more the ego attempts to establish and assert itself in a central, autocratic posture in the management of its consciousness, the more the compactness and richness of its being is diluted. On the other hand, the more the ego is conscious of being one among, with, for an infinity of others with which dynamic relationships are mutually maintained, the more the ego advances in recapturing the experience of its own abundant being. [15]

Whence, then, arises my assurance of my incarnate self as a global assurance? How is it that this assurance extends to my whole situation, that it is the existential indubitable?

Marcel answers that the infallible assurance we have of our own personal existence is founded on the experience we have of the indissoluble unity between our existence and ourselves as the existent subject. The pure immediacy expresssed by the "I exist" arises from the fact that my incarnation in my body—which is the rock-bottom of my being and actual self—has brought me and continually brings me into direct physical contact with existence in all its nakedness. [16] To make this point Marcel appeals to intimately lived experience and then turns etymologist in his analysis.

Take the image of the small child. He comes running up to us, eyes shining, face smiling, his whole being seeming to

[13] *MB* (II), p. 10.
[14] *Ibid.*, p. 18.
[15] *Ibid.*, pp. 18-19.
[16] *MB* (I), pp. 111-12.

shout: "Here I am! What luck!" To say that I exist in such a situation is to glimpse, more or less obscurely, that my being is present not only to my own awareness but that it is a being manifest to others. It would probably be more accurate to say "I am manifest" than "I exist." For etymologically the Latin prefix *ex*—meaning out, outwards, out from—in "exist" reveals a truth of the greatest importance. I exist is as much as to say: "I have something to make myself known and recognized both by others and by myself, even if I wear borrowed plumes." [17]

But eventually the philosopher in Marcel cannot be satisfied by the etymological analysis and he plumbs the depths of this lived assurance in the "I exist" and comes up with this deeper analysis.

My assurance of my existence has a global character about it. I receive as a *given*, beyond all possible doubt, the confused and global experience of the world as it is existent. This assurance appears to be *constitutive* of every knowing *subject*. It is not something *added to* or *provided for* a subject already in existence. Quite the contrary, without this experience of the global assurance, a subject ceases to be a subject, ceases to be anything and seems to be reduced to a logical shadow of itself. [18]

Infra-rational beings, far from existing as the logical shadows to which Idealists have reduced them, are actually like man, though in a far lesser degree, of course. Like man, beings enjoy rich density and concreteness; like man, objective beings are open and receptive to the action of other beings. Moreover, in their own analogous and diminished way, they ape man's varied and intensive transubjective acts of communion with all other beings. Marcel never tires of stressing the communal aspects of all reality.

Marcel lays much stress upon intersubjectivity because he wishes to emphasize a genuine metaphysical finding of his. It is that there is a presence of an underlying reality that he feels, that this felt presence is of a community of being which is deeply

[17] *Ibid.*, pp. 111-12.
[18] *MJ*, pp. 322-23.

rooted in ontology. Remove the presence of this underlying reality and you cut the roots of the ontological community of being. Take away this radical cohesiveness and human relations become unintelligible, mythical, even impractical. [19]

The ontological root that founds all being in communion and in community is, for Marcel, that underlying reality whose presence is felt and immediately known. And that reality is made manifest to me in my incarnational existence of I, my actual participation in being and my existential and ontological appetite for further, richer, superabundant participation in transcendent Being. To be sure, I enjoy an exclamatory awareness of my initial degree of this participation, but I may never be content with the gift-reception of being and must strive, in my drive for transcendence, to open myself with all that I am and have to the other, by the giving of hospitality to all other beings through creative acts of communion.

Blackham sees Marcel's thought as achieving the best in life through the resolution of the tensions existing between irresponsive sentiments and the will for creative activity. What is Marcel's program for resolving these tensions? It is as follows: Having is not eliminated but assimilated to being; one and the other are not opposed but conjoined as I and thou; science does not rebel but integrates with philosophy; autonomy and self-sufficiency is transcended in the liberty of participation; my body and the world enlarging and multiplying its powers are the places where I bear witness to Being, through fidelity, hope, love and an inexhaustible availability. [20]

Marcel, speaking of "the presence of an underlying reality that is felt, of a community which is deeply rooted in ontology," admits that the very nature of this presence, of this community is mysterious and can only be glimpsed. In what he calls his "metaphysics of hospitality" he insists that in this world of dramatic tragedy there ought to grow up between the knower and the known, between the ill and the well, between the secure

[19] MB (II), p. 19.
[20] H. J. BLACKHAM, Six Existentialist Thinkers (London: Routledge & Kegan Paul, 1951), p. 73.

and the unprotected a bond of loving respect for the sacredness
that lies at the heart of all reality. [21] This bond of love and
respect, that is meant to unite the precious and the precarious,
touches something that is essential in all being, and in the life
of man, something that is of absolute not of relative importance. [22]

There is no doubt in Marcel's mind that an organic
connection exists between presence and mystery, and to illustrate
his conviction that every presence is mysterious Marcel presents
a striking example.

There is a mysterious atmosphere that pervades the
situation where someone is sleeping quietly in one's presence.
This mysterious milieu is heightened with a reverential awe
when the sleeping person is a child. From the point of view
of energetic activity such as rising, running, grasping things,
the sleeping child is physically relaxed, completely unprotected
and *in the power* of the spectator. The spectator is physically
able to do what it pleases with and to the child. But from the
point of view of mystery and presence, the child's very
helplessness, its very vulnerability are its greatest guarantees of
loving protection. To the person who is present to this child
in slumber, the child is sacred. Only a sheer barbarism would
violate this sacredness. This sacredness of the unprotected lies
at the roots of what Marcel calls "a metaphysics of hospitality."
All great civilizations, all humane peoples have held the guest
in the highest regard as being the more to be honored and
protected, the more feeble and defenseless he was. [23]

Is it any wonder, then, that Marcel, in his examination of
presence, concerns himself with all being? As a dramatist he
has charged himself with being, both singular and plural; indeed,
he transcends the opposition between singular and plural.

Alive, complex, obscure, immersed in the realities of daily
living, Marcel's characters never present nor represent a pure
idea nor an abstract scheme. Virtues and faults coexist together
in them as they do in real, living men. Tragedy of thought

[21] *MB* (I), 266-67.
[22] *Ibid.*, p. 257.
[23] *Ibid.*, pp. 266-67.

passes quickly into tragedy of life, rising from the conflicts of man with his neighbor and with himself.

Theatre is for Marcel an art of communication, of communion. [24] A true tragedy is not an entertaining pastime. Marcel chooses to espouse the aims and visions of his characters, and not simply as abstract representations, but as concrete realities rooted in the very style of their beings. Marcel demands of his audience that each member adjust his plan of life to viewing reality with a free, unclouded view. To do this each play-goer must break down barriers that separate him from his own true being and thus, perforce, from other souls whom he really never gets to know because of his solipsistic imprisonment. Alienated man must reconquer himself; he must progress to that point where he willingly engages in a living exchange with others; he must foster and establish between himself and others the method of participation which the theatre, modeled upon authentic living, shows forth and attempts to inject once again into its audiences. This method, Marcel is convinced, is a necessary propaedeutic for the establishment of true charity. Marcel can say of his dramatic work:

> My theatre is the theatre of the soul in exile, of the soul which is suffering from a famine of communion with itself and with others. Interior illusion and self-deception play a very important role in it. [25]

The soul in exile is for Marcel the alienated soul, the person who has become a stranger to himself. Everywhere the dramatic thread of the plays is the same, only it shows up in an infinite variety of forms and in an infinite diversity of circumstances. Marcel gladly accepts, as a heading to his own dramatic works, the profound comment of the great dramatist Gerhart Hauptmann:

> Drama is one of the many attempts made by the human mind to create a cosmos from chaos, attempts which begin in early childhood and continue throughout life. [26]

---

[24] R. TROISFONTAINES, *De l'existence à l'être,* I, p. 33.
[25] *Ibid.,* p. 35.
[26] Gabriel MARCEL, *Three Plays,* p. 13.

The theme that dominates Marcel's plays is expressed as an ardent wish by Claude Lemoyne in the last line of "A Man of God."

Être connu tel qu'on est—To be known as one is... [27]

The central theme in nearly all his plays, indeed, in nearly all his work, is a living relationship as seen at work in particular situations. [28] It is quite normal for his drama to present situations that put obstacles in the way of communion, that strike discord where there was harmony and that turn joy into sorrow. For Marcel who is so delicate, sensitive and sincere, theatre reaches its heights when duplicity, harshness, pride, daily banality, treason or false fidelity fight against interpersonal communion and the limpidity of interior guilelessness. Whence the shocking portrayal—so true to life—of a thousand forms of egotism, of disappointments in love, of sorrowful misunderstandings which in some of the dramas scarcely enkindle a faint glimmer of any resurrection. However, in all these works, the most despairing sentiment of solicitude serves as a springboard to the highest hope.

Marcel acknowledges the harmonious intercourse between being and its existential situation that is vividly portrayed in Georges Bernanos' *Sous le Soleil de Satan*. What greatly impresses Marcel, above all, in the book of Bernanos is that the author himself exists, not after the manner of an object of art which tourists can circle, view, study and catalogue. The author, rather, exists as a being who is bound by a thousand undiscernible currents to the whole universe which flows back upon him to nourish and strengthen him. [29]

Marcel the metaphysician, who is constantly and anxiously bent over and absorbed in the mystery of being, appears as the guileless child entranced with all the wonders about him, his vision undimmed nor distorted by the veil of self-love. He looks out honestly and expectantly upon a community of being always fresh, always new, always coherent, a community of being in

[27] *Ibid.*, p. 114.
[28] *Ibid.*, p. 17.
[29] R. TROISFONTAINES, *op. cit.*, p. 38.

which every creature is unique and enthrallingly sacred. Nothing can be more alien to him than that an attitude of negation should be adopted toward this world of wonders. As a truly wise man, Marcel joyfully sings of his solidarity with every creature.

In more concrete language: *I concern myself with being only in so far as I have a more or less distinct consciousness of the underlying unity which ties me to other beings of whose reality I already have a preliminary notion.* In the light of the ideas which have not yet penetrated to the obscure regions in which we have tried to hack a path for ourselves, I should say of these beings that they are above all my fellow-travelers—my fellow-*creatures*—for once the English language can give us an expression for which there is no exact French equivalent. [30]

[30] *MB* (II), pp. 19-20.

CHAPTER IV

The First Thrusts Toward Community

The ontological seed-bed that nurtures all finite being is the infinitely mysterious and fertile soil of Primal Existence. Though Marcel, to my knowledge, has nowhere expressed this thought exactly this way, it is none the less in harmony with his mind and spirit to say that beings actually exist because Being Itself is externally and lovingly anxious to call forth and care for an innumerable variety of existents. The land of Divinity is more than adequate ground for the presence of concrete beings. But the existential situation is even more marvelous by far than at first it seems. When we recall from Revelation that the Ground of Being is not merely solitary Divinity but the unutterably loving Country of a Triune Community, then the insight that all being is called from a physical union in a natural community up to a spiritual communion in a transcendent community—this insight suffuses the soul of the Christian philosopher with a deep sense of reverence at the incomprehensible heights of the mystery of being.

Thus, though the community of created beings quite naturally reflects the Creator's openness to all creatures at the very outset of their departure on the adventure of existence, yet, in a certain sense, every being remains unique and still has to complete its own initial participation in the Ground of Being by a further mutual participation in the being of the created other.

We are back again to the Pauline "you are not your own." But this time we go beyond the fact of the givenness of our metaphysical existence. Not only are created beings not autonomous in their existence, but they are not even autonomous in many circumstances of their existence. The structure of our world, the structure of the very context of any single being cannot be located exclusively within the concrete being itself. For every single being is *de facto* conditioned by being outside of it; every finite being is situated in a milieu that is not of its own choosing, in specific temporal, topographical, meteorological and thousands of other relationships within the external world that, perforce, sustain it on its arrival and project it on its parabolic journey back to Being Itself. There are no self-centered monads, gateless and windowless, sealed off from participation in physical and psychical communion.

Every being must respond to the requirements of its position in being. Indeed, every being is implicated in the mystery of sociality. This mystery draws in, surrounds, and engulfs each individual. Eventually, in the relatively quiet harbor of community, the all-pervading metaphysical appetency for concrete communion that surges up from the depths of emptiness in every being is paradoxically ever exercised and ever sated in the perfect community of love.

Like being—itself the metaphysical root of communion—the first shoots of community are also given to man. They are facts imposed upon us. No man can choose his own conditions and terms for human existence.

We are not consulted about coming into this world. The time, country, family, social milieu into which we arrive are not subject to our choosing. Not even the physical and psychological structure of our being are initially under our command. A healthy or weak body, an attractive or unattractive countenance, a temperament and character that is pleasant or irascible, these are the first facts of existence that are imposed upon us. And Marcel calls this situation "existence" in the significance of that word which is rooted in the Latin *ex-sistere*, meaning to be outside of. Thus, we are conditioned by what is outside of ourselves. We never become conscious of ourselves except through experience of the outside world; outside lights, movements, surfaces, molecules in the air, vibrations are essential if we are to discover consciousness of our bodies. We are born dynamically related already to a multitude of things and facts in our make-up and in our milieu. Sartre calls this state of affairs "facticity," because these relationships are facts. [1]

I find, then, that I am aware of myself, but of many, many other things besides. My existence is dynamic and tendential, but it is also surrounded by other active and tendential existences. If I would come to terms with reality, I must admit that my existence is not presented with an immense array of ideal, stationary objects, static and neatly arranged objects of knowledge. The true state of affairs is such that my existence is constantly colliding with a kaleidoscopic infinity of moving and surging objects which exercise not only a physical magnetism of attraction and repulsion, but also act as moral obstacles or aids to the maturation of my own being. My own urges within me drive me on to confront both alien and benign forces without.

With equal immediacy I am aware of my active self and likewise of my friendly and inimical situations. Together with alien and amicable forces I exist-in-the-world, ceaselessly seeking the peace that comes only with the attainment of the plenitude of being.

But we must resist and conquer the habit of understanding the word "in" as a purely spatial insertion of being. My world is not a static spatial container, in which I and all others are stationed at certain fixed positions. John Wild, speaking from an existentialist's point of view, presents the true state of affairs.

He tells us that things exist not just out there in the world, as it were a mere sum of realities. Actually they exist "in a field of care or concern." The world is not just a sum of juxtaposed objects. Its order and structure are ontologically prior to the objects themselves. Our first experiences are never of mere things to be stared at, but rather of tools and instruments to be used and enjoyed. "Things are at hand rather than on hand." Things are first to be worked before being fully known. The

[1] R. TROISFONTAINES, S. J., "What is Existentialism?" *Thought*, XXXII, 127 (Winter 1957-1958), p. 523.

typewriter invites typing, the pen writing, the book reading or
study. Things invite action before contemplation. Things are
in or out of place if they fulfill or fail to fulfill some plan or
purpose. They are where they belong if they are where they can
readily be used. [2]

And yet Marcel refuses to admit that man is merely a Self
versus his situation. Other men do not occupy a spot out there
before me like mere physical objects. Of course, man finds
himself in place, but he also prepares new places, new situations
for himself; he participates in neighborhoods he has actively
formed in cooperation with raw nature and real men. Besides
being spatially located man spatializes himself in the projects
he initiates and brings to mature completion; his activities help
to reconstruct the structured world he finds at his birth and with
which he now moves and works. Existential presence is far
richer than mere spatial manifestation; it merges with time and
transcends both time and space as it progresses up the ladder
of participation toward the Absolute Thou. There is a psychic
as well as a physical location, a presence as well as a position;
there is a psychic as well as a physical distance, a distance unable
to be measured in miles or meters. A loved one, physically afar
off at this moment, is actually much closer to me than the man
who is presently speaking to me in such a manner as to remain
quite uncommunicative and coldly reserved. In fact, true
presence, once initiated, tends of its very nature to be timeless,
spaceless and eternal.

According to Marcel existence is emphasized as an absolute
presence. [3] Participation in act, in actuality, constitutes my
existential self which is founded by incarnation. Being is really
present in and around us. Relational structure enters into my
intrinsic being. This root aspect of being has been neglected by
philosophers of the past and there has been an "outrageous
oversimplification... of the relationships which bind me to
myself." [4]

[2] John WILD, *The Challenge of Existentialism* (Bloomington: Indiana
University Press, 1955), p. 75.
[3] *MJ*, p. 331.
[4] J. WILD, *op. cit.*, p. 170.

One of the most serious obstacles to the grasp of the sociality of being is the tendency to reduce the human body to the level of a mere mental object. It is, of course, possible for me to regard my body as an extended object among other objects, yet this certainly does not exhaust the whole mysterious phenomenon of its being and activity. I find that all my activities, even that of thought, are in some sense localized within my body. I can separate myself from all other objects, but my body is always with me and I find myself in grave difficulties when I attempt to conceive myself apart from it. Hence it is incorrect to think of my body as being merely an instrument, and Marcel proceeds to demonstrate the infinite regress that such a view of the body entails.

My body inserts me into the world of real existence. In so far as it is my body and not just any body, another among millions of others, able to be observed and described by anyone, my body cannot be an object for anyone, least of all for me. "I am my body" denies the reality of the gap that is inserted between me and my body whenever I look on my body as an instrument. Unfortunately, it seems inevitable for man to look upon the relationship of himself to his body as an agent-instrument construction. The body is something we use, something we have, therefore, a tool. Perhaps the emphasis on the community of natures between tools and bodies as extended realities explains this thought construct. At any rate, this pure construction leads to insoluble problems. For once we postulate this gap as really existing, we are caught in an infinite regress. The use of tools is an extension of body powers, an extension of the body itself. If the body is also an instrument, its use should also be the prolongation of the powers of some other body. Must the self which uses the body as its own extension be called a body also? If so, who possesses it and what kind of third body's powers is it extending? Marcel avoids this unintelligible regress by never equating the body with something he has. The act of having is spoken of in relation to the body itself. If the body itself is an act of having, by whom is it possessed? Actually the body is not something outside of me, external to me. When

I speak of my body, says Marcel, I speak of myself, expressing, from a position in existence that transcends the instrumental relationship, my incarnate mode of presence to the actual world. [5]

My body, precisely as mine, is present to me primarily as something felt. I am a being of feelings and, as such, my body has absolute relational priority to all I can feel outside my body, i.e., to the external world of being. Sensation cannot be treated, therefore, as something that takes place along instrumentalist lines, nor even as if it proceeded along the lines of the transcription and reception of a message. The reason is that every kind of instrument or apparatus *presupposes* the existence of my body, even as every kind of transmitter-receiver communication *presupposes* the existence of sensation. [6]

Sensation, therefore, is not a translation of something other than itself. Rather, it involves the immediate participation of the subject in the encompassing world from which it is separated by no real frontier. Sensation is one of the early operations that actualizes my incarnation in and with the world. It is, to be more precise, the second important way in which I am made to be, for it actualizes my presence to the world of sensible beings. I, as a dynamically existent Self—what we might call the first degree of my participation in being—am further actualized and enriched in the participation of other beings through sensation. Sensation helps to fill in for me the meaning of "I exist." My original mode and manner of immediately participating in being is my gift of existential transsubjectivity; I am at once in relation to all being, the instant I am. Sensation lifts me to a higher level of participation in being; it advances my original degree of incarnation to a richer, loftier, more self-conscious height of participation. It is here, in my primary operative acts, that it becomes immediately apparent that my human person is a being made for communion.

Thus my body is a co-immediate with the existential world. My Self, in its personal aspect, is seen as a co-immediate of my

[5] *MB* (I), p. 123.
[6] *Ibid.*, p. 133.

being, emerging within and together with the communion entered into and enjoyed in sensation. My body is given to me as presence in the world; my Self is given to me as presence in the original operation of sensation. *Esse est co-esse* is raised to the second power and is seen to be infinitely truer on the higher level of active communion in sensation than it was and is on the original level of spatial openness and the tension of intersubjective relationship among all things.

In effect, then, to be experiencing sensation is quite simply to be living in union with things. When I insist on what specifically makes my body mine I am actually accenting and emphasizing the act of sensation. To be sensing is indissolubly bound up with the fact that this body is my body, and not a "body" among other bodies. No discussion is possible with others who are not simultaneously experiencing my fatigue, my pain, my sorrow, joy, etc. When others say that they are undergoing the same sensations as I, they are actually experiencing these sensations within their own personal situations and their own unique contexts, and hence these sensations are not the same, for they are solely their own sensations.

There is in my body something that escapes every possible verification and every technical try at its conquest: by death, accident, etc. The secret strength of the existential position— namely the absolute mediation of my body—is, in effect, also the ultimate condition for all objectivity. Without incarnation, without the unseen substructures of an experience which I cannot completely convey nor communicate to others, even the dialectical and objective constructure would not be possible. In every possible hypothesis, the world does not exist *for me* unless I am able to act upon it, in which case, nevertheless, I constrain things to take me into their consideration. Sometimes the object is, by definition, thought of as not taking me into its consideration. Yet I do not act as a physical and bodily agent except through my body which is, in a certain fashion, homogeneous with all things. Nay more, I only act in so far as I am in participation with my body which then succeeds in escaping objectification. Thus the body itself accepts the I into its grateful embrace. This very conjunctive image itself, for example, directly entails a bodily modification. In the very degree in which the body does not take me into its consideration, it appears to me as not being *my* body. Thus, although I can think of the body as an instrument placed between me and all other objects, still it is metaphysically contradictory to treat the body in this way. I cannot legitimately cut the roots that ground objectivity in the soil of the purely sensed existence. [7]

Feeling is not an act of receiving; it is a further participation in being in an immediate way. The more intimately personal my living is, the more it becomes impossible for me to dissociate my immediate participations through feeling from their appearances of mediation and communication. This explains the metaphysically unintelligible elements in sensation. Thought is mediation in being; feeling is unthinkable; it is an indubitable given.

Besides being my body, there is a real sense in which I am my customary environment. Marcel speaks of the "laceration," the division from oneself that accompanies exile from one's home. Can I say, however, that I am more essentially my body than I am my habitual milieu? If I am not, then death or separation from my body can only be a "supreme exile," not a *reductio ad nihilum*. Truly, our experience is that we do literally *belong to* countries, towns, homes. And when we are uprooted violently or otherwise, we feel as if *adhesions* are snapped; the resulting laceration is an agonizing experience. [8]

But how are adhesions originally formed? It is in his inimitable descriptions and analyses of the most elemental human experiences that Gabriel Marcel contributes startling and inspiring insights into the first shoots of human community and communication. Surely, if sanctity is said to be attained by man through his efforts *adhaerere Deo*, may not sanity likewise be said to be attained by man via his efforts *adhaerere rebus et hominibus?*

[7] R. TROISFONTAINES, *De l'existence...*, I, p. 184.
[8] *Ibid.*, pp. 258-259.

Marcel often enough warns that a steady retreat from one's situation tends to erase even the subject-hood of the one experiencing the situation, for without an intersubjective commerce with one's existential surroundings, the subject, who is originally founded and grounded as *this* dynamic person in these dynamic circumstances, gradually breaks the existential ties that sharply delineate him as this unique person and, ceasing to exist as himself, he inevitably evanesces into a rootless shadow of himself. The displaced person is too often a tragically diminished person.

But we do not begin life by retreating from reality. The normal child is welcomed into a family that begot it in love and has been eagerly awaiting and preparing for its arrival. The child in turn reaches out almost frantically to embrace every member of the family and every object of the household. Marcel proceeds to contemplate a child's wide-eyed openness and charming acceptance of the world of beings. Within the intersubjective radiance there found, Marcel tells us, man can discover something of the rich mystery of presence. Presence is that mystery of personal immediacy that constitutes the main spiritual stem of society. When presence is felt, recognized and mutually cultivated, it develops as the sturdy trunk in the tree of community life. This trunk produces, via the innumerable interlocking and vital branches it forms and feeds, the rich foliage, flowers and fruits of a vigorously healthy intersubjective life of communion. Marcel presents the fascinating spirit of the child which excludes, ostracizes and excommunicates no being, but welcomes everything.

A child runs up to its mother with a handful of flowers freshly gathered from the meadow just for her. "Look, I picked these." Voice and gesture are triumphant in pointing out the unique doer of this deed. Surely the child offers himself as worthy of admiration and love. I who am before you, with you here, picked these flowers. Not Nanny, not my brother or sister. I and no one else picked these for you. The child spotlights himself, comes upstage for special and exclusive applause. The mother is called upon to be totally present to the child who is totally present to the mother. The child's presence excludes all others, none of whom had a hand in this wonderful deed. The mother must be present as a witness to this deed of flower-giving and exclude all other distractions, for these flowers are solely for her. The delighted acceptance of these flowers is the mutual acceptance and presence of each other by mother and child. [9]

The "I" of the child, considered as a magnetic spiritual headquarters, cannot be reduced to any specified part of the child—not body, brain, soul; the "I" is rather a total, a worldwide presence which gains a growing degree of glory and self-confidence by putting itself forward with the beautiful bouquet of flowers it donates to the other—the thou—together with itself. The bouquet and the child are a whole, a magnificent one. And the "thou" is called upon, appealed to as a qualified witness, to wonder and rejoice at the magnificent whole that is in the act of donating itself. The act which establishes the self of the child is the act by which the child attracts the attention of others so that they may praise—perhaps even scold—but at all events, notice and enter into communion with the child. In every production of one's self, Marcel tells us, "the 'I' is seen as a global and indefinable presence," [10] possessing something which it wants to share or withhold in the same manner and degree in which it freely determines to share or withhold itself. And to make this notion of presence clear, Marcel attempts to define it.

Presence in the world is by spatiality but for communion. To be alive is to be open to reality with which I must enter into some sort of commerce. [11] Thus, presence denotes something far more comprehensive and real than just being there. Objects, therefore, are never strictly speaking present. They are there but have no experiences. And presence depends on irreducible, vague experiences, on the sense of existing, of being in the world. Only human beings have this consciousness of existing.

[9] *HV*, p. 13.
[10] *Ibid.*, p. 15.
[11] Kenneth T. GALLAGHER, *The Philosophy of Gabriel Marcel* (New York: Fordham University Press, 1962), p. 22.

It is linked up almost from the beginning with the urge to stand forth and be recognized by another person, a witness, a helper, a rival, even an adversary, by anyone, for someone is needed to help man integrate himself consciously. The bond of communion and presence by which I give myself to others returns me to myself an integrated, conscious person. I really exist not in private but in transsubjective experiences. [12]

The "I," therefore, is in no way an isolated reality: nor is it an essence of a person that is closed and circumscribed by a sum total of characteristics. It is definitely more than this, or rather, infinitely beyond this because the "I" is always open to the infinite "thou." Strictly speaking, the "I" cannot be adequately characterized. As a matter of mysterious fact, the "I" is in itself uncharacterizable. For it should be obvious to the alert philosopher that any consideration of a human person as a sort of mechanism outside of his own I, with which he can tinker and experiment in the hope of finding and cataloguing the secret springs of its being and activity, will only lead to totally exterior data about the person of man, data which, in a way, are a very denial of man's real being because they "degrade him effectively." [13] The being thus characterized and catalogued is not an "I" but a depersonalized apparatus.

To reduce man, the "I," to a machine is to reduce the person to a segment of space and to mount an attack on man's "highly sensitive and spiritual enclosure" which dynamically seals him as an *imago Dei* who is on the move toward transcendent communion. [14] Again Marcel asserts that the "I" may not be regarded as "an atom caught up in a whirlwind" or "a mere statistical unit" or "an anonymous entity," because all these attitudes misuse man as a means to an end and impose on him a demotion from the status of spiritual subject-hood in presence to a condition of physical imprisonment in insular objectification. [15]

[12] *HV*, p. 15.
[13] *Ibid.*, p. 23.
[14] *Ibid.*, p. 16.
[15] *Ibid.*, p. 20.

Somehow I am present to being and being is present to me in a sense of plenitude that includes and encloses my being. Speaking as one who happily travels in the Platonic and Augustinian traditions of philosophy, Marcel seems to be obsessed by the ontological memory of being; he speaks as if he is haunted by the memory and the persistent, all-pervading presence of being. The inexhaustible concrete appeals to his affirmation of the presence of being. This side of his philosophy which is, perhaps, its most fundamental cornerstone—more fundamental even than the neo-Socratic aspect of his thought—is his primitive assurance of the presence of being, which is, for him, absolute.

Thus presence, far from being akin to the inertia of static conformism, entails an energetic and prolonged assault on the forces of inner disintegration and chaotic dissipation. For Marcel, presence is not merely an *idea*, but rather, presence as presence is unconfined; it transcends the diminished limits of the logical order; as a matter of fact it transcends the frontiers and even the vicissitudes of time and space; it exceeds its object on every side, like being itself; for true presence is involved in the mystery of being. True presence corresponds to a certain kind of hold which being has upon us. A presence is a concrete reality; it is a kind of influx of being; human persons will have to make it their business to maintain themselves in a state of active permeability to this influx. Nor must this influx be considered as a mere accretion of more being and more strength, for this would reduce the mystery of person to a problem in physics, whereas it is in reality a mystery that lies in the area of the metaphysics. [16] Marcel elaborates on presence thus:

> Whenever a being is present to me, I cannot treat that being as a mere object, placed out there in front of me. The reason is that a relationship has grown up between us which transcends any spectator's awareness of the other. The person is not only before me; he is within me; indeed, these categories *before* and *in* are left behind; they are now meaningless for this relationship. Perhaps the word

[16] *PE*, pp. 22-25.

"influx," purified of its physical and spatial connotations, can convey better the degree of interior accretion of being from within that the creation of effective presence begets. [17]

And presence is effective as soon as the "I" assumes responsibility both for the "I" itself and for everyone else. Presence is effective as soon as the "I" faces up to its obligations, as soon as the "I" holds itself accountable for what the "I" does and for what the "I" says. To whom is presence accountable? Presence becomes effective when the "I" holds itself conjointly accountable to itself and to everyone else. And this conjunctive responsibility is precisely characteristic of an engagement of the person. This is the distinguishing mark of a true person.

Marcel indicates how a person establishes himself. The assumption of responsibility for one's own behavior distinguishes the real human being from the dreamer. Dreamers reserve to themselves the power of modifying their dreams according to their whims. They are blithely unconcerned about the ramifications of such arbitrary modifications on the world of others. But a person who really believes in and is concerned about the existence of others, develops his own personality in a mature manner by allowing his belief and concern to influence his conduct. He realizes and acknowledges the existence of others for themselves and not only at those times when their existences conveniently or inconveniently intersect with his own. [18]

Marcel warns us not to fall into the temptation of thinking that presence can be only that of an object. This would be to drain presence of its mystery and to reduce it to the level of a problem. Effective presence raises its voice against this objective interpretation of itself and, in a spirit of ardent fidelity, speaks thus: "Even if I cannot see you, if I cannot touch you, I feel that you are with me; it would be a denial of you not to be assured of this." [19] "You—with me!" Carefully notice these words. "Behold," Marcel tells us, "a metaphysical value which can be

[17] *Ibid.*, p. 24.
[18] *HV*, p. 22.
[19] *PE*, p. 25.

reduced neither to a relationship of inherence, nor of immanence, nor to a relationship of exteriority. Presence is the very essence of genuine *co-esse*, the very heart of genuine intimacy." [20]

Is it possible to explain why some people reveal themselves as "present," who always seem to be at our disposal in any trouble or need, while others, despite a large measure of good will, never succeed in communicating to us this feeling of presence? Here is an undeniable fact and a puzzling mystery of lived experience. It forces us to admit that presence cannot be proved nor demonstrated. Like existence itself, presence reveals itself immediately in an exclamatory awareness at the action of its ardent welcome; presence is revealed unmistakably, immediately in a look, a smile, an intonation, a handshake.

It is through his quiet, meditative scrutinies into the mystery of presence and the value of genuine intimacy that Marcel opens up the new shining realm of what he calls "total spiritual availability" *(disponibilité)*. [21] To understand this characteristic of the human person, Marcel first warns us that the gift of personality possessed by each "I" cannot be strictly said to be a good in itself, nor even an element of goodness. For the truth about personality is much fuller, namely that the personality controls the existence of a world where is there good and evil. For example, take the person who remains shut-up within himself, who is the prisoner of his own feelings, of his own covetous desires, of his own dull anxiety that feeds upon himself, is he not beyond the reach of evil as well as of good? Has he not literally as yet not awakened to the presence of being? Is he not ruled by a sort of vague fascination which is localized in objects arousing sometimes desire, sometimes terror? Can such poor beings be directly judged as good or evil, or rather as pathetic blindmen? [22]

Well, whatever the verdict, it is precisely against such sleep-walkers that the spiritual condition of availability is opposed. But Marcel explains this condition in his own illuminating way.

[20] *PE*, p. 25.
[21] *Ibid.*, p. 25.
[22] *HV*, pp. 22-23.

Availability *(disponibilité)* cannot connote emptiness as is indicated in a "rooms for rent" advertisement. Availability is rather the attitude and aptitude for giving oneself, of binding oneself to anything which makes an appeal to us. Availability transforms circumstances into opportunities, into favors. It turns them via active participation into the personal formation and shaping of one's own destiny. Personality is often said to be a vocation. This is true if vocation is seen again as a response to a call. And a vocation must be recognized as a call which paradoxically comes simultaneously from within and from outside. In every vocation we become aware of the intimate connection between what comes from within the called one and from the outside caller. This connection is vital, strengthening; it is severed only at the cost of self-destruction. [23]

Availability also applies to the relationship which binds me to myself. I must perform those acts which will open myself up to myself, which will make me recognize myself and which will preserve me from becoming alienated from the dignity which is proper to my nature—*imago Dei*. This is a real danger and is exemplified in those who, from birth through adulthood, have allowed themselves, quite uncritically, to accept passively and to be ruled by a set of regulations that the circle of their birth and social milieu have rigorously imposed upon them. [24]

Availability is made much clearer when we say that the person who is at my disposal is the one who is able and willing to be with me with the whole of himself when I am in need; while the one who is not at my disposal seems merely to loan himself to me with patent reservations. For the former, I am a presence; for the latter, I am an object. Presence and availability involve warm reciprocity that is coldly excluded from the depersonalized relationship of subject to object or subject to subject-object. [25]

A further penetration into the meaning of availability is that the person who is imbued with this spirit and who lives

[23] *Ibid.*, p. 23.
[24] *Ibid.*, p. 24.
[25] *PE*, p. 26.

in this aura of self-donation is ready for anything and is not cluttered up with himself. He never thinks of his unfortunate brethren nor treats them as so many social cases that need organized help. In his eyes, there are no cases at all, but only the presence of the unique, spiritual and inviolable "thou." Thus he offers sympathy not only with his mind but also with his genuine feelings of compassion. The man that is available and at the disposal of his fellowmen is prepared to consecrate his being to a cause which transcends himself because it is greater than himself. These transcendent causes he makes his own. Far from being a pessimist, he has a perennial hopeful and upward outlook on life because he does not allow himself to be chained to the outward aspects of things and of experiences—to the world of the problematical—but he sees things from within and dwells in the world of mystery. In this world of the spirit, because he is at the disposal of others, because he is inwardly consecrated and dedicated, he is protected against the related evils of despair and suicide—evils that are the final product of that Luciferian *hubris* which moves the captive soul to misuse his freedom as if it were solely his own, and to dispose of his life as if he were the unique source of it.

As opposed to this devotee of *egolatry*, this cultist of the idolatry of the self, the man of availability possesses a feeling and an awareness of all things in a most grateful and unself-conscious way. In fact, he is aware of himself far less as a being than as a desire to rise above everything which he is and is not, above the very actuality in which he is truly involved and presently plays an active part. For the man of availability knows that each passing actuality cannot adequately satisfy him, because it falls short of the ultimate aspiration with which he identifies himself—the attainment of transcendent communion with the Absolute Thou. As Marcel puts it, the man of availability, the man who is at the disposal of others, takes as his motto: "Not *sum* but *sursum*." [26]

The person of presence, of dedicated availability moves in

<hr>

[26] *HV*, p. 26.

the order of creation, of power and of creative fidelity which bears in upon his personality a deeper degree of participation in transcendence. This creative activity must not be confused nor confounded with the mere acts of production that come forth as distinct and disparate from the technical man. What is essential in the creator is the act by which he places himself at the disposal of something which somehow simultaneously depends upon himself and yet transcends him and beckons him up to a higher level of being—the area of creative achievement. This creative process is inherent in the mysterious metaphysical and moral gestation and spiritual personal development of every truly mature man of presence. The man of presence and of availability is convinced of the necessity for incarnation.

Returning to a basic truth, Marcel points out how human personality is and can only be realized in the act of becoming incarnate. The author realizes his personality by incarnation in his book; the artist in his painting; the composer in his composition. Of course, the person must never become petrified into one particular participation or incarnation. For personalities are meant to participate in the inexhaustible fulness of being from which they emanate. To think of the personal and of personality necessarily involves thinking of what transcends both—of the supra-personal reality who presides over all personal, creative initiative because He is both their Alpha and Omega, their *causa exemplaris* and *causa finalis*. [27]

To sum up what has been discussed in this chapter concerning the first shoots of community, we should recall that, for Marcel, the ontological consists basically and centrally in the exclamatory intuition that all being exists in "ontological communion" and is metaphysically and morally called to ever higher degrees of participation in being, even unto transcendental communion in the Absolute. Secondly, my body actually incarnates me in this world of communal being, and sensation dynamically actualizes my presence to the world of sensible beings, thus raising me to a higher degree of participation

[27] *Ibid.*, p. 26.

in communion with beings that are tendentially and concretely
moving toward communion with me.   Thirdly, my existential
situation grounds me, surrounds me in and with being, and
evokes from me a unique response to its unique appeal for my
creative commerce in communion in this portion of the community
of being.   Fourthly, the person of the "I" becomes a true presence
to and with the universe of objects and persons in so far as it
donates itself conjointly with these universes to the person of
the "thou."   This presence is accomplished in the heights of
spiritual communion through the effective availability by which
the "I" offers itself to be at the disposal of the "thou" and of all
reality in an ascending dialectic of creative fidelity that corresponds
to a surging dialectic of hope and culminates in a total dedication
of full love.   Marcel alone can appropriately conclude this chapter
with the following words:

> Person—engagement—community—reality: there we have
> a sort of chain of notions which, to be exact, do not readily
> follow from each other by deduction...but of which the
> union can be grasped by an act of the mind.   It would be
> better not to call this act by the much abused term of
> intuition, but by one which, on the contrary, is too little
> used—that of synopsis, the act by which a group is held
> together under the mind's comprehensive gaze. [28]

[28] *HV*, p. 22.

CHAPTER V

The Risk of Divisiveness

The primitive fact of the community of being is, as we have seen, imposed upon us as a given which antedates every exercise of the free will of man. This universe of being is one vast complex, bewilderingly rich and amazingly confused in its elaborately interrelated and dynamically interconnected commerce in existence and activity. One of the first impacts of this galaxy of beings is to seize the senses of man and to sweep them up into a trance-like fascination at the brilliance of its own variegated beauty. Have you ever noticed a child transfixed and staring at the wondrous newness of its surroundings? Or again, have you ever noticed a child, under different circumstances, besieged and distracted by the countless happenings that evoke in him thousands of sensations? Fr. Roger Troisfontaines admirably uses the existential method to describe what the infant must be going through.

A baby may seem to be passive and doing very little. Actually he is working strenuously, much harder than an adult. He is building up a representation of the world within himself. By so doing he is educating himself, first his senses by catching and analyzing the sounds, colors, movements, odors, distances and pressures that envelop him; then, by synthesizing the same into integral experiences to be remembered for future reference. Thousands, millions of eye movements are needed to localize and focus colored objects. The same amount of incessant attention catches, sorts and stores the endless waves of vibrations striking against the eardrums. Parents, relatives, people in and out of schools, all rush to the child's aid to see to it that he correctly orders his universe. [1]

Slowly, painstakingly the process of analysis in the child—and in the adult for that matter, though in a far more scientific and objectified way—takes the world of being apart and lays out the many elements that go to compose it, much as the apprentice in watch-making takes a watch to pieces and lays out each of its parts for specialized study. Now it is in this hunger for knowledge and its consequent analytical technique for the dismemberment of reality that we come upon the basic risk of divisiveness. And there is no avoiding this basic risk for it is founded on man's essential condition and fundamental activity toward other beings which must be transsubjective, given the very nature of a community of disparate beings. Following, then, inevitably upon sense participation in being, analysis and criticism are necessary first procedures for man's attainment of a scientific knowledge of all he surveys. And this is all to the good, provided we have been forewarned about the fact that reality is risky for the reasons we shall presently consider.

The danger consists in stopping at and settling down in the process of dismemberment and it is a very real danger. Watch a child pull his toys apart to study the pieces. Perhaps you have gone seeking for sections that a child not only severed, but also quite effectively isolated, hid, threw away or even swallowed. You may have even tried to pry a child away from the useless, maimed remainder of his toy world. Chaos and chagrin wreck the harmony of both child and adult world. In the persistent and almost exclusive application of the process of atomizing the coherent harmony of the community of being consists the first degree of the evil of divisiveness. Intoxicated and exhilarated by the new-found power for separating and sifting reality, man, like an irresponsive child, decides to keep dismembered what he ought only to keep distinguished.

The blemish that mars the purely analytical attitude toward being consists in the abnormal desire the knowing subject has

[1] R. Troisfontaines, *Existentialism and Christian Thought*, p. 66.

to "objectify" the world and all reality so that he may be able to enjoy and utilize being without having to be committed to loving being. We read in St. Paul of a "concupiscence of the eyes" which is found, upon reflection, to be far more essentially a disease of spiritual vision than of one's ocular organs. Marcel calls this excessive penchant for objective analysis a process of "alienation" of all reality.

This process designates its devotee as a spectator of the universe as opposed to a participant in reality. And the spectator always remains a stranger to the world, for he invariably looks upon all things, and even upon all human beings, as mere modifications of being brought about by natural and scientific processes—by evolution and the thousands of methods used in technocracy. We have here a mad kind of objectification that leads to a madder kind of science. It begets a science in which all things, and especially man, tend to become dangerously isolated and abandoned to the processes of exploitation and utilization. The universe's primary purpose is taken to consist in being discovered, in being objectively organized and properly functionalized for its successful application to the purely objective and scientific ends of man. In a sense, Marcel tells us, this detachment of the spectator, this mere functionalization and utilization of being by the scientist are forms of desertion of reality because they prevent a genuine human participation in being. [2] The universe is meant far less to be known and utilized than to be contemplated and saved.

Moreover, the spectator-attitude begets a form of lust by which the knowing and greedy subjects enter into sharp competition to subdue and monopolize large segments of reality. Things are out there to be known, dominated, inventoried, manipulated, catalogued and expended for pleasure and self-aggrandizement. And this includes human beings, human things. Troisfontaines echoes Marcel's criticisms of this spirit of extreme objectification.

[2] *BH*, p. 20.

Reality often appears as a public show-place where everything can be inventoried in columns and added up in a perfect tabulation. This procedure tempts man to dominate all being as if it were a universe of inert beings. To be sure, this way one gets the experience of the *libido dominandi*. But despair soon overtakes the human soul. Inventorie scannot hold the interest of man; they will eventually afflict him with nausea. As for the pleasure of power, it gets man accustomed to the agonizing experience of teetering on the brink of emptiness. The more man emphasizes the objectivity of things by cutting the umbilical cord which binds the universe to his organically physical person, the more he affirms the independence of the world from him and its unconcern about him. The universe is then seen as being radically indifferent to man's destiny, to his purposes. Thus, the more the world is transformed into a spectacle, the more it is felt to be illusory, a sort of immense documentary film which appeals to man's curiosity but which, in the final analysis, cancels everything out because it rejects man, the personal subject. The universe, in effect, tends to annihilate itself in the same measure in which it suppresses the subjective person. This truth is forgotten each time one attempts to crush man under the weight of astronomical data. [3]

Are we to say then that Marcel anathematizes all objectivized thinking? Rather than snap-answer this question incorrectly, it would be well to follow Marcel's reasoning on the value and deficiency of objectivized, analytical thought. We have his own definition of the word "object" as expressed in the Gifford Lectures given at the University of Aberdeen in 1949.

I am here taking the word "object," as I shall always be taking it, in its strictly etymological sense, which is also the sense of the German word *Gegenstand*, of something flung in my way, something placed before me, facing me, in my path. [4]

[3] R. TROISFONTAINES, *De l'existence...*, I, p. 129.
[4] *MB* (I), p. 57.

Much the same is to be found in the *Metaphysical Journal* where "object" is something separated from me in some manner or other, which does not participate in my intimacy. A thing is an object for Marcel, then, only in so far as it delivers itself up to conquest by scientific knowledge and scientific know-how. Contrary to the badge of friendship or even to the work of art which is essentially destined for the "I" and to which the "I" answers through the spiritual heart of itself, the "object" does not arouse my care nor anxiety as such. It never occurs to me that the object is addressing me; it remains what it is, mysteryless, indifferent, changeless whether I regard it or not. The object, of course, takes no account of me, is neutral to, unmindful of and independent of whatever makes me a subject, a conscious "I."

Scholastic philosophy, often enough, has a wider meaning for the word "object," which is "whatever is real." Marcel's meaning is more restricted; "object" is signified only by that portion of the real which is *devant*, before the subject, separated from him and quite impersonal. Marcel opposes Descartes' doctrine in which the idea becomes the "object," the only thing directly attained through the act of knowledge—the senses, for Descartes, being incapable of arriving at knowledge. Marcel rejects Descartes' pure and distinct idea screens as the only true objects.

Spirit of Abstraction [5]

Marcel admits that objectification is really a form of abstraction which man must indispensably use to arrive at a determined end. Psychology is constantly enlarging in an excellent way the internal connections between abstraction and overt activity. There is a legitimate abstraction which constantly remembers the methodic omissions that are being practiced in order to attain a foreseen and legitimate end. With the type of philosopher who keeps these omissions in mind and in his conclusions Marcel has no quarrel.

[5] *MMS*, p. 114.

But there are others who, under some sort of spell and fascination for the art of abstraction, have lost all consciousness of the artifice employed in this method and end up by deceiving themselves about the true nature of that which is in itself a process of analysis. It is against this latter "spirit of abstraction" that Marcel inveighs; it must be sharply distinguished and not confounded with indispensable abstraction nor with the true spirit of analysis. He talks about the addiction to the spirit of abstraction being "a will for non-discrimination and for non-hierarchization" of reality. True analysis does not dupe itself. To give preeminence to the objectivized world over the conscious subject is to isolate arbitrarily the world of objects from the world of subjects, or rather, to reduce the world of subjects to a part of the world of objects, thus making all persons victims of the spirit of abstraction. We have here a transposition of imperialism into the mental world. [6]

Marcel tells us it would be useful to distinguish between the notion of abstraction as such, and that of the spirit of abstraction. To establish this distinction firmly, he admits, is not an easy matter. Nevertheless, he makes the attempt.

Abstraction, of course, is a perfectly normal and necessary human activity. It is a mental operation whereby a preliminary clearing of the existential ground of being is undertaken. Abstract knowledge is a substitute for intuition and strives to attain the unity of all reality. Our very exigence for integral knowledge begets abstract and conceptual activity. We have here a method for sifting out the stable in reality. But the mind must retain a precise and distinct remembrance of those methodical omissions which abstraction necessarily entails. Hence conceptual knowledge needs constant re-rooting and re-watering in the soil of concrete experience. This is true because conceptual vision is only partial vision. The danger is that the mind, yielding to the fascination for the abstract method, may cease to be aware of the phenomenological conditions that justify this logical frame-work. The mind may then take as the whole of reality

⁶ R. TROISFONTAINES, *op. cit.*, p. 79.

what is merely a methodical, expedient and partial representation of reality.

This mistake leads to the spirit of abstraction which is inseparable from a contempt for the concrete conditions from which abstract thinking arises. The contempt for the concrete approach is the spirit of abstraction. This spirit seems to be a transposition of the attitudes of imperialism to the mental plane. Gilson's evaluation of this attitude is apropos here: "Every system depends upon will more than upon understanding." [7] We have here a voluntarism that accords to the category of the logical the primacy of the ontological. This arbitrary and irreconcilable divorce between the concrete and the conceptual worlds is the worse effect of the unphilosophical spirit of abstraction. [8]

And Marcel proceeds to show how some abstractions become embodied without ceasing to be abstractions, i.e., they materialize without really becoming incarnate:

> "The masses"—this seems to me the most typical, the most significant example of an abstraction which remains an abstraction even after it has become real: has become real, I mean, in the pragmatic sense of becoming a force, a power. [9]

Technocratic Mentality

We are now in position to see what is wrong with the technocratic mentality. Its excess consists in extending to the whole of reality, and especially to man, a manner of acting and of thinking which belongs and can be justified only if used in relation to things, to "objects." For every technique presupposes a whole group of abstract preliminaries which condition it; every technique is a manipulation or discipline which tends to assure man mastery over a determined and definite object.

[7] Etienne GILSON, *Existentialisme chrétien*, p. 3.
[8] *MMS*, pp. 115-116.
[9] *Ibid.*, p. 118.

Technique is defined through its affinity for a certain kind of
domination which the objects offer it. Inversely, a being is an
object only through the holdings, the graspings, the dominations
which we can technically attain over it. The truth of this can
be seen on the most elementary plane of exterior perception.
Thus, we can see that there inevitably exists a parallelism between
technical progress and progress in "objectivity." But by the
same token a technique is impotent in relation to the question
of total, concrete being, for the simple reason that its efficiency
and its transmission demand of it a non-individual character.
A strictly personal "know-how" will not be called a technique,
but a gift, or an art. A technique is essentially perfectible by
the one who takes the trouble to learn it; it can always be made
more precise, more adjusted. Inversely, one can, without doubt,
only strictly speak of progress in the order of technique, for it
is here that a measure of progress is possible which corresponds
to efficiency itself.

Of course, Marcel recognizes the positive value of technical
progress just as he emphatically admits the positive value of the
true spirit of analysis from which the former arises and upon
which it thrives and advances.

Marcel consigns scientific knowledge to the realm of having
and of the problematic. He fails to wax warm over science and
technics because he views them as the products of the spirit of
abstraction. Even more, he sees that the advancement in technics
parallels the advancement in man's barbarism towards man.
Nevertheless, there is a proper place and function for technics.
Admitting that he has slighted their positive values somewhat,
Marcel is quick to make amends. The usefulness of technics
only a lunatic would deny. But there is a much higher value
to be found in them than the mere dimension of utility and
comfort. A technician applying his mastered technique
experiences a joy that is both innocent and noble, a joy bound up
with conscious power over inanimate nature which responds to
man's control. Techniques develop precision in exploration and
execution; there is a connection here between precision and
intellectual honesty. Technicians must have the virtue of

accuracy. In their world inaccuracy can be fatal and is often punished in terrible ways. Thus, awareness of his responsibility always haunts the technician. What is most positive in all this is that the technician is thinking not of himself but of his task and of his service to others. [10]

Yet, although abstraction and objectivization and technique are legitimate and indispensable and fecund within their limited and foreseen areas, it is all the more absurd and fatal to generalize them or to seek them for their own sakes. We cannot abstract, we cannot objectivize, we cannot technically handle all being. [11] The attempts to do so have led to drastic and tragic divisive results. [12] It might be well to point out some of the evil results of certain pernicious, abstract approaches to man and the universe. The positivists dethroned man from his position of honor in the center of the cosmos and demoted him to an insignificant point in an infinite and purely mechanical universe. Now the multiplication of his very instruments of observation and their very acute perfection, far from extending the scope of his liberty

[10] Gabriel MARCEL, *The Decline of Wisdom* (London: The Harvill Press, 1954), pp. 10-11.

[11] *MMS*, p. 48. Marcel is often accused of making only a token admission of the meaning and finality in technology. He fails to divulge the spiritual grandeur that arises with the adventure of man's technological conquest of the universe. To balance this one-sided aspect of Marcel's thought the reader could profitably read Walter J. Ong's *Frontiers in American Catholicism* (New York: Macmillan, 1957), especially Chapter 5, entitled: "Technology and the New Humanist Frontiers," pp. 86-103.

[12] See the penetrating treatment of this divisiveness by Nicolas Berdyaev in *Solitude and Society* (London: The Centenary Press, 1947), p. 69, which reads in part: "As long as a man does not feel himself at home in the world of his authentic existence, as long as he sees other men in the light of this alien world, he can only conceive the world, and the men in it, as objects reflecting the objectified world of necessity. But the objective world can never be the means of liberating man from the prison of his solitude. Thus the fundamental truth holds good: no objective relationship can help the ego along the path of freedom and communion, whatever their relationship. In the depths of his solitude, of his hermetic existence, man grows acutely aware of his personality, originality and singularity. He also longs to escape from his solitary confinement, to enter into communion with the other self, with the thou, with the we... The ego's solitude is experienced not so much within its own existence as in the midst of others, in the midst of an abstract world."

and from favoring his profound moral revival, only get him ready for imminent catastrophes, leaving him forever disarmed before himself and casting him under the blows of the very instruments and machines that he hoped would save him. Take the Marxist attempt to interpret the whole of human reality as taking its origin solely from economic facts; it reduces man to a machine whose sole purpose is economic output, man, in the words of Marxist abstractions, "that most precious of all capital." The result is that behind the prodigious effort to think objectively about the cosmos and the conscience, there is found to be nothing either in the one or in the other. Perhaps the most objective, and hence most damning, criticism written about the Soviet man is to be found in this passage from Helmuth Gollwitzer which Marcel quotes in his own *Decline of Wisdom*.

> This system neither recognizes any subject as confronting it nor as a result does it allow the development of any such subjects, whether individuals or groups, and this means exactly that here nothing is allowed to grow. If life is unfettered growth in conformity with its own laws, this is surely the gravest accusation that can be brought. And indeed, for the life of the community, both the spiritual and the economic consequences of this fact are terrible. There is room for nothing but pre-established plans and manufactured objects: anything that grows is suspect. [13]

Spirit of Suspicion

It is precisely this spirit of abstraction that begets the spirit of suspicion. For once men feel themselves objectified, isolated, abandoned in an abstract universe that presents itself in the dynamic yet calloused lineaments of technology, an attitude of fear, suspicion and consequent disengagement with one's human and concrete environment sets in. Naturally enough there ensues a breakdown in the organic growth of the person, the family,

[13] Gabriel MARCEL, *The Decline of Wisdom*, p. 13, as quoted from Helmuth Gollwitzer, *Und fuhren, wohin du nicht willst* (Munich: Kaiser Verlag, 1953).

the community and this happens not merely on the exterior level of feeling, but of belief, and of the formation of genuine communion in all its forms.

In this world of the barrenly atomized and the harshly alienated, every knowing person becomes suspicious of the other. Why? It seems that the individual and isolated ego is set free to foster his own self-delusions, to set himself up in defiance against others, to read everywhere nothing but the harsh struggle for existence and to plot stratagems for the domination of man and matter. In an atmosphere of such spiritually sub-zero frigidity, techniques, of themselves morally indifferent, are feverishly refined in a spirit of hubris, of wanton pride, and lethally brandished by a will to intimidate so that with them, in the words of Marcel, "there is not the least hesitation in doing violence to nature to carry out an abstract plan." [14]

There follow the complexities of the game of social hypocrisy. The egoist, prize product of the alienated world, is invariably unavailable to his fellowmen. Yet driven on by an idolatry of the self, while burdened with himself and plunged into this disturbing, sometimes friendly, sometimes inimical world, the egoist aspires to possess, annex, even monopolize by fair and foul means everything that can subserve his craving for power, position, pleasure, and public confirmation. Although unavailable, the egoist turns poseur, feigning preoccupations with others to project a favorable picture of himself. Unsympathetic, the poseur can yet flatter others, simulating affection in the cause of his own advancement to high places. Dishonest, he acts the part of a forthright counselor, whereas he is the basest of cowardly pretenders. Actually his every word, act, attitude is studied and adapted to produce a definite effect on his victimized listener. The adopted attitude, always subserving some selfishly clandestine purpose, controls every thought, every facial expression, every intonality, every sentence, indeed every word in advance. In the world of abstractions, life becomes a game played under the inspiration of boundless pride.

[14] *Ibid.*, p. 14.

The man of abstraction is incapable of presence because he is both preoccupied and encumbered with his own self. The immediate object of his preoccupation may be his health, or fortune or even his inward perfection, but what is important is the particular manner in which such a man is preoccupied. The manner reveals a kind of obduracy, a fixation, a definite pathological disquietude that constricts and degrades the will. This manner of disquietude, Marcel thinks, "should be identified with the anguish of temporality and with that aspiration of man not towards, but *by* death, which is at the heart of pessimism." [15]

In attempting to get at the bottom of such pessimism, Marcel asserts that pessimism thrives in the same soil as does the will to unavailability. The refusal to be at the disposal of others tends to grow in us as we become old and decrepit and approach the portals of death. Perhaps the explanation is that, as death moves forward, anxiety mounts in us to choke us. Protection against this onslaught is often sought in the vulnerable mechanism of self-defense. Yet hope diminishes the more the soul is enchained, fascinated with fear and desperately fleeing death, to the world of the problematical. [16]

It is in the world of the problematical that everything is planned, organized, dissected. In this abstract and alienated world there is no room for mystery; everything must be labeled and accounted for. And the means for doing this is lived experience which, because of its dialectical aspects, inevitably transforms itself into reflection, "that mental fuel that keeps a life alight from day to day." [17] It is because they restrict themselves to but one type of reflection that certain philosophers succeed in distorting reality. Primary and only primary reflection, that function of man whereby he succeeds in decomposing and analyzing reality as pure objects, is the level of reflection that these men have opted to remain upon. Is it any wonder, then, that in this diminished world of mere objects the friendship that formerly existed between the community of men and the

[15] *PE*, pp. 27, 28.
[16] *Ibid.*, p. 28.
[17] *MB* (I), p. 101.

community of objective beings has been tragically broken through this malignant work of those certain philosophers who, restricting themselves solely to the tool of primary reflection, first subjectivized, dissected and reduced man to a thing, and then turned this diluted thing over to the processes of scientific technology? Marcel warns us that it was through imprisonment first in the philosophical jail of primary reflection that man was degraded and then handed over to the prolonged abstractions of the industrial world, of the world of politics, of the world of the totalitarian State to be dehumanized and enslaved.

Roughly, the process takes place as follows. Primary reflection dissolves the unity of experience. Secondary reflection has the function of recovering and reconquering the freshness of the original unity of existential experience. Primary reflection must break the fragile link between me and my body, between my mental world and the concrete world. This type of analytical reflection assumes an attitude of radical detachment, of what appears as a complete lack of interest, towards the truth that this particular body is my body. [18]

Radical Detachment

This "attitude of radical detachment, of complete lack of interest" toward the whole man and its complete absorption with the naturalized, objectivized and actually pulverized subject tends to snuff out the source of brightness, the principle of radiance that is the mysteriously privileged being of a person. Knowing himself merely by the light of primary reflection, man can alone bring benefit to himself by a light borrowed from "objects." Inevitably, then, the techniques which will pretend to pertain to his own benefit will be constructed on the model of the techniques which are oriented toward the exterior world. Now the perversion of this procedure consists in the following illicit and unjust transposition—namely, the techniques which are

[18] *Ibid.*, pp. 102, 103, 113, 114.

useful and beneficial when applied to the "doing" or performance of objects are also applied to the "being" of consciously free and knowing subjects. [19] This perversion, known as pan-technicism, exposes man to the manipulation of mechanics as it obscures within him the feeling for genuinely concrete being. We do well to quote here from the admirable critique of C. Virgil Georghiu:

> The fact that we submit man to the laws and criteria of techniques—criteria excellent in all that concerns machines— this fact is equivalent to the assassination of man. Any man that is forced to live in the conditions and the milieu of a fish dies and, of course, the reverse is true too. The West has created a society that resembles the machine. It forces men to live in the bosom of this society and yet to adapt themselves to the laws of the machine. When men shall have so resembled machines that they identify themselves with them, then there will no longer be any men on the face of the earth. [20]

The technocratic man is incapable of knowing himself in the sense intended by Socrates, i.e., with a knowledge that is founded on the bond of a certain identity that should exist between the knower and the known. This bond is annulled by the technocratic mentality because such a mentality necessarily entails a process of specialization that first begets pure technicians and then imprisons these purists within their objectivized specialities where all questions about the unity of the world and of all reality are never openly broached nor professionally recognized as valid.

Corresponding to the abstract analytical dismemberment of man that is a necessary first step in the process of philosophizing, and to the technocratic break-up of the world that is but the transsubjective projection and impersonal concretization of the initial objective analysis, there stands the social pulverization of the subject which, as a logical and inevitable consequence of the two prior processes, extends and intensifies their explosive disintegrations into the field of human relations. To be somewhat

[19] R. TROISFONTAINES, *De l'existence...*, I, p. 82.
[20] *Ibid.*, p. 82.

simplistic for the sake of a quick summary, we might say that primary analysis produces abstract man, that technocratic analysis produces man the machine, that the analysis of pulverization produces the functionalized man. All of these men are really one, of course, in different stages of their logical development, which is to say, of their non-existence and, therefore, in different stages of their ever-descending degradation.

For every depreciation is in foundation what the French call a *"ressentiment"* and corresponds to a sort of fierce attack directed against the integrity of the concrete, the real, the authentic, which attack consists in holding up a fictitiously exalted counterpart that represents the displayer's prejudices about how the real being exists, ought to exist, acts and ought to act—and never mind the contrary eloquent testimony that such is not and cannot be the case from the nature of authentic things themselves. Thus the clear and tidy abstract man, the Cartesian fellow, is more real than this particular, concrete mystery-man before me who is an unpredictable enigma. Man the precise machine is represented as more authentic than a concrete temperamental individual, for the former is readily, easily and accurately usable while the latter is often obnoxious and may even be downright "sticky." The functionalized man is an existential joy to science for he can be accurately and meticulously catalogued, while his opposite number, the uninhibited individualist transcends all the scientific laws laid down for man and yet somehow manages to mature in all that is human.

Functionalized Man [21]

The demolition of the social subject begins in the appraisal of the value of each individual man solely in relation to his ability to perform certain "functions," to effect much "production," and to do both of these with high "efficiency." The key, perhaps the only, questions about any man now become: "What is your

[21] *Ibid.*, p. 82.

speciality, your function, your service in life?" Of themselves these categories and questions are not bad, but they pervert human relations when they restrict man's role in life solely to that of being a producer. This new anthropomorphism has its overarching dogma: every man is an "agent" whose production must contribute to the progress of a certain totality of man. What does it matter if this total community is yet in the far distant future and if its prophets are even now revealing that certain central aspects of this community are to be rigidly oppressive and even violently tyrannical? This synthesis of man and his universe is inevitable and hence must be accepted; it is "in the air"; it is "the wave of the future," and anyway, this particular drive for unity is incoercible, for unity appears to be the very foundation for man's thinking.

The result is that in countries that are crusading for this ideology of the perfectly functioning and perfectly functionalized community of the future we find that the populace is presently under the heel of police dictatorships, a populace that is registered onto thousands of paper documents from the moment of birth to the instant of death. And to see to it that everything continues perfectly functional and functionalized an anonymous bureaucracy is interposed between the masters above and upon the masses below. To be sure, in such an arid milieu every sense of what is personally intimate in man's life is obliterated.

Men are now identified with their cards in the file, with the aggregate of their functions, with the dusty, abstract, depersonalized details of their abilities. We are witnessing the "massification" of man; everyone becomes a "paper-man," or "a man of things," rather good at handling inanimate objects but woefully inept at handling human persons and human problems because all have either abandoned or are being prevented forcibly from pursuing concrete activities, creative activities, while they pursue and maintain the functional heaven. In this historically materialist haven men are looked at under different aspects at different times, as consumers, producers, political agents, etc. But the all-pervading aspect under these apparent changes never changes: men, whatever else they seem to be, are objectified things with certain objectified functions. Under these desiccated and artificial conditions the spirit of man is in jeopardy; his interior life atrophies; his functions of eating, sleeping, recreating and begetting devour the man and reduce him to the permanent position of being a chattel, an apparatus at the service of the herd community.

Marcel is at great pains to point out that the planned organization of all functions presupposes the ever-engulfing intervention of the State into the lives of its subjects. We see this invasion in the vast colossus of the totalitarian regimes that confront the West as some Super Moloch-State that arrogates to itself divine attributes and powers. [22] Music, art, religion, literature, science are all under its iron scrutiny and control with the consequent quenching of all genius and inspiration in these fields of creative activity. Even the activity of parenthood is interpreted as an activity of the State and is rewarded according to State laws. The father is just an instrument and the mother a channel through which the State gets the manpower it needs and will train for its own prolongation in economic, political and martial supremacy.

Part of the pulverization of the subject is that he is exposed more and more to treat his job as a sort of forced labor, a labor that begets him no joy and in which his heart is not. It may earn him his bread, but without love for his trade or business, he eats his bread in tears and tediously. Even the very notion of life is degraded since it is regarded merely as a technique and a very imperfect one at that.

With such a point of view, it is not astonishing that man has already claimed for himself the right to interfere with human life as if he were damming the onflow of a river. Before starting a baby "on the way," careful, economical calculations are entered into. What will the annual expenses be, the estimated cost of doctor's fees, the bills in case of illness, the budget for maintenance

[22] R. TROISFONTAINES, *op. cit.*, p. 82.

and repair of wear and tear? The child could just as easily be an automobile or motorcycle. Frequently enough a settlement is made for a pet as being more economical. Its cost, fees and upkeep are far less. And, should it become economically prohibitive, it can be put painlessly out of the way. [23] Today in Sweden, man has arrived at this solution in the case of sickly, deformed, small children.

We have here a social and spiritual malaise which is becoming more and more inhuman and leads to an inhuman philosophy, the philosophy of function which purports to explain all there is to man. A world which has surrendered to the primacy of technique takes as its human archtype the man whose production is objectively discernible, the man who is worth plenty of money, the man whose activity is most assimilable to the tireless, endless productivity of the machine. Marxists, unable to resist the fascination for the progress of materiality in this world, are also unable to think of man, their most precious capital, as anything but the most perfect and perfectible machine. In this technocratic atmosphere in which man is measured according to the standards of the machine, the man whose repair costs exceed his output is no longer useful and, according to the objective and functional view, must be done away with. He has served his purpose, the production of new capital. He is presently unable to continue this service, nor is there any hope that he will recuperate again to return to this service. By what logic, then, is he allowed to clutter up the earth and to consume the precious products of his vigorous fellow-workers? It seems monstrous and inhuman that he is to be done away with. Yet this methodic suppression of the infirm and of the incurables is being advocated in the West as euthanasia and a service to man, in the East as a necessary sacrifice for the coming millenium of the classless society. This is the road that leads to the new and frightful barbarism of the modern age—the barbarism of the implementation of the objectivized thinking with the engines of technocracy.

[23] *MMS*, pp. 44-45.

Techniques of Degradation [24]

But the engines of technocracy, for all their awesome and highly specialized power and efficiency in the service of the pulverization of man, are almost play toys, indeed the very friends of man, in comparison with the men who perfected unspeakable techniques of degradation against their fellowmen. Such men, besides being malevolent geniuses at ceaselessly thinking up ever new and more refined methods of spiritual pulverization, are also past masters in applying these methods of torture with such a spirit of delight and sacrilegious exaltation that one is constrained to see in these agents the very incarnation of the satanic. The sensitive soul of Marcel has suffered intense anguish over this scourge against humanity.

By techniques of degradation Marcel is referring to a body of methods coldly thought out and callously put into operation to attack and destroy in human persons their dignity and self-respect. The ultimate purpose of these techniques is to transform men of stature and standing, little by little, into "mere human waste products," to make them conscious of their degradation and thus force them to despair both on the level of thought and within the spiritual core of their beings. [25]

Some such procedures to degrade and disintegrate not only the spiritual whole and wholesomeness of the person and the community are recorded in detail by eye-witnesses of the techniques employed in the past and still being employed today in concentration camps. Every kind of cowardice is exploited; jealousies and hatreds of all brands are stimulated and encouraged; moral and physical weaknesses are cultivated and abused; spying, talebearing, blackmail, violence reduce humans to the state of cringing beasts. Conditions of physical dirt and disorder are consciously fostered as a principle that debases, humiliates and drags down into the mud the human dignity of man. Men that

[24] *Ibid.*, p. 27.
[25] *Ibid.*, p. 30.

live "plastered with filth" are calculated to be turned into monsters. But Marcel tells us the subtler end that the tyrants desired.

The torturers, of course, intended to immerse their victims in such abject conditions that the afflicted souls would eventually acquire the habits of animals. But even more than the physical degradation sought after, the torturers planned the spiritual annihilation of their victims. The victims were encouraged to spy upon one another; mutual resentment and suspicion were fomented among them. The wellsprings of human relationship and communion were poisoned. Prisoners, who should have comforted one another in their sufferings as brothers-in-persecution, became instead mortal enemies, demons, an incubus to one another. We have here the most monstrous collective crime in history. [26]

The techniques of poisoning the wellsprings of human relationship are perhaps the most violent spiritual catalysts to disorder and social chaos in the world today. They are the instruments that men imbued with the spirit of abstraction are constantly sharpening and making more precise in order to bring about, as realized powers and active forces, their own carefully planned abstractions for the domination of man and the universe. Upon investigation of these plans, we find that these elaborated and realized abstractions not only invariably turn out to be oriented toward human inter-destructiveness, but they also seem pre-ordained to aggravate ideological confrontations and to ignite them into hot wars of total destruction.

Propaganda [27]

Take for example the technique of propaganda. In itself it need not be classified among the instruments for degradation. Yet no technique in our day, perhaps, has actualized its potential for corruption more fully than has the activity of propaganda.

[26] *MMS*, p. 32.
[27] *Ibid.*, p. 38.

That there is a close kinship between propaganda and the techniques of degradation is incontrovertibly demonstrated by the historical fact, everywhere evident in the crisis of our times, that propaganda which used to be a method of persuasion has become instead a carefully developed system of mental saturation for the purposes of seduction.

Its real, deep purpose is to reduce men to a state so passive that they lose all capacity for individual initiative and constructive reaction. Propaganda degrades those whose thoughts, emotions, volitions and attitudes it seeks to shape and control. The masters and manipulators of propaganda are self-conditioned for their anti-human activity by a prior and permanent fundamental contempt for the rest of humanity. Propagandists beget that scourge known as "the single party," with all the fanatical and even religious adherence that this party demands of its members. Propagandists are the most radically and violently intolerant people on the earth. Marcel excoriates the arrogance of their attitude.

Propagandists are moved by a cynical refusal to admit the competence of the individual judgment. They are impatient with the "intolerable presumptuousness" of the private person. They must manipulate the minds and opinions of all men lower than themselves. By constantly imposing their own world-construction on the masses, propagandists, unconsciously at first, lose the sense of truth and, when this habit of imposition yields them the fruits of power and position, they consciously become convinced that *their* truth is the *whole* truth. This fanatical temperament is then used in crooked and devious ways and through the agency of renegades and traitors, to wind into the thought and under the thoughts of the unsuspecting masses to circumvent and subjugate them. [28]

Now the single party, once it becomes the established, intolerantly reigning abstraction, grows like a root from which the vine and the branches of State dictatorship climb and overrun every other legitimately competing movement of life and thought. This total State makes use of the renegade because he is the

[28] *Ibid.*, pp. 37-38.

precise personification of the propagandist of bad intent and
evil will. Renegades reconnoiter and skillfully exploit the
weaknesses of their enemies, all the while posing as friends
and confidants. They will put the means of communication to the
most satanic roles in the moulding of that most malleable of all
things human—the opinions of the masses. The renegade leader,
abandoning his people's genuine ideals and bending these people
themselves to his own ambitious abstractions, is so adept at
camouflaging his concealed purposes under some national aim
or purpose that he often enough succeeds in duping the masses to
accept loyally his so-called policies for peace and progress which
actually are policies branded with a most cynical imperialism and
aimed at the estrangement and subjugation of all men.

Commonly enough, the propagandist's procedure in his
drive to indoctrinate the opposition into peaceful conformity
is to make use of certain specific orthodox words and formulae
that are associated with the most revered and loved institutions
of the people. [29]   In what Marcel calls "a spirit of imposture,"
the communications media of radio, TV, newspaper, cinemas,
advertisements etc. are flooded with ideals that are not only
morally good but even Christian—ideals of equality, liberty,
brotherhood, progress, plenty for all, of economic and spiritual
reform. In this manner the single party with its single leader
wins first a hearing, then adherents and finally stable power. Once
consolidated in power, the ideological camouflage which covers
up the fundamental errors and the ruthless plans of the party,
slips away, leaving the populace painfully conscious that it is
confronted with a clique of organized and entrenched criminals
entrusted with power through its own cooperation in their
campaign of organized lying.

[29] Just as in the existential philosophy the original meaning of
words is revealed for the purpose of initiating the rebirth of a living philosophy, capable of coping with the social crisis of modern times, so too
does the propagandist of collectivism make use of the original brilliance
and fulness of Christian formulae to win the masses to his cause. Using
the phenomenological method, in imitation of Marcel, we are attempting
to explore this technique for social dissolution as it is used by some well-
known tyrants of our times.

We are reminded in recent history of the rise to power of Mao Tse-tung under the characteristic slogan of "agrarian reformer"; more recently still Fidel Castro's political apotheosis was accomplished under the aura of the god-term "*humanismo*" for all Cubans, when humanism is taken to mean reform and social justice.

It is only when the slogan-bearer is ensconced in power that his meaning of the charismatic expression is revealed and imposed upon the populace. Then the whole world becomes a witness to how the charismatic expression is purposely drained of any transcendental meaning, once it has been successfully abused as a shining symbol to seduce the masses. Mao's "agrarian reform" is emptied of any spiritual or substantial content and is today seen to mean the herding of millions of Chinese into cattle-like communes for the economic and military aggrandizement of the party and the State. Castro himself did us the service of interpreting his Cuban humanism by saying that any moderate force in Cuba is a weed; we can trust only the radicals.

The technique of imposture [30] is clearly seen to be based on objectivized thinking and the spirit of abstraction, if we analyze the above incidents. We might trace the steps somewhat like this. The manipulators of the mind thoroughly understand through psychology that no slogan will allure men if it is drained of all meaning; the meaningless standard is non-existent. But what are the meanings and the standards that are dear to the hearts of the people? First, then, capitalize on some attractive transcendental truth-content in a slogan or formula that is bound to attract the unsuspecting masses. Pour out perfervid rhetoric on every opportune occasion in behalf of this uplifting doctrine; this procedure besides stirring up the masses into fanatical supporters of your cause, will also hasten you to power. Then from your position of solidified power, garnered under this symbol as the bearer of transcendental truth, turn on your captives, indoctrinate them anew now in your own preordained meaning of this symbol. This will not be an easy undertaking,

[30] *MMS*, p. 55.

for you will now have to subvert the minds you previously seduced. But oceans of ink can now flow from your captured presses into print that will provide philosophical gloss for your new doctrines. The very means of communication, used to ascend to power on the capital of spiritual and Christian truth, can now be used to corrode these same truths and to turn fuzzy all former values in the masses, thus preparing the new human clay from which your new man and new community may be constructed. But you must annihilate as arbitrary and superstitious, all former meanings of these same terms that the ignorant masses believed in. Once accomplished, you have established a new, revolutionary, simplified and scientific significance to the identical verbal symbols, once so pleasantly subjective, but now so objectivized and idealized. Via this procedure of intellectual opportunism you can keep the mentally renewed faithful eager to sway with every nuance of your doctrine—with neutralism, pacificism, atheistic optimism, pessimism, etc.

Doctrinaire Humanisms [31]

So many parties of abstractionist entrepreneurs have spun out such a bewildering congeries of objectivized plans for man and his society that existential man has become almost hopelessly confused and skeptically divided, caught as he is in the proliferation of ideological systems all competing in the lust to reorganize and rule the human community.

Marcel is convinced that we are witnessing today the disintegrating solvent effects of a variety of abstractionist and atheistic humanisms. Secularist humanisms have already cut millions of men and many nations from their metaphysical and theological moorings. Marcel can write:

> It can never be too strongly emphasized that the crisis which Western man is undergoing today is a metaphysical

[31] *Ibid.*, p. 51.

one; there is probably no more dangerous illusion than that
of imagining that some readjustment of social or institutional
conditions could suffice of itself to appease a contemporary
sense of disquiet which rises, in fact, from the very depths
of man's being. [32]

And yet man continually succumbs to the temptation to
return to the formula of the Greek sophist: *Man is the measure
of all things*. Marcel rejects this formula not only because it
is strangely ambiguous but, above all, "because the moral
relativism implied in the formula puts us on a path that will in
the long run lead us to a degraded kind of humanism: a humanism
that is parasitic on nature, as moss is parasitic on a tree." [33]

But there are many species of parasitic humanisms and
if one were to make the anatomy of these his primary business, he
would discover much about the pathology of these abstractionist
and secularist doctrines. He might even be able to indicate how
these parasites might be killed, thus leaving the human mind and
soul free to mature spiritually.

This much, anyway, can be said about these doctrinaire
systems. It seems that all abstractionist and atheistic humanisms
win social acceptance for a time partly because they preserve,
often enough quite earnestly though illogically, some of the
attractive aspects of Christianity, striving to realize in man
some Christian values from their ever-diminishing capital of
Christian lore. We have seen that with some it is a studied
technique of imposture to use these values as spiritual fronts for
the calculated deception of the masses. With others, however,
the movements are sparked by good will and move forward in
good faith for the betterment of human society. Even so, Marcel
warns us, a general alarm must be sounded to warn the gullible
that such great values as these, once severed from their
transcendental source, become unreal and unrealizable. Divorced
from the divine, they are sterile, indeed, dead. To reduce the
good gifts and the good news of the participation in transcendent

[32] *Ibid.*, p. 27.
[33] *Ibid.*, p. 51.

being to the good news of the inevitable social salvation of society based on the innate grandeur of man is to present a distorted perspective of man's relationship to his fellowmen and to God. The lamentable result of denying the divine, transcendental dimension in man is that his noblest aspirations are blighted.

Once such humanisms drain and dilute the divine depths of charity and leave the soul in the shallows of humane sentimentality, all that remains is an effete and spiritually anemic humanity which responds oftener to the seductions of the secular cults of civility, culture, progress, plenty and survival than to the Christian challenge for divine growth in the cult of genuine love toward all. In the end, all narrow humanisms, victims of their diminished and empty abstractions, impatiently collectivize masses of men and compel them to enter their exclusive and privileged milleniums—a classless society, a limitless democracy, a borderless State, a religionless culture.

Despite their attractive aspects, such humanisms beget the dissolution of man. Marxist humanism is passionately concerned about the economic welfare of "the people," and yet confines the people to propertyless communes. "Liberal" humanists are obsessed with civil rights for all and yet expose society to the prowlings of unconvicted and unpunishable criminals; the humanitarian humanist is dedicated to the alleviation of the destitution of men and nations and to the material and cultural enrichment of the whole human fraternity, but he is unconcerned about the substantive spiritual advancement of these same people. A special breed of intellectual humanist, whose master-dogma is the denial of all dogma, advocates a form of catholic lecture and research that purports to smile neutrally on all academic positions, however irreconcilable, in an atmosphere of peaceful co-existence devoid of all dialectical divisiveness, but to men who beg him for the bread of truth he gives the stone of learning. His political twin is the humanist who, humanely founding his policies on the master-value of human survival, attains a peace that is the tranquility of moral paralysis, often standing by petrified while millions in friendly nations are liquidated.

Any abstract and objectivized humanism that guarantees

man complete emancipation from the transcendental, from God, from his fellowman, can only succeed in delivering man up to complete slavery to his fellowman. Without the transcendent man is no longer man; he is man against man, man in bondage to man. The metaphysics and religion of humanity leaves man without a metaphysics and without a religion or rather, what is worse still, it leaves man his own transcendent being, his own god, in bondage to self-idolatry. Such parasitic humanisms are inhuman, anti-human because they lead man not upward to genuine communion but downward to massive despair and to mass suicide.

The despair of the "robot-man," of the "fugitive from life," and of the "mass man" are specimens of that disease whose root is undue objectivization. Just as the world seems unsubstantial and inconsistent when men objectivize it, so does my life, so do the lives of my fellowmen, of my communities, once I cut them off from the subjects and persons that are concretely experiencing them. The *taedium vitae* of the masses is due to the rupture or more exactly to the loosening of the ontological bond which unites each being in particular to being in its plenitude. The mass man, frustrated because of the lack of meaning in life, is committed to nothing but comfort, security and pleasure and all these pall human existence. Idleness eats into all leisure hours like a cancer and eventually leads to despair. The mass man becomes the silent millions, kept in the dark about his future fortunes which are secretly forged at the power sessions of summitry. The fallout of a scientific rationalism has rendered him incapable of admiring or wondering at anything, for life seems to be entirely empty. The mass man is the millions of frustrated who cooperated in winning hot wars that seemed to have meaningful beginnings and who are helpless before the defeats suffered from a meaningless peace. Nothing seems of importance to him any more; the soil seems to have ceased to reverberate under his feet; the world has become trivial, even transparent. The mass man is now in the process of frantically mining the enormous deposits of atomic energy and secretly storing this cosmic force into rocket reservoirs labeled for destructive missions. There seems to be no longer any spiritual resolve or resistance in the will of the mass man. There is no longer any adaptability, no elasticity. The mass man is depicted as the end product of a massive, world-wide, centuries-old defection from the transcendent, from God. There is a distressing retreat from great deeds in the harrowing experience of living a functionalized life. Living in a society that is rootless and rudderless, man in the mass is that mechanical, depersonalized animal whose weary mind is so tenderized and confused by a constant stream of crafty propaganda that his will to resist is broken and he is easily enough dragooned into a hopeless acquiescence in his own defeat. Becoming thinner and thinner spiritually, the solid substance of mankind seems to be evanescing from the face of the earth. And yet though the pressure is on to pulverize man into classless equality, the mass man is still cosmic-conscious; he struggles socially to stay awake and alert because he hungers to have all the spheres of his life and human activity integrated and directed to some lasting, transcendent goal.

Self-centered techniques and humanisms try to twist man's activities to the glory of himself in this world. In all the domains of his self-centered activity there is an insensible passage from the insipid to the insupportable; victim of abstractive humanisms that make a travesty of living truth, that lower his sights from eternal, lasting to temporal, fleeting values, mass man, disoriented man, interiorly disorganized man has yet been able to arm himself with elemental cosmic fires that are capable of blasting his ever-expanding, yet ever-surrendering universe, right out of existence.

The rupture between man and the transcendent, between man and man, between man and God, which naturalized and secularized humanisms would establish into normalcy, has led Gabriel Marcel to give the following somber analysis of the modern world.

It is a world given over to fatigue. It is a world being eaten away by a parasitic mode of thinking which plausibly justifies all the evils it is perpetrating upon man. Every injustice is justified because it is done in the name and for the benefit of the masses. An idolatry of masses is the *idée fixe* of our generations. Man cannot be considered safe, nor human unless he is lost in the anonymity of the masses. The modern world lulls itself into a false sense of security by seeing the masses attaining in the near future a happiness never before known. The fulfilment of this happiness is to coincide with the fulfilment of man's social duty. But, in reality, what choice is man given in today's world-wide confusion? Marcel answers: A choice "between the termite colony and the Mystical Body." Man seems to be committing the greatest error he can commit; he seems to be confusing the one with the other. [34]

And here we would do well to attempt some sort of synthesis so that observations, previously discussed somewhat diffusively in this chapter, may be reviewed *in globo*. We have seen that the stage of communication is a necessary one for the maturation in consciousness of the ego. Yet it represents a real risk and, if the transsubjective propulsion of the ego is exercised in such a way that it handles all other beings only as all other "objects," then the stage of communication will never become the bridge to the stage of genuine communion, then man has yielded to the temptation to use everything, to cling to nothing, to break any living links he may have had with concrete reality. Such a sick attitude in man is called the spirit of abstraction, a spirit that emancipates man from speculative and contemplative knowledge of transcendent being and leaves him incapable and unwilling to respond affirmatively to personal encounter. The result of this attitude of disengagement is that man restricts himself to the activity of tinkering with objects and solving problems for merely utilitarian motives. Even other humans are cases and problems in different stages of partial solution. And when these other humans are looked at under the aspect of problems that can possibly threaten the comfort of the objectivized thinker, then fear and the spirit of suspicion injects the harsh note of competition into the area of inter-communication. In the struggle for domination that is enjoined, the lust for power,

[34] *MMS*, p. 140.

position, pleasure dictates the unrestricted use of the finest and latest techniques. The whole struggle is exacerbated by the spirit of imposture and resentment.

Now among such men who are irrevocably unavailable to each other, who refuse to be at each other's disposal, retrogression in human solidarity is speeded up and climaxed by the use of the techniques of degradation, i.e., by violence, lying, enprisonment, deportation, blackmail, subversion, propaganda and disloyalty—all such techniques being carefully premeditated, cleverly organized and cruelly imposed upon the masses. And the effective instrument of imposition is the skill of technology which is perverted to the goals of the will to intimidate and to dominate. To be sure, such techniques in the service of such technology do bring about a unity of a sort, but it is a false and pernicious unity, a unity of the masses that has nothing organic nor vital about it; rather it is an organized unity, a unity imposed violently from without and leading towards the unity that is found in the dissolution and the silence of death. Marcel especially excoriates and rejects this equivocation of true unity.

"Identity does not mean unity." The danger of a unification process that is undertaken by violent imposition is that it is a unification by reduction. Differences which confer on people their individuality and their unique, spiritual dignity are suppressed through this tyrannical process of amalgamation. There is no positive value in this sort of unification. Rather positive values are sacrificed in order to attain an inhuman conformity. This imposed conformity is identified with the opposite of value; it is the attempt to annihilate all spiritual values. [35]

Man, when he chooses to rest freely in the objectivized stage of inter-communication, when he refuses to go up higher to the stage of authentic inter-communion, though he thinks he is safely at rest in the protective shell of the former enclosure, actually does nothing but expose himself to the dehumanization of his being. Having placed himself in the hermetically sealed

[35] *MMS*, p. 124.

prison of objects, he can no longer breathe metaphysically; he can no longer hear the call and appeal of being that is persuasively beckoning his personal response, a response once given that would set him free in the transcendent world of inter-subjective communion. Finally, the man bogged down in the abstract world of objects, with concrete being all around him, is slowly starving to death from an acute hunger, from an insatiable need for transcendent being. And the tragedy of this situation is that, although he feels despair mounting as his hunger pains become more anguished, he actually does not seem to realize that his demoralizing decline toward death is due to his own refusal to convert from objectivized being to the being of participation. He will be sated and saved the moment he decides to open himself to participate freely in the personal encounter of the other created thou and, above all, of the other and only Uncreated Thou. He will be saved because he achieves communion in the transcendent.

> We must recognize that each of us, in order to "grow," must open out to other and different beings and must be capable of meeting them without allowing himself to be dominated or neutralized. This is what I have called "intersubjectivity." It cannot be considered a mere given fact, or rather, it only assumes value where it is more than a given fact, where it appears as a gradual victory over all that incites us to become withdrawn and self-centered. In short, intersubjectivity has meaning only through freedom. Nowhere perhaps does freedom show itself in a more positive and constructive light, whereas previously freedom appeared to us under a negative aspect, when it showed a tendency to detach itself from existence. [36]

[36] G. MARCEL, "Authentic Humanness and its Existential Primordial Assumptions," *The Human Person and...*, p. 90.

CHAPTER VI

The Achievement of Communion

From the plane of reflection we have thus far seen that a restrictive analysis, which consistently dismembers and merely isolates the constitutive elements in the infinitely rich complexity of being, inevitably leads to the spirit of abstractionism and this spirit, in turn, leads to deeds of atomistic disintegration on the plane of social life.

This will always be so whenever ideas are separated from and do not run with the concrete action of lived experience. For then they are usually patterned on some personal and unrealistic assumptions and tailored to form a tightly fitting absolutist system which, once it is imposed upon the human race, is supposed to lead the community of men to the promised land of some naturalistic heaven where he enjoys the perfect peaceful federation or classless society in the plenitude of human self-sufficiency.

But whenever the realm of reflection remains rooted in, feeds upon and grows up within the realm of concrete reality, then a true and fruitful planning for the advancement of the human community becomes possible, very probable and, indeed, sometimes actual. For, unlike the spirit of abstractionism which cuts all mystery out of reality by restricting the real solely to what falls neatly into its tightly-fitting thought-system, reflection that remains rooted in reality stands humbly open to all being, whether it is solving objective problems or meditating on reality's inexhaustible mysteries.

At this point we must consider Marcel's distinctive contribution to the field of philosophy—his classical distinction between

a *problem* and a *mystery*. A full understanding and deep appreciation of this philosophically fruitful distinction will enable a
reader to grasp the unity that exists in the ontological order
between object and subject, presence and position, I and it, I and
thou.

We have already seen that for Marcel an object is that which
is thrown in front of me, stands over against me, is external to me,
its etymological roots being in Latin: *objectum*—something cast
before. By a very singular coincidence the Greek roots of the
word *problem* correspond to the Latin *objectum*, for a *pro-blema* is
something thrown in my way, something I run up against.

A problem, then, for Marcel, is a mental investigation that
is undertaken in respect to an object. A problem bears on something completely outside of the investigator. The observer can
observe the problem from all sides. Not only that, but he can
obtain definite and sure solutions to the problem, so that, given
a certain amount of time, a period will eventually be put to the
problem, because all the objective laws involved in the problem
and all the agents and their proper relationships are discovered
and accounted for. Objectified thought is used to solve problems;
the person as person is not involved in the solution or make-up
of the problem; he can take the object in clearly, distinctly; he can
transmit, in a perfectly rational manner, the full clarity of his
solution to the mind of another person. The objects, and the
problems concerned over them and their solutions, all lead a
public life: they belong immutably to the public domain of knowledge and action. Scientific knowledge embodies, par excellence,
the problematic approach to objects. It is made secure and public
by the spectator-investigator approach to objects.

But there are other data in existential reality that cannot, as
data, be objectified, for the simple reason that the investigator is
dealing with an area of being which necessarily includes and involves himself. I cannot regard Being as outside myself, nor
myself as outside Being. Being, as such, is not an object, for it
also includes me, a subject. Here is the greater, the infinite range
of mystery. If I attempt to objectify Being, I lose the original
data of the Self which is included in asking about Being. Every

question bearing on a mystery recoils upon the questioner who is unable to give a perfect answer or to produce a perfect solution to the question because the area of the mystery being investigated is too vast to be fully comprehended by the limited and involved mind of man.

Ontological exigence in man cannot be compared with his search for solutions. Man's reality is built on the meta-problematic which is really participation in being. Genuine participation can never be a solution to a problem. For were it a solution, it would cease to be a participation in transcendent reality. It would be, rather, an interpolation into transcendent reality; this would be a degradation from the degree of being which participation really is.

Two inquiries are needed here. First, an investigation into the conditions in which participation can become thinkable. Both these investigations prepare and lead to each other. We will find that participation goes beyond the order of the problematic, and can never be stated as a problem. As soon as there is presence, we again find that we are beyond the realm of problem. Yet we also learn that the motives behind all thinking and problem-solving processes give a provisional aspect to every judgment we make. Thus even each presence may give rise to problems, but only in so far as the presence loses its value as presence. [1]

The one who asks about a problem may be any epistemological subject, but the questioner is not necessarily looked upon as a personal Self. Just about anyone is correlative to the object; the questioner, moved by curiosity, is rather neutral and non-existent as a subject. Any mind can approach this object, for the epistemological ego is correlative to the world of objectivity, of the verifiable.

On the other hand, however, subjects are not at all interchangeable in the area of mystery. Only a unique person, moved by wonder, seeks and affirms truth about a mystery. Here I cannot be purely an epistemological subject, but a wholly existential subject. No other can become me; my act of faith is unverifiable

[1] *BH*, pp. 114-115. See: *PE*, pp. 8-9; *MB* (I), p. 204; all of *PAC*.

by anyone else because it is not objectifiable. There is simply no criterion at hand for the positivist or rationalist with which he may test my act of faith. Now the unverifiable lies in the land of mystery.

But how are we supposed to think mystery, how participation? This is our second inquiry.

If a mystery is really irreducible to a problem, then is there a different way of thinking *mystery* than there is for thinking *problem?* Is there a distinction within the vital activity of thought? Marcel certainly makes one.

Mystery cannot be reduced to a problem. How, then, can I think about mystery? If thinking is seen solely as a way of looking, the question can have no solution. Whatever cannot be reduced to a problem cannot be looked at or treated as a problem. But this looking-at aspect of thought is inadequate. A distinction must be made within the thought process itself. There is a closed and open thought, what Marcel calls *pensée pensée* and *pensée pensante.* Concrete philosophy, in its immediate and vital pursuit of the real, is undertaken through the activity of *pensée pensante,* whose essence is to gain on mysteries but never to catch them completely. This kind of thinking cannot be represented but only grasped as such. It apprehends every representation of itself as truly inadequate. "The contradiction implied in the fact of thinking of a mystery falls to the ground of itself when we cease to cling to an objectified and misleading picture of thought."[2]

For Marcel there are two ways in which thought can proceed and within these ways he makes two minor distinctions and one major. His first minor is a return to Bergson's and Blondel's distinction between *pensée pensée* and *pensée pensant,* i.e., between closed and open thought. Philosophical thought, since it is ever pursuing being, is and must be open thought, engaged in the real and open to continual enrichment. The second distinction is between *penser* and *penser à,* thinking and thinking on, upon or about. Thinking focuses merely on objectified essences or structures; it is a type of depersonalized thought usually prior to full

²*BH*, p. 126.

personal consciousness. But to think on or about someone is very personalized and intimate thought. For example, thought about a beloved who is dead is not a mere passing in review of something structured; it is thinking through participation, a re-creation of participation in the being of the loved one.

Thinking bears on essences alone. However, depersonalization is impossible in the order of *thinking of*. Only a particular person can *think of* a particular being or individual thing. This truth is of the utmost importance. It is to be observed also that the more the thinker fills in the context of reality, the more he passes over from just *thinking* to *thinking of*. This helps us understand the sense in which the infinite is involved in the act of thinking or conceiving the individual essence. [3]

Marcel's major distinction within thought is between *primary* and *secondary reflection*. Nothing is more necessary to integral human living, Marcel agrees, than reflection. But reflection actually takes place on different levels of thinking, about problems and mysteries and in varying degrees of intensity. We have already seen that to handle the problems of life and to explore the complex objects of the universe man takes things apart via mental and physical techniques. These analytical prodecures tend to isolate objects and to insularize subjects. Thus primary reflection severs man from incarnation in the immediacy of his milieu. As purely analytical, its function and role in the elaboration of science and technology can never be underestimated. Yet, as a dissolvent, it does not further the relationship of participation; rather it emphasizes technical contact and commercial communication. Thus primary reflection is actually a retreat from participation and from involvement in lived experience. Certainly this scientific outlook attains its limited ends quite admirably, but philosophy recognizes its inadequacies, foremost among which is its inability to explain or appreciate the totality, unity or quality of the unqualifiedly actual.

Now secondary reflection does not give the lie to the findings of primary reflection, but it identifies, exposes and fills out the

[3] *Ibid.*, p. 31.

partial aspects of these findings which, were they allowed to be
exalted into absolutes, would become false idols.   Secondary
reflection re-establishes the immediacy between subject and object
and between subject and subject that had been ruptured by the
objectifying process of primary reflection. Thus secondary reflection is actually a new level of ontological participation and incarnation, superior to that of sensation in quality and intensity and
making use of the very skills and technical fruits produced by
primary reflection as instruments to a higher metaphysical communion.   Speaking of the different use made of concepts by both
primary and secondary reflection Kenneth Gallagher writes:

> After all, secondary reflection proceeds by concepts, just as
> primary reflection: what exempts it from the charge of objec-
> tification? Two answers may be suggested. First, Marcel
> must allow some legitimate role for the concept. Secondary
> reflection certainly uses concepts, and if all conceptualizing
> were invalid, his whole philosophy would be undermined.
> Secondary reflection differs not in the instrument of thought
> which it uses, but in the *direction* of the thought: primary
> reflection tends to reify its concepts and in doing so to ab-
> stract from existence; secondary reflection, in replunging into
> the oceanic immediacy from which its concepts are scooped,
> at the same time re-establishes the primacy of the existential.
> To say this much, however, is only to give half an answer. In
> order that secondary reflection may be moved to re-route the
> impetus of thought in the direction of participation, it must
> be that at some level of cognition that participation has not
> been lost hold of. Otherwise, a motive to initiate the new
> direction would be entirely lacking. This means that second-
> ary reflection lives off an intuition. Marcel, struggling to
> express the nature of philosophical thought, first called it
> "reflexive intuition" and then settled for secondary reflection
> as the less incriminating phrase. But it is still right to insist
> on the progressively intuitive character of this reflection, and
> indeed it would be inconceivable apart from the blinded
> intuition that underlies it. While this intuition can never be
> an object of thought, without it philosophical reflection
> would never begin to be. [4]

[4] Kenneth T. GALLAGHER, "*The Philosophical Method of Gabriel
Marcel*" (New York: Fordham University Doctoral Dissertation, 1958),
pp. 81-82. Later published as *The Philosophy of Gabriel Marcel* (New
York: Fordham University Press, 1962).

Primary reflection interprets a way of having; secondary, a way of being, of participating; the latter is a new immersion into being, for it transcends the antinomies that primary reflection perforce sets up—such antinomies as: I am the master and possessor of my body—my body is my master and I am its slave; faith gives me knowledge of reality—faith is merely an interesting subjective experience; sensation apprehends the world—sensation, being merely subjective, is cut off from reality. By a deliberate conversion back to the immediacy of lived experience, secondary reflection surmounts, transcends these antinomies and attains a higher spiritual incarnation and communion with being.

There is a magnificent connection and correspondence between Marcel's view of knowledge, his epistemology, and his philosophy of intersubjective communion, his social philosophy. Roger Troisfontaines exposes this relational insight when he writes:

> To the primitive complex corresponds the *community*, which imposes itself on us as a fact anterior to our free will. To analysis corresponds the stage of *communication*: man takes note of his personal autonomy and it rests with him whether to break his relation with others or on the contrary to accept and deepen it. And according to which he chooses, he will either shut himself in the *isolation* of egoism and pride, or open himself up to communion with God and men whom he can meet in faith and love. [5]

Somewhat analogously to the way in which primitive being is caught up in the community of original creation, primitive man is caught up in the ancient tribes that impose upon him his original community. A specific clan, family, nation, civilization begets each person and continually moulds him in the community it constitutes. But, unlike the mere physical and evolutional advancements of irrational beings from the initial complex confusion to the harmony of a higher elemental, geological and biological synthesis, man is free to go up higher from the imposed

[5] R. TROISFONTAINES, *Existentialism and...*, p. 68.

community into which he arrived to a personally planned and perfected communion of a far higher spiritual synthesis. The effective power of freedom decides whether men will communicate harmoniously among themselves for the establishment of the life of spiritual and social communion or whether they will break off communications and, from their isolated strongholds, compete violently for a total domination which, not only fails to attain any communion, but actually succeeds in destroying whatever communities of value men had previously enjoyed.

The stage of communication is thus seen to be intermediate between the original, unconscious complexity of community and the much-desired, fully-conscious completion of communion. [6] In the previous chapter we considered, in the light of Marcel's thought, various reasons why men both choose to break-off harmonious conversation and communication with all subjects in pursuit of an all-object universe, and why they choose to vitiate these same channels toward communion into avenues that lead straight to the armed-camp community. In this chapter we follow Marcel in his consideration of the alternative course that is open to freedom vis-à-vis the community—namely, that human freedom, besides facing the risk and danger of opting for divisiveness, is also offered the marvelously creative possibility and challenge of choosing union and communion.

Far from being a datum, the stage of communion among men, because it is a challenge, must come into existence as a human achievement, an accomplishment that can only be won through self-donating human choices. But before we can clarify the mystery of the achievement of communion, we must attempt to throw more light on the mystery of the question, "Who am I?" We are in the land of spiritual incarnation here and must seek the immersion in reality that comes from secondary reflection. Immediately it is evident that if I attempt to answer the question for myself, my answer will not be accepted, either because I will be deemed unqualified to answer this question or because, being too involved,

[6] *Ibid.*, p. 70.

the legitimate answer will be expected to be forthcoming only from somebody else. Are these objections valid? Marcel says:

> All of us have at times had the feeling of being lost in ourselves as in a maze; in such a case we do count on somebody else, the nearest friend, the truest comrade, to help us out of the maze, or in a word to do our reconnaissance for us and help us toward self-recognition. "You who really know me better than I know myself, tell me, is it true—am I really such a selfish, heartless person...?" [7]

But another difficulty arises. The person chosen may really be qualified to enlighten me about myself. But I chose him and thus I decided he had the qualities to enlighten me; I legitimized him to tell me who I really am. Perhaps I am counting on his friendship to get the answers I want to hear about myself. Or the opposite may be true; I have chosen an enemy to tell me about myself. But again his credentials as judge on me come from myself and, once I remember that I am the source of my judge's authority, I will always be tempted to call his judgment into question, whether it be a judgment of commendation or condemnation. [8]

Is a valid answer to the question, "Who am I?" possible? Marcel answers in the negative and gives these reasons.

"Who am I? What am I worth?" These questions have no answers. We have here a riddle that simply cannot be solved on the human level. For no group, no society can give us a plain answer to these questions. Why? Because these are not really questions but appeals sent out beyond the circle of one's own associates. These appeals are supra-empirical; they are sent out to the Absolute Thou, above and beyond the limits of our experiences. These are calls made upon the Absolute Thou to witness, as a last and supreme resource, the needs of the troubled human spirit. [9]

What Marcel is telling us is that every endeavor to throw light on the mystery of "Who am I?" orients us towards what transcends our own personality—towards the world, towards

[7] *MB* (I), pp. 182-183.
[8] *Ibid.*, p. 183.
[9] *Ibid.*, pp. 184, 187, 188.

others, ultimately towards God. [10] We have already seen that, through incarnation in the body, through primary participation in sensation, through primary reflection on lived experience, man partially lights up for himself the reality of the datum of his experience in a community of being and simultaneously sets the stage for his freely-chosen re-immersion into the immediacy of experience with its consequent spiraling activity, via secondary illumination, into the higher mystery of his becoming in being and of his ever-deeper and fuller participation in transcendent being. To understand the achievement of communion among men, we must study man's indispensable bond with his fellowmen, we must study what Marcel calls man's "encounter with the other."

Needless to say, on the plane of existence and within the initial cosmic and social milieu, the "I" of the newly arrived human being is dormant. Moreover, even with the passage of some time and while still on the biological plane of development, while primary reflection still dominates its communication with the other, the "I" will continue to emerge merely as an objectified "it," or "him." Marcel has found that man never attains his being, his "I" until he freely and generously enters into the tension of an intersubjective communication with the other which ceases to treat the other as an "it" or "him," but accepts the other as a "thou."

Intersubjectivity

Now the human act which posits and establishes the "I" always implies a reference to the other. I only think of myself as myself by distinguishing myself from all others, and by conceiving of myself as being other than they. In demonstrating that the "I" can neither be auto-sufficient nor an absolute headquarters unto itself, Marcel makes analytical use of the immediate and simple experience of feeling tired and the judgment formed on it.

"I am tired." We have in this statement a pure, simple feeling, an absolute, something not related to something else, not

[10] R. TROISFONTAINES, *De l'existence...*, II, p. 9.

mediatized. In this judgment the non-relation functions as a *him* or *it*. The feeling, having become a predicate, depends on this non-relation. The dialogue would proceed as follows: "Someone is tired. Who is? I am." But to have meaning, this whole dialogue must be directed to another interlocutor for whom the *I* is a particular person. Thus I only become a given person to myself through the mediating idea of the other to whom I am a given person. In principle and quite literally, I am never a given person for myself. I am even the negation of a person. The *I* seems always postured, and hence must be postulated, in confrontation with a *thou*. *He* or *it* can be meaningfully defined only in function to this dialogue. [11]

Could it be, Marcel queries, that the answer to the question "Who am I?" is to be given by my life, by my whole life of lived experience? But what exactly can I mean when I talk about my life? It cannot be the sequence of episodes lived along a certain time-line that I can detail or even summarize for you, since I can never recapture these events just as I lived them. The documentary reproduction of my life can only be a narrow, fragmentary condensation of its lived richness, a sort of cinematic "slice of my life" issued and stamped with the defects and limitations that are native to my mental and memorative studios. Moreover, diaries, journals, histories of my life suffer from the same inherent defects; even works of art, of literature, of music—my deeds and acts— cannot fully reveal the meaning of my life to me, much less to the other. Somehow my life seems to transcend all these efforts to capture it. My life cannot be my past, for when I talk about my life, I am still committed to living, I am still caught up in living now, at this moment, in the present deed. My life at this instant seems to be focused in the purpose and the goal I am definitely aiming at, since this purposeful activity actually heightens my awareness of being alive. Marcel writes of this experience thus:

The more oriented a man's life is towards a definite goal, the more vividly he is aware of being alive. Where a person is concentrating all his energies on something, he is living to the fullest of his capacities. What is the nature of this plenitude of living? It seems we must conclude that my life cannot be really separated from the quality of interest I take in my life. This leads to a more ultimate question. What is my interest in my life based upon? On the mere prolongation of its span in time? This would be a curling up into one's shell to extend mere survival. It is, to be sure, one possible course of action. There are hundreds of people who "keep fit" and are interested solely in the perfect functioning of their bodies. This narrow self-enclosure reflects the deprivation of their lives. The more encumbered, the more self-concerned, the more loaded down a man is, the less intensely he lives, the more poverty-stricken his life is. [12]

Availability

In the previous chapter we had seen that the self-centered person is unavailable or rather uncommitted, unhandy. He is unable, because unwilling, to respond to the call made upon him by life, his own and fellowmen's; he refuses to answer appeals for sympathy, shutting himself up in his shell, not daring to go beyond the secluded circle of his own petty experiences, engrossed in the trivialities that hold him enchained exclusively to his own sterile existence. Such a person succeeds in depleting his life to the point where it shrivels away into a negativism that rejects anything that can extend or enrich his experience. How can the unavailable give his life when he has not as yet discovered the inner coherency of himself? And how can he give his life before he gives himself? But how can he discover, or rather create, himself as a person without giving his life? The paradoxical truth is that the act of giving himself, i.e., the act of self-sacrifice, is the essentially creative act that constitutes the life of the person. The act of self-sacrifice is the act of self-fulfilment, to be sure, on a higher and invisible level of being.

[12] *MB* (I), pp. 199-200.

For Marcel, the man who gives his life, and is fully aware of what he is doing—namely giving himself without any hope of a return—this hero or martyr performs what on the surface seems to be a sacrifice of madness, but on deeper, on secondary and recuperative reflection, is seen as the inestimable madness of love. The martyr who is carrying out the act of self-sacrifice has the incontrovertible conviction that he *is* reaching self-fulfilment. He has the inner assurance that he *is* most completely, transcendently in the very act of giving his life away. Marcel handles the paradox at hand with wonderful insight.

Have we not run into a marvelous paradox? It seems ridiculous to say that I attain plenitude of being for myself by the very act with which I dispatch myself. Here a careful distinction is in order between the physical effect of the deed of self-sacrifice and the deed's inner meaning. Doing away with oneself has only to do with the obvious physical effects: one more dead body on the hands of society. Sheer insanity would claim that self-fulfilment is the effect of becoming a corpse. Fulfilment is realized on a higher, on an invisible level. A man's life infinitely transcends any possible grasp of it by himself at any given moment. Fundamentally and essentially personal lives refuse to tally up neatly. One of Marcel's characters says, "My life is the realm of yes and no, the place where I have to say at the same time that I *am* and that I *am not*." [13]

Eventually, then, I am fully aware that my life eludes me on all sides; I am forced to admit that my life is too full of mystery to be grasped or comprehended fully by me. I see in a blinding flash that even on the natural plane of living he who willingly loses his life here for the other, somehow regains it more richly hereafter for himself, and that on a much nobler plane of living. To sacrifice one's life, to consecrate one's life for and to someone else is to bring to mature consummation the "I" that is more totally concentrated and alertly aware of the other than of itself, the "I" that dedicates its life and itself to living, here and hereafter, for someone else, to the eternal living of someone other than itself.

[13] *Ibid.*, pp. 205-206.

It seems to be a natural example of John the Baptist's supernatural dedication: "You must increase and I must decrease," where the very culmination of his life is attained in its apparent total self-destruction for the advancement of the life of the Thou to the summit of its perfection.

The act by which I consecrate myself to some "thou" resembles the bursting of my life from the bud of mere existence into the flower and fruit of intersubjective union and communion. Unlike the shy young man or woman who is caught in the dungeon of his own self-consciousness, the dedicated "I" has entered into a genuine encounter or conversation with the "thou." The self-conscious subject, on the other hand, feels himself the cynosure of hostile eyes; he imagines every word as a barb against his person; every glance is a malevolent light exposing his inadequacies; every laugh is a joke about his stupidity; every gesture aims at ridiculing his awkwardness; the whisper is a whip that lashes his hyper-sensitive soul; the wink is a signal to execute the plot that has been planned to bring about his downfall. Thoroughly preoccupied with himself, in a tension of fear, insecurity and outright panic, the poor introvert is incapable of becoming himself because he is rapidly becoming alternately the persons he suspects others think he is. Because he is on the defensive, because his guard is always up, because his gates are barricaded, the introvert is incapable of a genuine encounter *with* the other; under these psychological conditions conversation with a "thou" is impossible, for conversation is seen, under a murky Sartrean suspicion, to be merely an instrument of domination. Thus the introvert remains juxtaposed near others, alongside people, precariously beside them, timidly beside himself, but never *with* anyone.

For the relationship expressed by the preposition *with* reveals the splendor of what is eminently intersubjective in man's life. This relationship is simply never verified in the world of objects. Objects are never *with* each other, but merely juxtaposed. A chair is *alongside* a table, or *beside* a bed, or *by* a window; chairs never are really *with* any of these or other objects. [14]

[14] *Ibid.*, p. 218.

When the ice of suspicious objectivity is melted "between the stranger and the shy young man," [15] there is a relaxation of inner tension, a spiritual strait-jacket is shed and the liberation that ensues is the creation of a bond of communion that links the two together in a mysteriously intimate way. An insight of Marcel that keeps constantly recurring in a variety of descriptive experiences is that "ego-centrism is always a cause of blindness, a blindness that cannot be localized," but that falls like darkness on an ever-widening area of reality.

Obsession through an ego-centric preoccupation sets up a barrier between the one obsessed and all others. There is simply no exchange of life and experience between the egocentric and his fellowmen. The egoist is self-confined; his very restriction of himself to his own thought is the act that blinds him about himself. He is ignorant of his real needs; he is unaware that he is betraying himself to the very extent that he curls up within himself. But there is an equally true and important corollary to this truth. Complete, concrete self-knowledge cannot be heautocentric; it must be hetero-centric. We only find and understand ourselves by finding and understanding others. Only in this perspective can a legitimate self-love be fostered. [16]

I cannot, if I am honest with myself, discover any evidence in lived experience that will validly give me the conviction that I must be superior to others and hence worthy of superior treatment from others. Actually, only in so far as I am open to others, only in so far as others are open to me, only, that is, in so far as I trans-exist for others and others trans-exist for me in the mutual activity of welcoming, serving, surrendering and loving can the "I" and "thou" co-exist as co-presence in communion. My trans-subjective life with the "thou" gives me my personal life of the "I." The only way I can fully discover and express the "I" of myself is through communion with the "thou" of the other, for "I" am fully realized only in the "thou" that responds to my appeal and crosses the threshold of my mind and heart.

[15] *Ibid.*, p. 219.
[16] *MB* (II), pp. 8-9.

"Who are you?" is the only legitimate question that may be asked of the "thou," and, like the question "Who am I?" it is not a plea for statistical information. For even as the documentary and statistical reproduction of the history of the "I" would never touch, much less grasp, the transcendent substance of the "I," so too the narrative or the question-and-answer approach to the superabundant richness of the "thou" will fail to capture that mysterious person. What is produced by these methods is merely a sum of objective characterizations, judgments, descriptions concerning the talents, background, experiences of an absent third, of a him, and nothing is known about a present "thou." Such information reports the findings of the collisions that take place between a questioner and the one questioned on the level of being where the commerce of mere communication holds sway, a level that is far below the plateau of presence, of communion, of the genuine encounter with the other. The filing-cabinet relationship is not a genuinely personal relationship but, as a matter of fact, is an objectively depersonalized approach to man. The truth is that the "thou" is beyond all inventory; a "thou" cannot be founded on new knowledge. The "thou" is discovered only in an exchange of persons, in an encounter with the "I" that arises from a bond of mutual interest, concern, consideration. A moment of clarification bursts forth between the "I" and the "thou," a "flash of clarity" in which the "I" grasps the presence of the "thou" and the "thou" embraces the co-presence of the "I." Both "I" and "thou" in this moment are uncharacterizable, infinitely meaningful yet infinitely mysteryful; both transcend all categories; both are presences, presence (I) and co-presence (thou).

"Who am I?" "Who are you?" These are not questions: Despite their interrogative apparel, they are actually appeals! Be present to a thou! Be present to me! Not only are "I" and "thou" mysteries, but they, rather "we" are the same mystery. The uniqueness of the "I," my uniqueness, my unutterable person is constituted by the co-presence of the inestimable "thou." The towering transcendence of the "thou," thy ineffable person is based on the presence of the "I." We, "I and thou," mature as actual persons as we enter ever more generously and intensely into the living and mystical body of communion with each other. Communion is the co-presence of the "I" and the "thou" in which the essence is to be more than an essence in participation which transcends frontiers.

But what are the concrete attitudes and what are the solid deeds that successfully achieve communion, that project persons into what Jeanne Delhomme calls "participation without frontiers?" [17]   Marcel does not hesitate to designate them as the profoundly primary experiences of fidelity, hope and love. Enamored as he is with E. M. Forster's aphorism that "It is a personal life and it alone which holds up the mirror to infinity," [18] Marcel adventurously explores these three avenues of intensely intersubjective activity.

The Man of Encounter

The man of encounter is a friend because he addresses himself to a "thou" with whom he enters into living communion. He admires, enjoys or sorrows with his friend.   His friend is not merely an animated information bureau whom he consults for facts and figures and trends and indices.   The man of encounter is a man of co-presence; he shares truth and love with his friend; he *adheres* to his friend and *abhors* using him.   Long ago he has crossed over to his friend and is always "with" him in an enduring act of free and total commitment.   The attitude and actions of the man of encounter achieve in him the spiritual maturity of being a man of communion.

If I may use a personal example to close out this aspect of interpersonal communion, whenever I read columnist Arthur Krock, I feel that I am being invited to share with him his own genuine and secret analysis of some important event whose truth, he intends, will bind us together and bring us all greater good.   On the contrary, whenever I read Drew Pearson, I experience a suffocating attack on the free respiration of my mind, an attempt to

[17] Etienne GILSON, *Existentialisme chrétien*, p. 174.
[18] *RI*, p. 191.

abduct me to the mills of propaganda for some clandestine purpose, some secret, that Pearson will not reveal to me. I am "with" Mr. Krock because he sends out an urgent appeal to me and invites my free response. I resist Mr. Pearson because it seems he invades my mind and attempts to seduce my will to purposes which are either indifferent or even hostile to the well-being of my person. With Krock I know I am a person; to Pearson I fear I am an intended victim, a dupe to his art of obscurantism.

Charm

Then there is the quality of charm in the man of interpersonal communion, a quality that, like mercy, is not strained. For the man of encounter, of presence, is also a man of charm; he is unconstrained in his behavior, free from all self-conscious ego-spasms. In fact charm vanishes the moment a person attempts to employ it with conscious intent. As a matter of experience, the charming person has wide margins to his personality; plenty of spiritual space is allotted to his fellowman and to himself so as to allow for a full and free expansion of their own individuality in the life of spiritual communion. The man of charm refuses to be tensed-up himself or to allow his fellowman to be squeezed into tightly-fitting mental, moral or social boundaries.

Charm is immediately felt as coming from a thou and seizing upon an I, but the seizure is one of spontaneous naturalness. To charm us a person must overflow expansively around and beyond what he says and does; [19] he must have the quality of remaining alive in us and even with us after he is no longer physically present. Only a person in direct communication, or rather communion, with another person can experience the initial radiation and warmth of charm; it is a question of an immediate revelation of the "I" in a certain intimacy with the "thou." We have no charm for ourselves, but only for others and it grows with the gratuitous element in our communion with others. [20] Marcel boldly links

[19] *MB* (I), p. 254.
[20] *MJ*, p. 300.

up charm with all that is most metaphysical in the personality and claims "that I only become a complete individual through the infinite credit which I grant to other individuals." [21] Charm is the soul of the infinitely gratuitous act that generously extends this credit.

But how do persons become complete individuals in deeds? How do they manage the successful passage from merely extrinsic communication with others to intimate personal communion with them? In other words, how does this important procession from the peripheral contact with the existence of the "him" ascend to the full communion of the being of the "thou?" From an inexhaustible supply of actual and possible examples, we will choose one of our own, modeled on the Marcellian method of analysis, to illustrate the rise from communication to communion between persons.

I am next to a fellow plane-traveler in the seat to my left. We have never seen each other before. Certainly, I am not *with* him at all, for not even a word has, as yet, been spoken between us. Eventually our roving glances meet; there is a nod, a smile and a random conversation on trivia ensues. We are now communicating with inter-crossing verbal signs that represent to each other things out there to what we presently are to each other, "someone" out there; weather, food, comfort and similar reports are interchanged. Gradually the unknown world of our lives begins to focus as a conversational movie-tone of information flows on between us. It turns out that we are enroute to the same continent —Europe, to the same country—Italy, to the same city—Milano, to the same section of the city—the environs of the Duomo. *Mirabile dictu!* We know the same family—the Corellis! And the unbelievable! We are actually distant cousins!

Long before the blood tie is discovered, most of the outer barriers to intersubjective communion were down. From being "someone out there," we were transformed into someone advancing rapidly up the corridors of participation toward ever-more-intimate communion with each other. By the time we arrived at Milano in our conversational journey, we had left the thin state

[21] *Ibid.,* p. 302.

of the "him-relationship" far behind and forever out of sight and
were moving vigorously on the level of the life of the "thou." "You
too know the Corelli family!" Is it any wonder that the discovery
of the blood tie erupts into the exclamatory effusion of the conti-
nental embrace. We are as one with each other.

The essential truth to be grasped here is that the other becomes a thou for me in the measure in which I open myself to his
reality. To open myself means to cease drawing a circle around
myself, a circle outside of which the other person never becomes
more than an idea, never more than an idea which is merely a
disintegrated, disjointed and diminished "him." To open myself
means that the other ceases to be for me a "someone," a "third"
in a dialogue with whom I am reflecting in a triadic relationship.
For in every objectification this remarkable event takes place: the
more my interlocutor is exterior to my person, the more I am, by
the same blow and in the same degree, foreign and exterior to
myself; in the face of a "someone," I become even to myself
"another one." I become conscious to myself not of what I am,
but rather, self-conscious as to what others must think I am. I
lose myself. On the other hand, as intimacy deepens and
flourishes, there no longer exists the face-to-face opposition of a
"someone" toward "some other one"; there simply is "we" in a
dyadic coalescence that is the life of a unity grounded on the interior unification of love. [22] I have discovered myself in the thou,
and we live in the truly created intimacy of authentic and transcendent co-presence of love.

We have arrived at this unity of love from different levels of
the appeal. There was the first, timid, extrinsic *con-versatio*
toward each other that was motivated by the hunger and curiosity
for communication; we might name this the "call to communication." As this initial plea was heard and answered, the mysterious *co-esse* of the interlocutors in existence deepened through
the togetherness attained through communication. Spatial proximity began to be complemented by the awakening psychical
proximity; position began to be transformed into presence. When

[22] *Ibid.*, p. 146.

some common element, some common secret, some common experience or bond, however tiny, is discovered and shared, we have at once the "call to communion," the invocation, more or less clearly enunciated and heard, "abide with me." Once heard and freely answered in the affirmative, the boundaries of merely thinking of someone, of speaking to someone, of dealing with someone are crossed; we are beyond communication; we have entered the promised land of communion and the chosen community of love; we are *with* a thou, *with*, in a felt and ever-increasing intimacy of communion. I have invoked you so that we may always be together, mutually present in love. There is a void in us both which appeals to one another and permits us both to answer each other with the gift of self-donation.

We see, therefore, that to pass into action in response to an appeal, to say "Yes," freely, generously, in word and deed, to a vocation and an invocation is to engage the whole person of the "I" actively in the person and fortunes of the "thou." This acceptance, this total commitment demonstrates clearly that freedom is bestowed upon man both as a gift and as a conquest. Whenever man succumbs to coercion, which is nothing else than force imposed from without, he ceases to be present to himself; he becomes a stranger to himself. The intimidated and the tyrannized move through life like sleep-walkers as witness the apathetic, humdrum endurance of millions behind the iron curtain.

Engagement

But the response of *engagement* lifts a man from the dull anonymity of being a mere individual to the vibrant reality of being a spiritual person. This is so because the response of *engagement* is a spiritual response to the prior, interior spiritual action of the appeal, the vocation and the invocation. In some mysterious manner the response of *engagement* to the vocation restores the person to himself, especially when a person is explicitly conscious that he could have rejected the appeal. In any event, whether consciously or subconsciously entered into, the response of *engagement* delivers a person back to himself in the very action in which he is acting as a deliverer to a thou whose appeal he hastens to fulfill. We cannot engage in the fulfilment of the persons of others without simultaneously fulfiling our own persons.

Instead of shutting himself up in a selfish, proud and isolationary "No," a man with the attitude and spirit of *engagement* opens himself up, opens his heart up to the appeals from God and from his neighbor in an overflow of humble friendliness, receptiveness and generosity. This action is often arduous and not infrequently calls for heroic virtue. To become engaged in a thou and his fortunes, will often demand that I must overcome fears of compromising myself. I have to be willing to run the risk of provoking trouble and enduring hardship. I will have to overcome the temptations to cowardice, disloyalty, pretension and mediocrity. This calls for the exercises of courage, loyalty, veracity and of outstanding service. For the attitude of *engagement* is thoroughly opposed to the pusillanimous posture of the man of half-measures, the man who is always questioning whether decisions and action here and now are possible, the man who is constantly enumerating obstacles to, and predicting horrifying effects from any action save inaction. Marcel analyzes the trouble with this thin man of velleity with an acuteness that is worthy of comparison with the Ignatian scrutiny of the first pair in the meditation on the Three Classes of Men.

To make a positive act of the will is to refuse to question the possibility of what is willed to be done. Certainly, possibility is not of primary consideration here. To will means to transcend the point where possible and impossible confront each other. The man still wondering whether he is able, still enumerating and weighing actual and possible obstacles, is not willing at all in the strict sense of the word. "He would like to, but...." Whereas vigorous willing ignores *buts.* "I only will from the moment I make a *tabula rasa* of all *buts:* though strictly speaking I know them, I know them as suppressed." [23]

    [23] *Ibid.,* p. 184.

The man of *engagement*, then, is a man of strong will, convinced he can effectively change adverse conditions for the better with the aid of grace and via his self-application to these conditions. He is prudently, yet boldly, determined; he wills his decisions and actions wholeheartedly and expects to assume personal responsibility for all he says and does. A man of knowledge with a hunger for moral goodness for himself and his fellowman, the man of *engagement* commits himself to work for a morally good order and against a morally evil counterfeit of order. He eschews a spirit of neutrality toward the good order and condemns this spirit for what it is in reality, a degrading and immoral social opportunism; he has a spiritual sense of smell that detects the corruption of cowardice under the wrappings of prudence; his vision can pierce the labels for liberty that front for the actions of traitors.

Unlike the dedicated criminal who in some external aspects resembles the man of *engagement*, the true and full man of *engagement* is gladly willing to stand up for the consequences of his actions. His motto is not so much, "Truth or consequences," as "Truth *and* consequences." The man of *engagement* has entered into a pact of solidarity with his acts, as if he and his actions were members of an interior and spiritual community. The mere individual may be likened to the anonymous and impersonal French *"on"* as he goes about breaking life up into little pieces. On the other hand, the man of *engagement*, as a mature person, confronts life integrally; he assimilates it to himself, reflects upon it, moulds it, chooses it and synthesizes its apparent disparate and unconnected events into a shining harmony of a crusade for a communion of loving collaboration here enroute to a communion of loving happiness hereafter. This explains why the man of *engagement* is radiant, a promoter of all that is good, and animated with a will for that type of justice that transcends the abstract, static justice reigning in the world of abstractions. His justice is embodied in the Absolute Thou.

To contract a valid engagement, the whole soul of the man of action must be in complete control of herself, must be intellectually awake and volitionally uninhibited, in a state of conviction that will never admit the possibility of alleging in the future that she was not responsible for her actions. Her commitment can never be extorted through constraint or blackmail for it would then be as valueless as an oath extracted from a man in a drunken stupor. The man of *engagement* does not await nor demand exhaustive, comprehensive knowledge of a situation before proceeding forthrightly to a decision and to action. He knows that this exaggerated demand is often enough a thinly veiled dodge of one's responsibility. And anyway, in cases in which he is personally implicated this procedure is impossible.

To be sure, theoretically before a man opts to engage himself, he should first know himself. Practically, however, we have seen already that a person will really discover himself as a person only when he first becomes involved as a man of dedication in effective action for the thou of his neighbor, his country and his God. Too many people grope their whole lives away among the data of their private existences, stalking back and forth on a beaten path that moves through the heavy furniture of their private chambers. They never burn over important issues of the day. Quarantined as it were in a protective shell they seem to secrete around themselves, they claim they can support, or rather endure life if they are allowed to unroll themselves in the anonymity of a world that is engulfed in semi-darkness; they contentedly become acclimated to a foggy obscurity. They have chosen a state of non-vision, of unconcern that is slipping dangerously toward non-being. [24]

But the man of *engagement* lives the exact opposite type of life. His enthusiastic enlistment in events that are crucial for himself and for others becomes his creative work, a work whereby he transcends mere existence and becoming and penetrates into eternity. His decision for *engagement* is his decision to become an authentic being; it is his decision to collaborate actively in becoming what he aspires to become, an eternal being. He commits himself to strive to become what he wants to become. His very living deeds affirm the solidarity that exists between the philosophy of his being and the philosophy of his freedom: "I am—more

²⁴ R. TROISFONTAINES, *De l'existence...*, I, p. 356.

exactly—I will be what I aspire to be." [25]   The man of commitment, who holds to his pledge, dominates the course of history, creates his real being, not merely for time but for eternity.   More than this, through the radiance of his goodness and the love emanating from his person, he gives positive and inspiring meaning—transcendent and invisible meaning—to the human enterprise, meaning that alone can justify and make it worth living.   He is creative because he has bound himself, as it were by vow, to accept and to participate wholeheartedly in the human enterprise of intersubjective communion.

Communion

Earlier we stated that inferior modes of contact and union proper to the inferior realms of being were multifarious.   We also considered some of the preliminary modes of communal contact attained through the gift of human existence: incarnation, sensation, primary reflection, secondary reflection and communication.   As we ascended the scale of participation from the material toward the spiritual and transcendent communion, we were able to suspect the truth of Marcel's statement that the aspects and attitudes of interpersonal living are infinite.   In the previous chapter we followed Marcel in his analysis of some anti-communion techniques that are presently threatening to dissolve our long-established social institutions.   Thus far in this chapter we have considered some of Marcel's suggestions for the development of communal attitudes that will act as antidotes to the disintegrating poisons in the body social and can help restore the social community to a healthy and vigorous life of communion.

But as we look closer at some of these attitudes, it becomes clear that, in themselves, they do not constitute union nor valid communion.   True, they effect "spiritual touches" that can blossom into full-blown communion with the other.   But even these touches are but the material out of which communion is

[25] *Ibid.*, p. 357.

woven, the bricks out of which the house of community is edified
Yet such spiritual stones as the following must be inserted into the
foundations of the community, if we are ever to inhabit the happy
home of communion: self-donation to the thou, the spirit of
encounter, co-presence, *engagement*. Following Marcel we intend
now to explore how the person freely ascends, through these spiritual attitudes, from the alienated plane of the community in
communication to the radiant plane of the community in communion.

All "touches" between persons on the level of communication
initiate between them a contact that embodies the stage of "social
acts." Communication with our fellowmen through promises,
contacts, commands, requests and other such actions brings men
into the "interpersonal space, the unique medium which exists
between spiritual persons and is analogous to the space of the outer
world between creatures." [26] My command or request on the
level of this new rendezvous presents the other with something of
objective content. I am asking him to become my partner over
this object in this spiritual situation. Social acts, therefore,
concentrate not on the persons involved as thou's, i.e., as persons,
but on the thing to be communicated between them. By their
social acts persons do not directly reveal themselves; they are
reflected only indirectly and obliquely in the content of their
mutual communication. Persons are not the primary nor direct
objects of social acts; facts are.

Presence

A new and higher plateau of spiritual contact is chosen when
we arrive at the intersubjective union of the revealed atti-

[26] This analysis of the graduations of spiritual contact is treated
in an enlightening manner by Thomas J. Owens, S. J., in his doctoral
dissertation in philosophy: *The Problem of Interpersonal Relationships As
Posed in Contemporary Thought* (New York: Fordham University Press,
1951), pp. 157-188.

tude. [27] This is a level of confrontation that very much resembles what took place on the high mountain of the third temptation of Christ by the devil. It is a battlefield upon which an issue, important to two persons, must be decided one way or the other. A person must choose either egolatry with the passing rewards it gives in an alienated world or he will choose adoration or *engagement*, as the case may be, according as the thou accepted or rejected is God or one's fellowman. In any case, there is an eternal reward of love for the decision to dwell in the world of transcendental communion. On this high plateau of presence, persons, formerly enemies or acquaintances or perhaps even strangers, plainly reveal themselves to each other in their spiritual nakedness. Real "entering into" the other and direct spiritual touching ensues. Hatred or love flash forth. The outcome will most certainly be either a "Begone!" of rejection or a "Come!" of communion.

It is with the concrete expressions of the "Come!" of communion that Marcel's whole philosophy is obsessed. Three of the most intensely "engaged" and revealed attitudes that Marcel never tires of investigating are those of fidelity, hope and love. The purpose of his "rigorous and sinuous" researches into these spiritual activities is to locate himself more centrally within the mystery of being so as to participate more intensely in the treasure of communion that is found there in an inexhaustible profundity.

Fidelity

There is a directly unveiled revelation of the self, a real touching and entering into the thou of the other person that is achieved by

[27] The gradations of spiritual contact expounded here represent in summary the substance of the thought of Dr. Dietrich von Hildebrand as it appears in his *Metaphysik der Gemeinschaft* (Augsburg: Haas und Grabherr, 1930), pp. 23-37. In private conversations with Dr. Hildebrand, I learned that, although he does not use the exact same terminology, Marcel is in complete accord with the Hildebrand explanations of these gradations. Both eminent philosophers have frequently discussed their interpersonal philosophy tête-à-tête. They have been delighted to discover that they have arrived at the same conclusions quite independently of each other. In this connection, cf. an article by Dr. Alice Jourdain, "Von Hildebrand and Marcel: A Parallel," pp. 11-35.

these attitudes of fidelity, hope, love. Once a person is steeped in these spiritual commitments, he cannot be concerned with the *fact* that he has faith, hope and love for the thou of the other. His spiritual action is far nobler; it so far transcends any self-centered or objective position that it is psychologically impossible of bending back upon itself. The fact is that the man who is suffused with the spiritual action of faith, hope and love is in full *execution* of his revealed attitude. He is *in* his faith, *in* his hope, *in* his love for the present thou. He is lost to himself in these actions and all present and accounted for to the thou of the other person. Only in the presence of the thou is he spiritually naked to the thou as a friend, a witness, a brother, a co-lover. For the revealed attitude can only be achieved *coram te!* The person present by faith, hope and love is a whole and unified being to the thou, uttering the "inner word" of his total being in commitment to the thou. And upon experiencing that he has been accepted, there arises from this reciprocal utterance and acceptance of "inner words," an intense mutual love from this union and communion in transcendence.

The "thou" exists for me and "I" exist for the "thou" only to the same degree that we exist for each other. Our being in communion, which the knowledge and experience of our reciprocal engagement created, cannot be sustained by me alone. Once I have collaborated in the creation of our being in communion, I, nevertheless, remain free to annihilite this colloquy *in esse* by merely denying my former promise and dedication, thus severing my spiritual bond with the being of the "thou." I always have it within my power, in the face of temptations, that may be either attempts at seductions from my enemies or tests to virtue from my friends, to choose to snap the tie of communion, that binds me to my friend. The same spiritual situation confronts the "thou" in his relationship to the "I."

An historical example may help our analysis. We have in the situation of Peter, confronted by the servant girl over his tie to Christ, an elucidation concerning the ontological role of fidelity. "Thou also wast with Jesus the Galilean!" As a matter of fact,

Peter was *"with Jesus"* in the richest, most spiritual and intimate senses that Marcel has wrung from this intersubjective expression of communion. Yet Peter denied the bonds of knowledge, of co-presence, of collaboration, of natural and supernatural communal living that had been mutually enjoyed by him in the company of Christ. Formerly, these bonds had riveted the two to each other in a communion of sublime love. Fidelity on Peter's part called for his public avowal of his tie with Christ; it demanded his public prolongation of the presence of his friend in himself; it urged the open defense of his friend and the promulgation of his friend's many benefactions to himself and to others. Had Peter performed—which he will do in an heroic degree in the future—these acts of *engagement*, had he been faithful in this trial, he would have been acting in a spiritually creative way. His fidelity would have creatively multiplied and deepened within himself, while testifying before others to the unfathomable goodness of his friend, the presence and goodness of the one who had chosen him on the day he enlisted and eloped with Christ. His communion with Christ, his ardent re-assertion of his "we" with Him, originally rested on the first instant he crossed over to Him. It could only survive and wax strong on the instant to instant renewal of his confessing of Christ before men under fair or foul circumstances.

All men are tempted at times to fall back upon themselves, to consider themselves as an autonomous center for demanding claims to things from others. This comes down to treating the "we" relationship as though it were not real, as though it were non-existent. One of the weaknesses of the "we" relationship is that it is bodyless, without any organs proper to it. It only exists and catches hold of itself, as it were, across the spiritual space that exists between the "I" and the "thou," and only when the "I" and the "thou" reject the temptation to deny the existence of the "we." The tendency to deny the we arises from the fact that each person suffers from the ambiguity of a divided will. This interiorly disjointed articulation of the will is a central mystery in man that tears him simultaneously in two opposite directions. One pull of this double will opts for the egoistic "I" which is incapable of attaining any durable satisfaction. The other drive of the will aspires to communion and seems capable of opening the way to peace and joy.

Yet fidelity cannot be reduced to constancy in the will and in conduct. The immutable permanency of a certain state or attitude in man may never be identified with fidelity. For fidelity by nature possesses a certain creative and inventive spontaneity. Marcel is not too impressed when someone assures him, with the best will in the world, that his feelings and sentiments towards Marcel will never change. A reward for constancy may be in order? Yes. But fidelity? That is another question entirely. For if I ascertain that the constant one was not really *present* to me in a situation where his friendship would have been precious to me, I will certainly hesitate to speak about his fidelity. Peter, though physically present, chose to be away spiritually when Christ needed his friendship before Caiphas.

Marcel insists that a true friend is one that is never missing, one who overcomes every trial against friendship. Far from stealing away to some safe hideout, he is always found present in adversity. [28] And present here does not merely mean manifest on the spot like some official mourner at a funeral. It means that in all adversity somehow my faithful friend manages to communicate to me the feeling and conviction that he is *with* me. Marcel claims that the terms "friend and faithful," if deeply understood, will be found to be incapable of dissociation.

Not even the keeping of one's word constitutes the essence of fidelity, for fidelity is not an affair of honor, nor of self-respect. This would reduce fidelity to fidelity to one's self or to one's image of oneself. Such a spiritual subterfuge only returns the man to the bondage of narrow ego-centricism. Peter's ego-centricism was the malady that brought him down. "Even though all shall be scandalized because of Thee, *I* will never be scandalized." [29] Peter was more concerned about the figure he cut in his own and others' eyes than about the valid depth of his fidelity to Christ, than about

[28] *RI*, p. 200.
[29] Matt. 26:33.

the real danger of his rejecting and losing the presence of Christ. When the mysterious perfection of *presence* is missing, fidelity, drained of its essence, evanesces and some counterfeit form fronts for the real virtue. Constancy, honor, self-respect have as their objects not a thou but an absent third.

A constant person can drive a thou to distraction, perhaps even despair, by the very meticulous observation of all his obligations toward the thou. But because presence is wanting in this relationship, because the thou is looked to as an exterior judge whose approval is sought, the friendship of fidelity is rendered impossible. In reality, then, fidelity is possible to and can be appreciated by that one alone to whom friendship is sworn. Only in this intimate type of a human relationship is there present the element of spontaneity that is radically independent of all volitional and self-conscious tension.

Fidelity must be the spontaneously offered presence of an I to a thou; it cannot be exacted nor constrained. Sterile the irritation that is entertained because others do not respond to my appeals. Fidelity and the promised attachment cannot be the outcome of a popular mintage for they can never be vulgarized. Perhaps, indeed, fidelity could never express herself unconditionally if she did not suspend herself in Faith, if she did not rise to the more than human, to the Will that is in us both as the hunger and the testimony of the Absolute itself. All fidelity aspires to unconditionality, challenging men to found themselves in the eternal and unqualified meaning beyond the congeries of passing conscious states.

All fidelity is founded and constructed on a certain deeply felt commitment to indefectibility. Even though a man knows his feebleness and even though he realizes that the other often enough is the cause of weakness in him, for this very reason his oath of fidelity is accompanied with a prayer for strength. Would that Peter had heeded the exhortation: "Pray, lest you enter into temptation!" The man of fidelity prays somewhat like this according to Troisfontaines:

> Heaven grant that I do not give in to temptation, that is to say, that future or present events do not incite me to believe

myself free and authorized to break off my former engagements, under the pretext that the conditions that were
implied when I undertook these engagements are now so
changed that, had I foreseen them, I would never have
contracted this commitment. [30]

To be faithful I must fight successfully against the temptation to
renege.

Even though I may release others from the obligations that
are too heavy for them, I must guard myself, as far as is possible,
from breaking the bond of commitment that constitutes me a
being. I must keep myself resolutely enlisted in the way of interior
creation; I must actively maintain myself, despite all circumstances, in the state of a gift and of permeability. Fidelity, even
under these circumstances, again reveals her true nature which is
that of being a witness, a voucher. Creative as fidelity is, it
transcends, like liberty, the limits of the prescriptible. Without
any constraint, without any pressure, fidelity reveals herself to be
capable of mysteriously renewing the person who cultivates her in
his life. And sometimes fidelity is capable of rendering another,
no matter how unworthy he may be, permeable finally to the
inspirations that produce true life in souls that are interiorly
consecrated souls. Fidelity is a concrete approach to intersubjective communion because as Marcel states:

> Fidelity asserts herself never more truly than when she is
> challenging, defying, confronting an absence, when she is
> triumphing over this absence and, in particular, when she is
> conquering that absence that presents itself to us, doubtless
> falsely, as absolute absence—the absence known as death. [31]

Hope

By conquering the absence known as death, fidelity is at once a
witness to the exigence for being in all men and to their hunger
for participation in Absolute, Eternal Being. Now hope, like
fidelity, is one of the most fundamental of human experiences, a
"concrete approach," par excellence, to the mystery of partici-

[30] R. TROISFONTAINES, *De l'existence...*, II, p. 35.
[31] *RI*, p. 199.

pation and communion in being. The distinguishing mark of hope is that it almost immediately and unequivocally orients and projects the hopeful person towards participation in transcendence. The reason for this is that hope is always situated within the framework of tribulation. And the hoper, agonizingly conscious of his own inadequacy to extricate himself from the darkness of his trial, calls upon the Absolute Thou for deliverance.

No man escapes the cloud of calamity; sooner or later each is confined by some trial that must be endured or escaped, whether it be sickness, failure, exile, separation, slavery or death. Hope is about matters that constitute these tragic captivities, about matters each person cannot help but take seriously to heart. In a general sense the whole of human existence, as an arena of trial and struggle, takes on the atmosphere of a captivity that must be endured until a day of final liberation. Hence the whole of human existence is basically subject to hope or despair.

But hope is not concerned with the trivial, nor with things I merely desire or fear. I desire a good mark in class; I fear I'll miss my train. These things are problems exterior to me; they are not mysteries rooted within what I am in my being now nor in what I desire to be perennially. It would be a mistake to make fear, which is opposed to desire, the negative correlative of hope. Despair is contrary to hope—despair, that stark defeatism which paralyzes life and freezes it at its source. It is true, however, that the same conditions that call forth despair as one possible response in a time of trial are simultaneously the very conditions that challenge a man to respond in hope. In the dark interior night of the soul that is caught in the confines of catastrophe, the "I hope" surges up with a vehement aspiration for deliverance and salvation. Despair, on the other hand, makes no attempt to appeal to that Someone who is able and willing to accompany the sufferer through his trial to a brighter plane of participation in peaceful communion in being and life. Despair makes a man capitulate, go to pieces under trial, quit before the inevitable which is a certain *fatum* laid down by the quitter's judgment. [32] The person without

[32] *HV*, p. 37.

hope succumbs to the inevitability of captivity, thus raising the impotence and impossibility of all being to save or be saved to the universal and over-arching law of all reality. Availability is the indispensable predisposition to hope: it is the spirit of rudimentary opening up to the Infinite Thou in the interpersonal communion which seasons souls for their ultimate consummation in communion with the Absolute Thou.

If there can be no hope except when the temptation to despair exists, then hope will be the act by which this temptation is actively and victoriously overcome. [33] Hope is humble, is patient; hope does not rebel, is not anxious, is not high-handed, is not demanding, is not rushed nor panicked. Hope works no violence, rejects no grace, but accepts all with gratitude. Hope bears all trials and accepts them as integral parts of itself; hope considers itself as destined for absorption and transmutation into the joyful fruition of the liberty of the Absolute Thou. Hope never fails, but radiates towards an incomparable intimacy with the transcendent. Hope is never complacent, is never weakened, for it is animated by a love that urges it on, in all its tribulations, "to hope beyond hope" in the goodness of the Thou to whom it aspires beyond the limitations of space and time. Thus hope never succumbs to an inner determinism; it never is cramped into degrading positions of immobility of thought nor of paralysis of will; hope never sags with the spiritual bends under the sudden and rude pressures of adversity. But hope is supple, is docile, is always basically joyful, is always advancing through its tears by the inner workings of a sure creative process, and with a veritable resonance of prophetic assurance of victory ringing in its soul, toward the Thou who proclaims: "Have confidence, I have overcome the world."

Hope is centered on spiritual goods and, as such, constitutes an enduring affirmation of eternity and of eternal values. Hope, then, cannot be self-centered, but bears upon what is quite independent of the one hoping. I hope for the return of someone long

[33] *Ibid.*, p. 36.

absent, for the defeat of the enemy, for peace for all, for the guarantee to all peoples of their liberties.

Classic examples of hope always reveal hope's tie with salvation, hope's involvement through the events of closed time and
its surge beyond them toward the open time of eternity. These
examples also reveal hope's passage from the surface of "gradual
becoming" to the depths or heights of eternity. A distraught
mother named Monica, chasing a wayward Augustine down the
labyrinthine ways that captivate man in the luxury of lust and
the fascination for heresy, finally saves her son through her per-
severing hope and her ardent love. The wise Ambrose expresses
the essence of her hope in the words: "It is impossible for a son
of so many tears and prayers to be lost irrevocably." Nothing is
impossible to the appeal of hope. The hoper is one who will
meet no insurmountable obstacle on his way to transcendence.
Hope and salvation, hope and heroism, hope and sanctity are
ineradicably intertwined in the temporal process of growth; hope
is absorbed into the Absolute Savior, Hero, Saint via a transformation through a communion of love in the eternal peace of the
Absolute Thou.

To illustrate the opposition between the closed time of
despair and the open time of hope, the example of the father of
the prodigal can be explored. The boy has left home like a rebel,
taking his inheritance along. A long time passes and no news is
received; the worst fears possible arise in the father's imagination.
Yet buoyed by hope, he is on the nearby road every day, scanning
both directions for a returning boy; the mails are eagerly awaited
and devoured for news of the boy. Nothing. A dreadful anxiety
that all is lost tugs at the heart of the father. How will he pass out
of this crisis?

Above all he must not succumb to despair. The monotony
of the daily disappointments must never induce him to form these
judgments: "My wound of separation is incurable; death alone
will end this senseless vigil when it ends me too; destiny will cure
me by killing me." [34] This way lies despair which hypnotizes its

[34] *Ibid.*, p. 42.

victim with the dismal repetition of its disappointment, eternalizes
the situation of separation, anticipates nothing in the future but
the day to day renewal of this bitter trial and finally, fascinates
its victim with the solution of suicide as the only way out.

The dispersive, immobilizing and paralyzing action of
despair acts like a malevolent wind that blows out the flame of life.
Whereas life that is vigorous and arduous is meant to devour all
obstacles to the becoming of its person and to thrive upon them,
the evil spell of despair turns life back to feeding upon itself and
to destroying itself in the process of self-consumption.

Of course, the hopeful father rejects the temptation to dwell
upon his own sorrow, to prey upon himself in the dismal context
of his *hic et nunc* disappointment.   He transcends the morbid
phantasms of his imagination which attempt to present the closed
time of his trial as a sort of counter-eternity, an eternity turned
against itself, an eternity of hell.   For that is what despair is; it
is hell. [35]

By denying the negations of closed time, hope delivers the
father from the captivity of despair.   Hope ascends, transcends
in the opposite direction.   While the process of becoming perpet-
ually dismembers the self through a relationship to the self,
hope aspires to communion through the reunion, the recollection,
the reconciliation both of the dismembered self and of the disjointed society of the I-thou.   Instead of closing itself up within
its own self-consciousness, hope opens up time to allow the light
of eternity to shine through.   By this action hope seems to display
a memory for the future and quite spontaneously reveals its prophetic character.

To be sure, hope does not claim knowledge of the future,
yet hope affirms the future as if she saw it already.   For hope
anticipates the future whenever the soul rejoices, grows sad or
worries about coming prospects.   This very anticipation receives—
pockets as it were—the future in advance.   Such appreciation of
the future infinitely transcends action which is the mere application
to the present moment.   For such appreciation rests on a judgment

[35] *Ibid.*, p. 44.

about eternity. It is eternity that gives time its fluidity, whereas any anticipation of fatalism, because it already contaminates the future with the dismal past or present, actually petrifies both, tending to render the whole of life impossible.

It is in this betrayal that despair becomes the source of, nay rather, is itself a serious sin. Every man must categorically refuse every species of fatalism, must wage war upon every variety of catastrophism, private or public, for these, in one manner or other, state that all reality, and specifically life, is nothing but a sordid joke. [36]

Any father, then, can consume and dissolve the disappointment of a son's apparently irrevocable loss only by transcending beyond all conditions of time to the presence of the Absolute Thou. There absolute joy joins absolute fidelity. Both are mature, concrete responses of the creature to the infinite Being to whom the creature is conscious of owing everything it has, everything it aspires to be, and upon whom it would shrink from imposing its own demands or conditions. The "*fiat voluntas tua,*" that situates the creature in filial submission before the Absolute Thou, seems to forbid the temptation to despair ever to arise again. [37] The very thought of accepting the possibility of despair is rejected as a first step toward treason. For hope rejects the deepest meaning of despair which is the treasonous avowal that God has withdrawn Himself from me forever, is unconcerned about me in my trials, nay far worse, is incapable of bringing me through these trials to a higher being and, in its most satanic form, this avowal proclaims that God simply is not good enough in Himself to cure my physical ills, nor to forgive the immensity of my moral miseries. These accusations would destroy the very nature of the Absolute Thou. The despairing accuser, setting himself up as judge over God, actually claims the right of becoming God's executioner. The man of despair has fled God to the camp of the enemy.

Against this shutting of the door on God, on time and on himself so that a devitalized future, drained of all mystery—since

[36] R. TROISFONTAINES, *De l'existence...*, II, p. 179.
[37] *HV*, p. 47. The whole book treats what Marcel calls a "metaphysic of hope."

such a future can only be the pure repetition of trial and tragedy—stares man in the face as a "dirty joke," there is only one remedy—the remedy of hope and of communion.

Jean Paul Sartre, in his play, *The Devil and the Good Lord*, has pushed the sordid-joke philosophy of human existence to its ultimate sordid conclusion. Goetz, a German cavalry officer of the sixteenth century, revels in doing evil. And his rationale for his attitude of *ressentiment*—this attitude of hatred against all light, all goodness, hatred against God, hatred against other men, and the higher their moral rank, the greater his hatred [38]—his rationale for this attitude is that he wants to make "God's heart bleed." "God who is the only adversary worthy of me." But when the direct attack against God fails to bring him the total isolation in himself that he is seeking, Goetz discovers a new light in his effort to find the best way to be *alone*. He quits fighting God because there is no God. Goetz says:

> Now I know the answer: it is nothing.... You see the void above our heads? That is God.... Silence... that is God. Absence... that is God. God is the solitude of man. There was only me: I alone determined what was evil and I alone invented the good. *I*, man. If God exists, then man is nothing: but if man exists... Heinrich, I'm going to let you in on a big joke: God does not exist.... He does not exist.... Joy, tears of joy, Alleluia.... I have liberated us. No more heaven; no more hell; just earth. Farewell to the monsters, farewell to the saints. Only men exist. [39]

The only remedy to the infinite varieties of man's trials as they afflict him under innumerable forms of privation, exile, captivity, is his rise to personal communion with the transcendent through fidelity, hope, love. Hope already foreshadows this communion with its ardent "I hope in Thee for us." [40] *Spero semper habitare Tecum*, where the Thou is the guarantee of the union

---

[38] Dietrich VON HILDEBRAND, *Christian Ethics* (New York: Mc Kay, 1953), p. 443.

[39] R. TROISFONTAINES, "What is Existentialism?," *Thought*, XXXII, 127 (Winter 1957-1958), pp. 526-527.

[40] *HV*, p. 60.

which holds us together—holds me integrally to myself against
the temptation to go to pieces under trial, holds me to my fellowman against the temptation to agree with Sartre that: "Hell is
other people; original sin is the arrival of others; others steal my
world and cause my universe to leak away," [41] holds me to my God
in a transcendent community of love between us.

Hope not only foreshadows, but is also the outcome of this
union, the very cement that effects the union of us all in one.
The Absolute Thou is also the absolutely necessary bond of my
being *with* myself and *with* others. He is at the heart of every true
city, the city I form with myself and with others. To deny him
is to deny myself; to despair of myself is to despair of him; to
isolate myself is to take the road to self-destruction. *Sui vivere,
suicidium.*

Hope is a mysterious gift that, like all gifts, can be accepted
or rejected. But to reject this gift is to reject the invitation
"*habitare mecum,*" in a community of self-control, dignity of
demeanor and peace with oneself. To reject the gift of hope is to
refuse to participate in the infinite number of creative activities
that life, as a center of communal intelligence, love and service,
would actualize not only in me and in others, but also in time
and for eternity. To despair is to refuse—Judas-like—to live and
collaborate in the vineyard of the Absolute Thou, in the vineyard
of *presence.* Whereas to hope is to be liberated in a creative manner
through a time of trial not merely back to the status quo of our
beings, but, much more, to a transfiguration upward.

To hope, then, means essentially to be available, to participate freely—in the very teeth of the specters of trial, despair and
death—in the experience of communion which, in this life, is the
precarious adventure aimed at the exaltation of the community of
us. The hopeful man knows that no stable peace can be founded
within himself nor among others, unless men candidly and with
serious conscience accept the fact that they are itinerants in time,
called to establish here a community of fidelity, hope and love

[41] R. TROISFONTAINES, *loc. cit.,* p. 530.

which hereafter will be taken up into the community of the Absolute Thou. Hope cheerfully comes to terms with this condition and the *homo viator* of *engagement* and encounter rises above the trials of time, moving perseveringly beyond the criticisms that would destroy hope itself. For this is hope's very intelligible core—"the very movement by which it challenges the evidence upon which men claim to challenge it (hope) itself." [42]

However hopeless a situation seems, the hoper never arrogates to himself the right to affirm this hopelessness. He knows that the flight of despair is fatal and leads to fatalism. To declare that war is inevitable, already increases, in a subtle yet indubitable manner, the chances of actual war. But the hoper also avoids the roseate flight, for this is foolishness and may well lead to tragedies that need never have befallen him. To declare that war is unthinkable already increases, in quite another subtle yet indubitable manner, the chances for actual war. The man of hope is a realist. By squarely facing unpleasant situations as they exist and their even more sinister possibilities, the man of hope performs the positive act of preparing a salutary confrontation and a transcendent response to any tragic eventuality. The goal and consummation of hope is beautifully expressed by Marcel in one of those felicitous musical comparisons for which he has a penchant:

> ... from the moment when we open ourselves to these infiltrations of the invisible, we cease to be the unskilled and yet pretentious soloists we perhaps were at the start, and gradually becoming members, wide-eyed and brotherly, of an orchestra in which those whom we so aptly call the dead are quite certainly much closer to Him of whom we should not perhaps say that He conducts the symphony, but that He *is* the symphony in its profound and intelligible unity; a unity in which we hope to be included only by degrees, through individual trials, the sum total of which, though it cannot be foreseen by each of us, is inseparable from his own vocation. [43]

[42] *HV*, p. 67.
[43] *MB* (II), p. 210.

Love

Love is the most dynamic concrete approach to intersubjective reality, for it is love that most effectively breaks the tension and crosses the barrier that exists between the self and the other. Love Marcel asserts, might be called "the essential ontological datum" which alone can deliver philosophers and philosophy from the rut of objectification and the prison of problematization. The fact is that in all being love comes first. [44]

Just like fidelity and hope, love cannot be contained in a closed essence. Nor can love be caught and merely restricted between the subject-object boundaries, for love besides opening up on the being of the other person, also opens onto eternity, onto infinity. Hence love will never be captured in capsulated characterizations, pithy judgments or precise tabulations about other persons, for love touches the being of the other person, and is not contained solely in ideas about them. Thus love cannot be the act of the previously constituted self; love creates the self—the presence that is ontologically inexhaustible. Real loving alone creates real lovers, for real love is loved love. The only way to taste, to reflect on, to recognize love correctly is by reproducing within ourselves the sympathetic, compassionate and creative condition of loving, just as the only way to recognize genuine faith is to believe.

Although fidelity, hope and love are essentially one, love may be considered at the crown and climax of the interpersonal communion achieved by lovers through a whole process of concrete approaches to being. Any fluctuation in one of these approaches to reality causes a corresponding rise or diminution in all the other concrete attitudes, depending on whether the concrete situation is strengthened or weakened. It is love which most strikingly and fruitfully makes man conscious of the transcendence and plenitude of being. There is no activity of the person which elicits a more intense free choice and a more ardent involvement in the presences and lived experiences of others than the activity of love. Such

[44] *BH*, p. 167.

activity of love is absolutely necessary for a grasp and an assurance, and above all, for a joy in the mystery which is the communal participation in the created and Uncreated Thou.

Thus, what would love be without fidelity? Some sort of lie, to be sure. Or hope without love? The fear of a serf and not of a son. Hence the deeper a love, the more it is pervaded with hope and fidelity. Love is now seen as the splendor and the superabundance of fidelity and hope and of all concrete, intersubjective approaches and experiences. Communion is founded on love, is love. The experience of communion is the foundation for the experience of the I. The thou in communion founds the I. Love founds communion and every perfect community, for love is the most complete and deepest intersubjective act of mutual self-donation. Love creates communities in the highest order of transcendent freedom.

We have previously said that love comes first in all being and this is true whether we consider the creative source of Absolute Love as the *ab aeterno* ontological origin of all being in existence, or this same divine love as collaborating *hic et nunc* with creative human love as the ontological advance to fulfilment of all being in participation. "I have loved you with an everlasting love, therefore have I drawn you, taking pity on you," says the Absolute and ever-present Lover to His chosen people. But this is His relationship to every man. This same love, absolute and created, absolute and participated, continued to draw the person of the thou from the abyss of nothingness, of isolation, of objectification, of alienation, yes, if need be, of spiritual satanization. And the divine and human drag of love is ever upward toward communion with the creative I of the Absolute Lover, the Speaker of the "inner word" of love, toward the Absolute Thou.

It becomes patent, then, that love grounds man simultaneously both in communion and in transcendence. Love is a manifestation of the person's participation in being and transcendence. Love finally works out the full meaning—never comprehensively, of course—of the primitive creative intuition of being which is deep within us. To be sure, because of man's itinerant state, the other presence is both a thou and a that at times. Man's

love is never pure and perfect; he never experiences the other as
the Absolute Thou. But in so far as I love the other, he is a thou.
We may doubt that our love for another is totally unconditioned,
for we never achieve perfect co-presence. But our tendency
towards the absolute purification of love actually reveals our need
for transcendence and for absolute being. In so far as I am related
to a thou, I rise above the order of things. It makes no sense to a
lover for a beloved being to cease to exist. In so far as love of
persons bears on other persons, love tends to break away from
the categories of place and time and to enter into transcendence,
into dimensions beyond the here and the there.

To love a person is to say, "Thou at least shall not die." [45]
Love only addresses itself to what is eternal, above the entire order
of genesis and vicissitude. Marcel's point is precisely this: Within
the participation of love and communion this beloved thou is
exempt from the penalties of things; fate may prey upon things, it
can never overtake that by which thou are a thou, a being, a plenitude in participation in being. The more I love a person as an
authentic being, the more I grasp the summit of existence as
indistinguishable from being. At the height of communion where
total assurance is attained in love without any threat of fear or
error or doubt we would experience the presence of the beloved as
assumed into the Absolute presence of the Supreme Thou. Only
then will we be able to love in the climate of eternity. Actually
Marcel takes as his proof for the existence of God this analogy
of presentiality. The loving presence that founds the created
I-thou relationship overflows and transcends in every direction
into the loving presence of the Absolute Thou. Love at a certain
point must reveal the transcendent dimension of being, of
presence, of participation, of communion, of the Thou. The
very prophetic affirmation of love: "Thou at least shalt not die,"
is already a faith and hope in the power, the goodness, the love
of the Absolute Thou who is invoked as always present, always
concerned, always willing and able and determined to sustain
in the communion of love every created thou who is alive or

[45] *MB* (II), p. 171.

apparently dead. Of course, the assurance man gains through his faith, hope and love must always be renewed, intensified and strengthened against the betrayal, rejection and seduction to which he is forever being tempted.

Marcel also holds that faith, hope and love are not only affective realities, but that they also release certain cognitive insights into the person, insights into being, participation, transcendence, spiritual communion. Yet with all the profound appreciation these experiences reveal to us, they always spur us on to go ever deeper into the mysterious depths of spirit and being. The more I open myself to a finite thou, the greater is the faith, hope and love that is shared with this spiritual presence and the more I simultaneously become open to the Absolute Thou in whose presence and companionship I experience a superabundant fruition in faith, hope and love. One arrives at the summit of communion and enters into the supreme I-thou love-relationship only through the lived experience of the finite I-thou love-relationship. What you do to the least of His brethren is done to Him. One arrives at the bottom of the "slough of isolationary despond" only through the freely rejected I-thou relationships. We have here an insight into the solidarity that exists between the Absolute Thou and the finite thou. What we choose for or against the finite thou, we choose for or against the Absolute Thou. The solidarity is one of fidelity, hope and love.

Thus a super faith, hope and love—those of divine Revelation —cannot get through to a world of purely problematic knowers. Such knowers refuse to become lovers. Such knowers, pure technicians, high priests of scientism, positivists in all branches of learning, and devotees of despair have purposely closed themselves off from the metaphysical, from the metaproblematic, from the transcendent, from true and spiritual intersubjective communion in the presence of others.

In concluding this chapter, we might summarize thus. The effect of faith, hope and love, and indeed of all concrete approaches to being, is to develop the initial gift of created incarnational community of being into the radiance of the intersubjective community of communion. Faith is one of the primary "spiritual touches" whereby man successfully bridges the river of unreachability that is developed by the highly competitive processes of communication which tend to isolate men into suspicious anti-social islands. Faith takes man into the vestibule of communion, leading him toward the hearth of love; faith is the adherence to a friend under all circumstances, especially under the dark conditions of trial; faith is a witnessing for a friend at the cost of any personal sacrifice. Hope is a deeper, stronger adherence to the thou; it is the bond that welds friends together through the torch of trial; it binds and rivets friends together who have come through the shock of adversity together. Much more than a spiritual "touch," hope is the spiritual experience of a campaign having been fought together to victory. Love is the climax of faith and hope, the indwelling of the lovers within each other, their co-presence at all times and in all places. Love is the superabundant radiance of incarnational fulfilment, the free, graceful and limitless achievement of communion in the natural and supernatural company of God.

CHAPTER VII

Transcendence Through Tragedy

Theatre fulfilled Gabriel Marcel's quest for communion even as music satisfied his hunger for recollection. "Very early in life," Marcel notes, "I experienced a kind of intoxication not only from calling forth persons distinct from myself but also from identifying myself rather completely with them so as to become their dragoman." [1] His vocation for the theatre took root and thrived in the soil of his naturally sensitive dispositions and in the social isolation and discontent of the milieu in which he was raised. His father had an innate sense for the theatre and was an incomparable reader of plays. Then, too, the delicate, gifted Marcel was an only child and he tells us that "the theatrical persons with whom I was delighted to share dialogue held for me the place of the sisters and brothers whose absence I cruelly deplored." [2] Moreover, from infancy the precocious Marcel was involved in the diverse family strifes, sufferings and temperaments that obstructed communion and harmony among his relatives.

Music had already offered Marcel one type of suprarational unity that allowed him to transcend the agony of his studies, the distressing trivia of daily life. Music restored him to himself as a consciously free person aware of a loftier reality that synthesized and fulfilled the fragmentary limitations of sensory experience. Perhaps play-writing could be another avenue to a mysterious, spiritual recuperation from the fragmentizing contra-

[1] R. TROISFONTAINES, *De l'existence...*, I, p. 30.
[2] *Ibid.*

dictions of incompatible humans? Marcel discovered it was. He
relates that the plays in which he presented subjects as subjects,
i.e., in all their concrete reality without any philosophical premed-
itation, transcended objectivity and yet captured and conveyed
to his audiences and readers the vibrant authenticity of full-
blooded life.

Good drama is not likely to be written in the service of
philosophical prepossessions, although Sartre's diabolical *No
Exit, The Flies* and *The Devil and the Good Lord* are exceptions
that prove this rule. Now Marcel's theatre pieces are excellent
dramas, but they are never "thesis-dramas." Paralleling his out-
spoken contempt for closed systems of thought that arbitrarily
contract and desecrate the plenitude of reality is Marcel's abhor-
rence of didactic dramas that artificially destroy the mysterious,
complex, sublime and unpredictable freedom of human persons.
His plays illustrate no preconceived doctrine that his characters
must emit; nor is there any fatalistic destiny they must undergo.

Not that there is no connection between Marcel's drama and
his philosophical thought. There most assuredly is. "I have
been a philosopher-dramatist," writes Marcel, "and I insist on
their bond of union within me." [3] But his dramatic activity,
begun as early as age five, was initially an autonomous creation.
Long after his dramas are written, read and staged, his philosophic
reflection—as another, maturer, independent response to his
exigency for being—completes and elaborates the truths already
seminally incarnated in his ambiguous characters and their
complex conditions. Thus, drama holds a central position in
Marcel's work. The exact reverse is true of Jean Paul Sartre who
is, above all, a philosopher first and whose drama is purposely
derived from and subservient to this thought. Marcel insists on
the priority of his dramatic vocation over his philosophic
profession. He warns that "every attempt to expound my philosophic thought is condemned to serious failure if it does not include
a study of my dramatic works." [4]

[3] M. M. DAVY, *Un Philosophe itinérant: Gabriel Marcel* (Paris:
Flammarion, 1959), p. 76.
[4] *Ibid.*, p. 74.

Gaston Fessard, writing of the bond between drama and metaphysics in Marcel's work, says: "Here the bond is substantial. And to such a degree that his dramas cannot surrender their deep meaning to one who fails to discern the metaphysical intuition residing at their core. Moreover, it is as if the reflections of the *Metaphysical Journal* realize their full and true meaning only when referred back to the dramatic personages from whose lips they first emerged full blown." [5]

The reader, therefore, is not to see in the plays particular illustrations of themes previously expressed in abstract terms. The dramas present concrete situations more felt than conceived. Their deep significance is hidden behind the enigmatic faces of the persons embroiled. Even Marcel, their creator, may never capture the full significance of his own creatures. The way his protagonists respond to the trials in which they are intensely involved often enough surprises the author himself and Marcel admits that his heroes become clear and explicit to him only after years of philosophic reflection. And even then some of them remain obscure and hidden in mystery. Thus, if Marcel's philosophizing about existence is not always concrete, his dramatizing of it is always compact. His philosophy is complementary to his drama and in elucidating this bond between them Marcel can say: "It is in drama and through drama that philosophic thought grasps and defines itself *in concreto*." [6]

Alive, complex, inscrutably immersed in the realities of daily life, Marcel's characters never represent pure ideas or abstract schemes. Virtues and faults agonizingly coexist in his characters as they do in real people. Their dialogues do not lead the spectator to intellectual acceptance of proof-supported truths. "My theatre," says Marcel, "is the theatre of the soul in exile, the soul suffering from a miscarriage of communion with itself and with others." [7]

The characters are confronted with what is obstructing communion in themselves and others. They are at times lucid, dis-

---

[5] G. FESSARD, "Théâtre et Mystère," *Etudes*, April 5, 1938, p. 738.
[6] Quoted by Fessard in *La Soif*, p. 7.
[7] R. TROISFONTAINES, *op. cit.*, p. 35.

oriented, scattered, interiorly coherent or unreasonable; their lives are somber and tensely drawn-out; the tragedy of their interior alienation may eventually be illuminated by a sudden clairvoyance that pierces protagonists and spectators alike, permitting both to perceive the barren state of their own souls. Such "tragedies of thought" involve both actors and audiences in the mystery of man and of his existence. "The tragedy of reflection quickly becomes a tragedy of life, evolving from the conflict of man with his neighbor and with himself." [8]

There is little of the lyrical or poetic in Marcel's plays; they are obsessed with the seriousness of the human condition. Perhaps this is an excusable excess. After all, Marcel is not writing *drames de divertissement*. By his own admission, his theatre is an art of communion and communion is its all-pervading theme, but, more often than not, under a negative aspect. For Marcel is a living witness, and has been for over sixty years, to the tragedy of a violently desecrated and broken world in modern times. His theatre, therefore, trenchantly exposes contradictions rather than concords, sadness rather than joy. Troisfontaines notes that "for the sensitive and sincere Marcel, drama arises when lying, harshness, pride, daily banality, treason, false fidelity thwart interpersonal communion and interior guilelessness. Whence arises a frightful picture which is, nevertheless, so true! Thousands of forms of egoism, rejected love, saddening incomprehensions which scarcely illumine some of the dramas with even a glimmer of resurrection." [9]

Yet, unlike Sartre, Marcel does not abandon his audiences to despair, with "no exit" from the "sickness of being." In Sartre's existentialism, "Hell is... other people," [10] in the sense that the other always threatens his being, his freedom. Men are cursed with personal freedom and with the predatory presence of other free men who are threats to each other's integrity. Man's ideal is to be alone, completely self-sufficient, his own creator. But

---

[8] J. P. Dubois-Dumée, *Existence chrétienne*, p. 272.
[9] R. Troisfontaines, *op. cit.*, p. 35.
[10] J. P. Sartre, *No Exit*, p. 61.

man's dream and drive to become his own God is the primordial idiocy, for the very idea of God is contradictory. "The first duty, then, of the creature, is to deny its creator." Thus, Sartre's plays turn out to be propaganda pieces, attempts to popularize the philosophy that "man is a useless passion" [11] whose fundamental, metaphysical experience is that of nausea and whose noblest goal is the exaltation of his self-sufficiency in antitheistic humanism. *The Devil and the Good Lord* dramatically rejects a God who has already been metaphysically constructed as impossible. *No Exit* demonstrates the pre-determined fatuity of intersubjective communion. *The Flies* proves *a priori* that antitheistic humanism is the only possible authentic humanism.

Quite contrary to such dramatic ventures in ideology, Marcel's theatre is an experiment in metaphysics. It turns up a far more hopeful and sublime reading of reality, despite the omnipresence of tragedy. If hell is man-made—and there is a valid sense in which it is—it is created by man's willful refusal to pass from the initial reception of the love-gift of existence to new participations in being... in the world, in other men, in the Absolute. For Marcel, communion with others, not domination over others is at the heart of metaphysics. The unique, yet difficult, vocation of *homo viator* is to achieve his being in depth by gladly cooperating with other men, consciously making himself available both to them and God. Such transcendence in Marcel's dramatic work consists in exalting interiorization and acceptance of the way of communion, no matter what obstacles must be hurdled to persevere on this way. Marcel is ambitious in his plays to send the reader or the spectator back into his own soul, not isolated, but with compassionate love toward the souls in exile depicted on stage, so that with a renewed glance at himself and his companions in real life, his taste for being may be revitalized and blessed with a mysteriously new degree of expansion. This sense of reality, this superior grasp of one's life and destiny is attained in the consciousness of communion.

[11] J. P. SARTRE, *L'être et le néant*, p. 708.

The student of Marcel's drama is struck by the author's extreme sensibility to the anxieties and trials of his times. The climate of impending doom—political, social, economic, scientific, artistic and, above all, moral—permeates his drama. His early dramas, before World War I, reveal his apprehension over the coming destruction of Europe. Between the major wars, his theatre demonstrates that Marcel was never taken in by the post-war illusion that the millenium of perpetual peace and plenty had arrived. He tested the deceptive euphoria of the Western leaders in the fire of their alienated masses whose primary attitude was one of hateful indignation and whose favorite activity was violent revolution. His later dramas are rooted in the human anxieties that have become even more acute since the liberation of Western Europe. Some of the burning controversies his dramas portray are: resistance or collaboration with the enemy *(L'Emissaire)*; racism *(Le Signe de la Croix)*; socialism *(Le Dard)*; procreation *(Croissez et multipliez)*; voluntary exile from one's fatherland *(Rome n'est plus dans Rome)*; the twilight of a common meaning *(La dimension Florestan)*; the laceration of the modern conscience *(Mon temps n'est pas le vôtre)*.

Thus dramatic persons and tragic human situations embody Marcellian themes of communion years before Marcel ever gets around to understanding the persons themselves or developing the themes fully in his reflective, more mature philosophic distillations. With Marcel persons are always primary; he usually places them in situations which he himself has critically experienced; his living persons encounter and react towards each other in collisions of opposed instincts, minds and wills; the outcome of these encounters can never be accurately predicted. Troisfontaines, who has been privileged to peruse many of Marcel's unpublished works, relates that "there are a great number of unfinished plays in Marcel's files: for he has not been able to resolve the situations. On the other hand, sometimes he takes up and continues a play which he began years before, because now he finally sees the way in which the characters should develop." [12]

---

[12] R. TROISFONTAINES, "What is Existentialism?" *Thought*, p. 527.

We have here an indication of the reciprocal development of Marcel's theatre and his metaphysics. By a profound insight Marcel has come to realize that his feeling for tragedy is founded in the bosom of being. The tragedies that fill daily life constantly challenge men to transcend the temptation to restrict themselves solely to the possesion, problematization and systemization of all being. Tragedy and dialectics are engendered at the core of each personal life where the surge *to be* is confronted by the lust *to have*. This pulsating dialectic between *being* and *having* is the point of departure for every human drama. When *having* is victorious, the subject has surrendered to the temptation of self-alienation, self-objectivization, self-abandonment. Estranged from himself and others, such a "soul in exile" has lost authentic existence. Authentic existence consists in *being-with* others, not in *having-against* others. Even to attempt to possess oneself is to lose oneself. I can neither have myself nor my self-knowledge; I am both of these. To objectify myself or my knowledge of myself into the category of a possession is to problematize the essential mystery of my existence by freely abandoning my subjecthood.

The mode and milieu of man's existence is such that every man is tempted to flee himself through some form of objectivization. Some men identify themselves with their ideals, others accommodate themselves to the image demanded by the pressures of their circumstances; still others freeze themselves into postures they imagine are perfect for their professions. For Marcel, drama and philosophy, tragedy and dialectics are mutually created in this struggle to achieve authentic existence by conquering the temptation to flee into objectivization. It follows that Marcel's plays are a series of unmaskings of personages who have subtly, often even sincerely, succeeded in hiding themselves from themselves, and thus sealing themselves off from others. The dramatic roles lived by Marcel's characters, in their attempt to synthetize the metaphysical polarity between being and having into an inner peace of being, are as varied as real life itself. Here we will restrict ourselves to four major categories of human activities that attempt to surmount this ambivalent dialectic: religion, art, morality and love. In our analysis of these activities, we will

consider six of Marcel's dramas, taking two from each period
of his creative activity in the theatre. The three periods cover
more than forty-two years of work with publication dates appearing
from 1911 to 1953. The periods are divided into pre-World
War I, between the major wars, and post-World War II.

Pre-World War I Period

La Grâce (1911, a play in five acts)

The time is 1910. Françoise Thouret is typical of the newly
emancipated young women, endowed with a rigorously logical and
uncompromising mind. A student of medicine, she is an ardent
devotee of Dr. du Ryer, psychophysiologist and positivist par
excellence. Under a pseudonym, she composes and stages a
scandalous play which is a huge hit. Olivier, her brother, discovers her authorship and breaks down in *une crise de larmes*.
Amused at his naïveté, Françoise is, nevertheless, deeply moved
by his sense of decency. At twenty-three, characterized by a
thirst for moral and intellectual clarity, Françoise is in revolt
against pharisaism of any kind.

 She is also passionately, physically in love with Gérard
Launoy, dilettante and "mama's boy," who is endowed with an
astonishingly tender temperament and also stricken with tuber-
culosis. Françoise rejects maternal advice against the marriage;
she refuses Gérard's offer to break the engagement and rushes
plans for the wedding. As to the warning that happiness can never
ensue from this union with a sick man who has just severed a
liaison with a paramour, Françoise retorts that she does not expect
happiness, that silly, arid nothing; she will discover something
better. Sick or not, her Gérard "is handsome because I love him,
and I love him... because I am I." [13] So they marry and off they
go to the mountains to regain Gérard's health.

 But, to Françoise's horror, a spiritual abyss begins to yawn
widely between them. Gérard's illness becomes the occasion for

---

[13] G. Marcel, "La Grâce" in *Le Seuil invisible*, p. 31.

his conversion to Catholicism and his evolution in grace. For her part, Françoise is consumed by a double lie, the lie to herself—she has married to sate her violent passion—and the lie to her beloved —her marriage to the dying Gérard is not an "act of supreme charity," as she allows him to think. And the lies are rendered more unendurable to her because Françoise can truly say of herself: "... Sincerity is perhaps the only duty I have understood, the only duty I want to fulfill." [14] Her friend, Antoinette, attempts to console Françoise, justifying her lie-life with rationalizations on an ever-recurring Marcellian theme: "At bottom what difference does it all make? Aren't people always impenetrable to each other anyway? What good is it to desire to be known as one is? Do you really know yourself and what you actually are?" [15]

Will love dissolve the life of double duplicity that ensnares Françoise? Grace is offered to heal the conflict. Gérard accepts this "unexpected gift from a spiritual and unfathomable power who has heard the appeals arising from my misery and defilement." [16] But Françoise, invited to participate, remains obdurate, becoming instead her husband's temptress. Olivier, repelled by positivism and envious of Gérard's conversion, confronts his sister's pride: "Even if such faith as Gérard's were an illusion, it is far more honorable then your truth." [17]

Their opposition on faith seems final. At this point, Père André is called in and attends Gérard. Françoise sums up the situation in a letter to her mother: "It is the last station; grace will soon accomplish its destructive work. Whatever I loved, whatever I desired... everything has been torn from me." [18] Gérard, for his part, realizes the emptiness of his past life, of his ventures in illicit love as a man of the world; he is haunted by the ruined rakes he has known. Some persons, it seems, must bound up to God from the springboard of iniquity; he sees in Père André the long-awaited sign of his salvation. The priest quiets his final worries:

[14] *Ibid.*, p. 79.
[15] *Ibid.*, pp. 79-80.
[16] *Ibid.*, p. 86.
[17] *Ibid.*, p. 95.
[18] *Ibid.*, p. 107.

"Put no credence in a hell for the predestined." And Gérard exclaims: "My God! Save me from giddiness in the presence of the hereafter!" [19]

The impasse against communion locks into a spiritual rigidity. Gérard is almost over the threshold of the hereafter; Françoise is left behind and below. Daily, unavoidably they hurt each other. In desperation, Françoise admits her lie to Gérard: "No! I didn't foolishly throw myself into your arms for your sake, not for your sake. Nor was it to save you from despair that I refused to put off this mad marriage. It was for myself... I loved you... And now this sacrifice! My God, it is very simple: I desired you... Shall we end our sojourn in cloudland? Reality is not so noble... but it is much better, indeed, than idle myths which make men tipsy." [20]

The dream life between them is ended; grace can continue to grow. It begins to touch Françoise: "Do you believe that I have failed to follow the progress of your illumination, that I have not realized that its growth coincided with the growth of your sickness?" "Sickness is the instrument...," responds Gérard, "nature is always ignorant of its own capabilities; nature always acts as if it is everything, self-sufficient, forgetting that its source is outside, beyond itself, as is also its goal." [21]

But Françoise is still in revolt. Though rejecting faith, the struggle has shaken her loose from scientism. Bitter and in agony, she visits professor du Ryer and denounces him for playing at positivism which is "an illusion of science, a diversion, a screen erected to seal off men from reality." [22] Yet isolated and lonely, deprived of love and certitude, she throws herself at the old professor, her illicit surrender seeming to fulfill her need for suicide.

Almost miraculously, Gérard recovers. What is more, he is taken with a physical passion for his wife. But his response is too late. Françoise confesses her infidelity; she has given her body to a man she does not love and cannot share herself simultaneously

[19] *Ibid.*, p. 116.
[20] *Ibid.*, pp. 136-138.
[21] *Ibid.*, pp. 143-145.
[22] *Ibid.*, p. 159.

with others. And yet her old love is still aflame. "You do not see that you have reconquered me! The passion which rages within you consumes me also. Ah! Why was I destined to lose you at the moment I found you! I was bewildered, in despair... you spurned me... the first revenge life offered me..." But Gérard, all forgiveness, sees divine providence in her betrayal which restores his moral composure. "Don't try to explain... your crime is not self-explanatory, but it can justify itself... Pick yourself up." But Françoise will not succumb to grace even now. "No! Not the insult of your pardon!" Gérard attempts to belittle his pardon and her crime. "I have not pardoned you... the cause of your deeds is beyond you." But Françoise continues to flee anywhere, away from forgiveness, even toward the grave. "No, not that!... rather death!" [23]

The shock of final separation brings Gérard to a serious relapse. On the threshold of death he regains his faltering faith. Olivier, unable to enjoy the religious certitude of his dying friend, exclaims: "The intensity of one's faith is surely the measure of one's being... Perhaps He (God) is only man's supreme longing." "God is free!" exclaims Gérard, raising himself with effort. [24] Then he dies. Françoise, in tears, hurls herself on the body of the deceased, while Olivier, seeking the secret of the profound peace in that immobile countenance, murmurs reverently as the curtain falls: "Nothing remains but this look... and only on our faith in this look..." [25]

How did it all finally come out? Was Françoise converted? Did Olivier regain his lost faith? Is there a place beyond the barrier and mystery of death where love and faith can meet, where Françoise may accept the gift of faith and thereby attain communion with Gérard? Marcel, in a lecture years later on this play, admits of three possible answers. The objective answer is No! But this naturalistic response is utterly untenable; it misses the metaphysical, mysterious, miraculous dimensions of reality, hence it is superficial. The neutral answer is also inadequate; Olivier

[23] *Ibid.*, pp. 200, 203.
[24] *Ibid.*, pp. 207, 208.
[25] *Ibid.* p. 209.

personifies that; he recognizes the reality of faith and grace, but refuses to become involved in either. Gérard's response is the only authentic answer, founded on the transcendent truth that man's aspirations for immortality are not the mere illusory flames of hearts on the verge of extinction, but divine dimensions of their mysterious existence. [26] Grace is far more than a dream, than a sublimated delirium for eternal existence; it is the experience of an abiding presence and communion with the loved one beyond the visible grave, beyond the invisible threshold of transcendence, within a living intercourse with the Absolute Thou.

Le Palais de Sable (The Palace of Sand), (1913, a play in four acts)

Roger Moirans, rightist politician, nationalist pro-clerical and champion of Catholic morality against Laicism's freethinkers, is receiving the plaudits of enthusiastic backers when the curtain rises on a French provincial town shortly before World War I. He has just routed the forces favoring secularistic public education in a meeting of the city council. High comedy and satire permeate the scene.

Quite understandably, Moirans is adamantly opposed to the divorce which his eldest daughter Thérèse, caught in an unhappy marriage, is contemplating. Besides the religious reasons for this opposition, there is its threat to his political career. Moirans' pride and joy is his baby Clarisse in whom he sees the spiritual reflection of himself. But now Clarisse shocks her father by announcing her intention to become a Carmelite nun. The dramatic conflict revolves around Moirans' attempts to deflect Clarisse from the cloister.

Moirans is aghast at the possibility of witnessing the convent-burial of his spirited, intelligent, beautiful daughter. Clarisse, for her part, is amazed at her father's implacable resistance. How can her father's opposition to religious life be compatible with his political work as champion of Catholicism? Ironically, Moirans

[26] M. M. DAVY, *op. cit.*, p. 116.

learns that he himself is the inspiration of his daughter's vocation. His walks with Clarisse to the Carmelite convent one day moved him to speak so reassuringly about religion that he quieted her fears of death. Clarisse now wants to live where she can rise every morning with the peace she then experienced. But Moirans proceeds to eclipse her spiritual sun with the clouds of his reasonings.

He accuses Clarisse of running away to a peaceful refuge, of avoiding temptation and evil, the inevitable lot of all men. But Clarisse denies seeking mere repose; her entrance is not a flight, but a confrontation; the struggle is most terrible at the summit where life's value is measured by agony and fervor; ecstatic immobilization in adoration is not her goal, but rather combat and victory. As for Moiran's position, Clarisse has some accusations of her own. Her father's faith is not authentic; he does not believe in a future life where her sacrifice will find fulfilment; his life has been one long lie, an imposture, a fraud that has utilized religion merely as a necessary restraint on human excesses. He has been a skeptic dabbling in religion as a pragmatic dilettante, professing a faith founded on no transcendent Being.

The shock of confrontation in this *crise de foi* brings father and daughter to a reciprocal clarification. Moirans is disgusted by what he sees in himself; he would seek deliverance through death, were he that courageous. He agrees with Clarisse that he must abandon his role of *defensor fidei* to which he does not really adhere. He will retire from politics, thus completing the severance with his life's central lie, as a first step toward moral integrity and salvation.

But Moirans' doubt has now contaminated his daughter. Suddenly Clarisse is in a storm of confusion. Was her vocation, after all, only a dream? Was is not really a temptation to escape? Recourse to an incompetent confessor only compounds her confusion. At this point, Moirans cynically adds a diabolical condition to his retirement from political life: that Clarisse abandon her determination to enter the convent. [27]

[27] G. MARCEL, "Le Palais de sable" in *Le Seuil invisible*, p. 346.

A sudden emergency arises in which the Church needs Moirans. Monsignor Vielle petitions him to remain in public life, but Moirans counters that he is no longer a Catholic, has, in reality, never been one. The bishop's masterful rationalizations fail to hold Moirans at his post. Ironically, the bishop becomes for Moirans what Moirans has already become for Clarisse, a stumbling stone in the path of an authentic vocation. But where the bishop fails, Moirans succeeds. With the help of Clarisse, Moirans conquers the bishop's temptations. However, destroyed when his own faith collapses as "a palace of sand," the father now drags little Clarisse down with himself. Using his own sacrifice as a sort of blackmail, Moirans continues to urge Clarisse to give up her vocation. She gradually succumbs to the contagion of his incredulity. The priest had made some fatuous statements about convent life, making it appear frightful. In disgust, Clarisse decides her father is right and fulfills her end of their bizarre bargain. Moirans appears triumphant, but the price of his victory is that he has blinded with his own sightlessness the only being in the world he really loves.

Her paradise of prayers and peace gone, unhappy, alone and drifting, Clarisse drags out her existence "between heaven and earth... too low to live with God, too high to live among men." [28] When Pierre Servan asks her to marry him she replies: "... Because you will make me happy, I cannot accept... Some beings are born to be unhappy." [29] Though she really loves Pierre, Clarisse is suffering from the nostalgia for her lost paradise; now she will never be like other ordinary humans who marry and have children. But Pierre goes down fighting: "If you would not cling to your hope in the hereafter, you would not destroy the source of happiness, the origin of life itself... Your attitude is hideous. Had you seen, as I have hundreds of times, the life of the dying flickering like a frail flame on the verge of extinction, you would realize that this life is all there is that is precious. But no, hypnotized you walk toward mirages. True, you do not realize this. The dead

[28] *Ibid.*, pp. 385-386.
[29] *Ibid.*, p. 374.

do not repent... Allow me to unburden my whole soul as we will no longer see each other. I cannot even admire you, for, though the path you follow is certainly harsh, it brings you salvation; though its gate is narrow, it opens up on heaven." [30] "What do you know about heaven? What do you know about salvation?" replies Clarisse. "For you, these are but words or silly mirages. But the kingdom of heaven is within us. It is not a land of miracles promised for the day after death. It is a place of benediction where inexhaustible faith grows; eternal life is not a hope; it is not a future; it is today, the present." [31]

In the end Clarisse condemns her father for the spiritual murder he committed in bringing her to doubt her faith. "It was you who made me doubt and in doubting I became a different person... The spirit of pride was my master. Father, here is your crime. In wishing to explain my faith, you killed it... Never does faith die a natural death; in the realm of the spirit, there are only suicides and murders." [32] Life now becomes banal and intolerable for Clarisse; she is exiled and moves in a world of chimeras. One final blow falls. Her old, irksome, despotic mother, who has been away from home for a long time, is returning. Clarisse had some communion of thought with her father; her mother imposed the solitude of the tomb. But perhaps her mother could now help. "Mama, listen... I am here, Mama..." Clarisse is on her knees. "You are praying. To whom are you praying?" [33] demands Moirans. Clarisse can answer nothing. Their loss of faith has closed off all communication between father and daughter.

Was the life of grace recaptured? We cannot say for certain. Grace, for Marcel, renders liberty possible. Speaking of the meaning of this liberty, Marcel says: "The fundamental difference between Sartre and myself is that I have never been able to consider liberty as an absolute, that, in my eyes, liberty can only exist on condition that it be joined and connected with grace

[30] *Ibid.*, p. 378.
[31] *Ibid.*
[32] *Ibid.*, pp. 381-382.
[33] *Ibid.*, pp. 393, 398.

considered as such." [34]   Françoise and Gérard, Clarisse and
Moirans certainly demonstrate this Marcellian affirmation.   Intersubjectivity, communion are demanded for the heart of man by
ambiguity, by the invisible threshold that grace and liberty alone
can transcend.

Period between the World Wars

Un homme de Dieu (A Man of God), (1921, a play in four acts)

Claude Lemoyne, a Huguenot pastor, is an ideal shepherd in the
service of the holy gospel.   A cultured man of the cloth, he feeds
his parishoners on solid, well-reasoned sermons, eschewing superficial twaddle.   His dedication is total; he mounts every breach,
counsels, aids, consoles, relieves whoever is in need.   And his wife
Edmée is an excellent apostolic assistant.   Into this relationship
of family harmony an unexpected dissonance is sounded.   A
message arrives from Claude's brother, Dr. Francis Lemoyne,
stating that Michel Sandier, the real father of the pastor's child,
Osmonde, is dying and begs to see his daughter before the end.

Twenty years before, shortly after their marriage, Edmée had
as lover Michel Sandier; Osmonde was the fruit of their adulterous
union.   But Edmée had confessed her crime to Claude and
begged his forgiveness.   At the time of this shocking confession,
Claude was in the throes of a prolonged temptation to abandon his
ministry.   From the depths of a soul blacked-out by his wife's
treason, a mysterious grace illumined Claude and he found the
strength to forgive the betrayal.   His surrender to forgiveness
marvelously expanded his soul and inundated him with a renewed
sense of the dignity of his mission.   He related the experience to
his mother: "Yes, I forgave her.   And I shall never forget what
that did for me, the inner peace it brought, the sense of a Power
working with me and not instead of me, strengthening my will
but not supplanting it.   Since that day I've seen my way clear.

[34] M. M. DAVY, *op. cit.*, p. 123.

Before I was groping in the dark... The test, Mother, the test. Before those terrible months the word sounded hollow to me. But after what I went through..." [35]

Edmée's infidelity, by mutual accord, was erased and never beclouded their conjugal union. Osmonde was shielded from the sorry story. Yet the consciousness of this reality did disturb Edmée's relationship to Osmonde. Edmée is worried over Osmonde's frequent missions of mercy to the children of the tenant upstairs whose incurably sick wife has virutally rendered him a widower. Osmonde resents her mother's suffocating surveillance and appeals to her father for a life of normal freedom from suspicion. It is into this minor friction that Michel Sandier's petition comes as a catalyst for disintegration. Will Claude grant his plea to visit Osmonde? How can Claude justify a refusal? Would not a refusal to this legitimate request be an act of cowardice? Would it not prove that the past was not really dead? Where does forgiveness begin and end? As for Sandier, how brief his time for grace! Besides, refusal would undermine the foundation of Claude's apostolic mission!

But Edmée is terrified. How can Claude be so coldblooded! Dare he invite her companion in adultery into their home? "I'm sick of your tolerance; I'm sick of your broadmindedness. It nauseates me... Yes, you forgave me, but it wasn't because you loved me... What was your forgiveness for?... What good is it to me?" [36]

So his charity towards Edmée these twenty years was all a professional gesture! He had only been playing the role of the good shepherd and reaping personal profits from that stellar performance. Claude's magnanimity, the cornerstone of his renewed life with Edmée, is now undermined. And Edmée's distrust infects her husband. The home of the Lemoynes totters on the sands of suspicion and falls before the winds of confusion and uncertainty. Claude loses his sense of spiritual direction, his sense of mission; he questions the genuinity of all he has done in

[35] G. MARCEL, *Three Plays*, p. 47.
[36] *Ibid.*, p. 59.

the past, of whatever he is presently doing. An interior withering of soul plagues the entire family. Edmée is no longer sure of the sincerity of her remorse. Did she return to Claude for security reasons only? Did she ever love Claude, Michel or anyone else besides herself? Osmonde, estranged from her distrusting mother, is contemplating elopement with the married father upstairs.

Without awaiting an answer from the pastor, Michel Sandier appears at the Lemoyne home. He confronts Edmée and her husband. But Claude is temporarily called away, leaving the adulterous pair alone with each other. The ensuing dialogue is tense, coldly embittered, psychologically brilliant, one of the finest demonstrations of Marcel's skill as the dramatist who reveals the "inside" of souls in exile. Its temper is passionate; its pace swift, sure; not a useless word is uttered; the articulation of its various thoughts and emotions mounts to a crescendo of intersubjective agitation that is quite devastating. On the edge of the tomb, Michel wounds Edmée, despoiling their idyllic love of long ago. Edmée has only loved Edmée; pity, love, fidelity happened solely to her, never to *us;* jealousy is her canker; calculated cowardice her escape-hatch from moral insecurity. Edmée is terrified at being the guilty cause of Michel's dereliction. But, Michel, who has "gone to the dogs" on her account, refuses "the signed certificate of innocence" [37] she is desperately seeking. "If only you'd had more guts and less virtue, who knows . . . we might have made something of our lives together." [38]

Michel has scarcely left when Claude returns to find a gravely shaken Edmée. Quickly they are again pitted against each other. Edmée's adultery is laid at Claude's door. Had he loved her more as a husband, less as an evangelist, she would never have been unfaithful. As for his forgiveness, he was using a marvelous opportunity for "saving the soul of a poor sinner." As the curtain falls on Act Two, a livid Claude has jumped to his feet and is shouting at his envenomed wife: "Be silent, you are destroying me!" [39] The spectator is overwhelmed with tragic pity at the

[37] *Ibid.,* p. 74.
[38] *Ibid.*
[39] *Ibid.,* p. 79.

spiritual disintegration that is mutually inflicted by all the characters involved.

But the ultimate poignancy is achieved when Claude's last link to reality—Osmonde's trust and love—is snapped. When Claude eventually reveals to Osmonde the truth about her paternal origin, the girl is stunned. She reacts quickly and violently against her mother. "Oh, how I hate her!" [40] Towards Claude she feels the utmost compassion until she learns that, in a moment of shame, he lied to her about just having learned of Edmée's infidelity; he had known it all these many years. Now there is nothing left for any of them. "The three of us without any illusions left about one another." [41] Osmonde, determined to break away from this maze of detestable compromises with false conventionalities, throws herself at the married man upstairs; Claude sighs for self-presence or suicide. "To be known as one is... or else to sleep." [42] Edmée is frightened at the impending future of loneliness. In the end the poor pastor, touched by the kind act of some good parishoners, turns to prayer for the answer to his question: "Who am I? What am I? What am I worth?" Other sources had given him the lie; his family, his flock, he himself cannot solve this riddle. "To be known as one is..." is his agonized appeal to the Absolute Thou. And the drama closes on the hope that this man of God will rediscover his spiritual center, regain his metaphysical balance, reactivate his transcendent mission in the refound presence of the divine Thou to whom the grace-seeded tragedies of his life have driven him.

Le Dard (The Sting), (1936, a play in three acts)

As the clouds of World War II gathered over a Europe that was attempting to appease the Nazi beast by feeding it small, helpless neighbors, Marcel's dramatic work changed its focus. His "dramas of ambiguity" now echoed the heightened moral confusion that darkened the souls of men and nations. Everywhere the

[40] *Ibid.*, p. 91.
[41] *Ibid.*, p. 108.
[42] *Ibid.*, p. 111.

sickly spirit of surrender was corroding the spiritual stamina of Europe; the umbrella had supplanted the cross as the symbol of salvation. It was in this milieu of international illusion and treason that *Le Dard* was composed.

The play's conflict concentrates on the substance of human dignity; its clash occurs between Professor Eustache Soreau and German singer Werner Schnee. Eustache Soreau is an embittered, exasperated teacher of working class roots who is bound to an affluent politician's daughter, Beatrice Durand Fresnel, by marriage, money and munificence. In his student days, he worked in the Socialist party with Gertrude Heuzard who was dismissed from her teaching post for seeding her students' minds with revolutionary propaganda. Eustache learned his lesson well and rose, not without great personal effort, from proletariat to patrician status. This accomplishment and accommodation earned him the caustic contempt of his former radical comrades. Unstable, suspicious, hypersensitive, Eustache is plagued by a bad conscience that justifies itself in violent, anti-rightist rhetoric. His very success is the source of his bitter resentment, for it reveals that he is living the life of a lie, that he is a traitor to the social ideals of the revolution which still attract his allegiance.

Earlier in his career, as a lecturer at the University of Marburg, Eustache and Werner Schnee had met and become fast friends. Werner, a singer of *lieder* of consummate artistry, has quit Nazi Germany, much to the displeasure of his wife, Gisela, in a venture of fraternal solidarity with his friend and accompanist, Rudolf Schontal, a communist Jew who has been severely maltreated by the Nazis and lies dying in Switzerland. From the moment the Soreaus opened their home to the refugee Schnees, the dissolution of their friendship began. Eustache is a devotee of ideology; Werner despises abstractions. Much as he hates Nazism, Werner refuses to join any parties; he will not even associate with other German political refugees so as to avoid succumbing to the constricting emigré mentality. Above all, Werner aims at being a man; he rejects slogans and labels as vulgarian dilutions of the mystery that is man. On the other hand, Eustache's preoccupation with remaining loyal to his proletarian origins vitiates his whole personality. He accuses Werner of being an individualist, blames his wife for addiction to her privileged, bourgeoisie surroundings and scolds his mother for her fawning servitude towards her rich daughter-in-law. The partisan spirit is his moral disease and, as it metastasizes within him, it moves him to reduce all universality to ideology. Werner accuses Eustache of insufferable narrowness, of insolently judging others, not by their intrinsic, universal qualities, but by the categories into which he has imprisoned them. Eustache jealously resents his wife's concurrence in Werner's conclusions; the hostile struggle between them mounts. Finally, in a spirit of meanness, Eustache betrays Werner by revealing to Gisela a secret his friend had committed to him under the strictest confidence. A government emissary from Germany had invited Werner to return to his Nazified fatherland where he would receive top billing in an opera house, provided he espoused the Hitlerian cause. Werner categorically refuses this invitation to self-degradation. His superficial and light-headed wife, Gisela, explodes at his secrecy and refusal; she quits Werner and flees with a rich German baron from the intolerably harsh life of a refugee to the comfort of her homeland. Ironically, Eustache, who is haunted by a fear of treason against his proletarian masses, succeeds in committing the crime of treason against his friend.

But it seems as if no alienation occurs without some compensating communion and, thus, a bond of affection is born between Werner, who is endowed with the gift of moving hearts, and Beatrice who has lost her husband to the cause of ideology. Yet Werner refuses to exploit his gift for arousing sympathy, even when Beatrice, who has discovered Eustache's love affair with Socialist Gertrude, throws herself at him. Werner, uncertain that he can resist his love for Beatrice, decides to return to Germany, but not under the conditions offered by Hitler's henchmen. A scruple of conscience moves him to do something heroic for the political slaves in the Nazi concentration camps. Perhaps he can sing for them, become for them not so much a political ally as a companion in their suffering; he can give them the benefit of his presence, of his love. Has Werner been tainted by Eustache's

guilty conscience? Perhaps. But he has no illusions as to his
fate: arrest and deportation or execution. But before he goes, he
must do his best to save Beatrice, to lift her to his own heights, to
convince her that salvation springs from transcendence. Somehow
he must make her see that his departure is not an act of suicide.
Suicide! "Not in the least," Werner protests, "suicide is a crime...
I am simply putting myself at the disposal..." "Of what?" asks
Beatrice. "Of the cause? Of the revolution?" "I am not interested in the cause," Werner replies emphatically, "I am interested
in men." [43] But Beatrice desires to hold him. Will not her husband Eustache abandon her and flee with Gertrude, that tart,
that barbed dart who has speared him? Werner exhorts Beatrice
to remain at the side of her husband for she alone can save him.
"You cannot abandon him. You must always remember that you
are the wife of a pauper... Poverty is not a deficiency of money,
nor an absence of success. Eustache has had money; he has been
a success. Yet he has remained poor and grown poorer still.
Without doubt, he will never be cured of his poverty. This is
the greatest evil of our times; it is spreading like a plague. No
physician has yet been found to take care of it. Nor has anyone as
yet been able to diagnose it. Doubtless, the artist will be spared,
even if he fasts and starves. And, to be sure, the true believer
who gives himself to prayer...All other persons are in danger." [44]

Beatrice protests that Werner is asking her to live with a
leper. And Werner replies prophetically: "Leper colonies are
going to multiply on earth, I fear. To very few people will grace
be granted to live there knowing they are among lepers and yet
not finding them repulsive. Much more than grace, they will need
a viaticum to sustain them on their way." [45] Beatrice contends
she lacks the bravery to face life without Werner. In the end,
Werner exhorts her to find strength for the struggle where he
himself is finding it for his coming ordeal in Germany—in
communion with the beloved. "You will think of me as I think of
Rudolf. Later I shall be in you a living presence, as Rudolf

[43] G. MARCEL, *Le Dard* (Paris: Plon, 1938), p. 115.
[44] *Ibid.*, pp. 117-118.
[45] *Ibid.*, p. 118.

dwells on in me. You will remember then what I told you a few weeks ago. If there were only the living, Beatrice, I think life on this earth would be altogether impossible." [46]

Commenting philosophically on this drama from the Harvard University platform of the William James Lectures in 1961, Marcel said:

> What *is* this poverty which is neither lack of money nor lack of success and which, we are told, is going to spread like leprosy? It might be said, I think, that it is the spirit of abstraction which finds in our own day—and we must not hesitate to say so—its most terrifying, though not its only, incarnation in communism. But this spirit of abstraction cannot be separated from a certain lack of love, and by this I mean the inability to treat a human being as a human being, and for this human being the substituting of a certain idea, a certain abstract designation. The leper colonies which are going to multiply on earth (let me recall that this was written in 1936) are the popular democracies, to the extent that they are committed to the spirit of abstraction in its Marxist form. [47]

Le Dard leaves this fateful question yet unanswered: Which shall prevail—the rationalistic, ego-centric, resentful spirit of equalitarianism (Eustache's ideology) or the realistic, hetero-centric, neighborly spirit of fraternity (Werner's agapeology)? The nations, indeed the citizens, will have to make a dreadful decision between the determinism of ideology and the liberty of agape. Marcel expects the salvation of man's dignity solely in that free life of transcendence which strengthens man's consciousness of his living bond with his fellowmen.

[46] *Ibid.*, pp. 87, 118.
[47] G. MARCEL, *The Existential Background of Human Dignity* (Cambridge, Mass.: Harvard University Press, 1963), pp. 122-123.

Post-World War II Period

L'Emissaire (The Emissary), (1945-1948, a play in three acts)

Marcel was dejected at the excesses perpetrated by the Resistance in France's post-war purification program.   During what he calls *"des années noires,"* the spirit of suspicion, fear and vengeance pitted Frenchmen against Frenchmen.   Each citizen felt called upon to prove he had not collaborated with the enemy; blackmail became the common weapon to bring down your adversary.   The careful reader will notice that the existing state of confusion allows the characters involved to reveal themselves very gradually, like spies making contact with other unknown spies in enemy country. It is well for the reader or spectator, of this play especially, to recall Marcel's warning: "No more here than elsewhere did I start from abstract ideas to be dramatically illustrated afterwards." [48]

Clément Ferrier returns home after spending sixteen months in a prison camp in Polish Silesia.   He remains ominously silent, displaying no sign of joy at reunion with his loved ones.   People attribute his petrified silence to the intense sufferings he must have undergone, for he returned a wasted skeleton scarcely alive. But an uneasiness beclouds the minds of his neighbors.   "How did he manage to return?   Did he escape?   Did he collaborate?" Clément refuses to see the press, to answer any questions, to make any statements.   Yet to the congratulations of Antoine Sorgue, fiancé to his daughter, Sylvia, Clément explodes: "No, no, not joy; don't use that word, I beg you." [49]   Poor Clément seems to be reliving a nightmare, destined to die with these frightening words on his lips, words that are constantly haunting his wife: "Mathilda, don't ever have a doubt about this...you are speaking to a dead man!" [50]

[48] *Ibid.*, p. 117.
[49] G. MARCEL, "L'Emissaire" in *Vers un autre royaume*, p. 32.
[50] *Ibid.*, p. 41.

Some time later, a letter arrives at the Ferrier home from a doctor who was Clément's companion in captivity. Dr. Van Doren saved a Nazi leader's life in an epidemic which was raging in camp. The grateful leader offered Van Doren his freedomt but, in place of himself, the doctor persuaded the Nazi to free Clément whose condition was very grave and who had already attempted to poison himself. "I am sure," writes the doctor, "that he (Clément) is torturing himself on my account; no doub, he told you of this incident. He was unwilling to accept my proposal. But I felt I could hold out until the end, while he would doubtless have perished within a few weeks or even days." [51] So Clément was understandably ashamed. But how could he justifiably reject his family?

Mathilda belonged to a generation which still believed in conscience. Somewhat of a religious simpleton, she managed to confuse everything and confound everyone. To her the Resistance was rank sectarianism; she expected Clément's traumatic condition to be cured by a radiologist or an occultist as easily as one wipes away squalor and coal-dust from a miner. Sylvia, Clément's youngest daughter, is a very ambivalent person. Shortly after the beginning of the war, she worked for the Resistance together with her friend Noémie Vitrel. But she quit, after attending some secret meetings, to become engaged to Antoine Sorgue. Not long after this, Noémie was arrested and deported for working the mission originally given to Sylvia.

Antoine is a forthright, faithful, lucid Catholic, but hardly likable. Yet he is the one who lays bare the ambiguity of this drama. At first, Sylvia, who is strongly pro-Resistance, attempts to dissociate herself from him. But she eventually falls in love with him for the maturity and profound compassion with which Antoine understands the tragic condition of all the characters caught up in the maelstrom of the Resistance and the hateful collaboration. Antoine himself had been a prisoner of war, interned for a year in Saxony. Evacuated as sick, he later learned that he was freed through the intervention of a collaborator. Early

[51] *Ibid.*, p. 88.

in the occupation, he had worked for a publishing house that
printed German propaganda. Anne-Marie, an older daughter of
the Ferriers, and her husband Bertrand Sorel, had been very
active members of the Resistance. Together with Roger,
Bertrand's atheistic brother, they suspect Antoine of being a
collaborator and oppose Roland and his mother Madame de
Carmoy for banking on a German victory. After the armistice,
Roland is arrested as a collaborator. He hangs himself in his cell;
his mother, on hearing of this tragedy, commits suicide. What
was Roland's crime? A sincere young man, he had remained
in the Holderin Philosophy Circle even after it had fallen under
a "mixed patronage." It was Roland also who had intervened
to help free Antoine. Moreover, he disapproved of the harsh
methods of the French purification and was actually looking for
a rapprochement with the Germans through the mediation of
the intellectual elite on both sides. Roland may certainly have
been naive, but he was not a traitor.

The double suicide shocks a chastened and sympathetic
Sylvia back into the arms of Antoine, even though she feels that
her original convictions against the collaborators are still valid.
"Hundreds of thousands of men," she had told the collaborating
Madame de Carmoy, "have known hell...hell, Madame! I
suppose there is scarcely any mention of this word, which brings a
smile to your face, in the elegant and reactionary parishes where
you attend services. It would be improper, in bad taste...Never-
theless, hell exists...persons of your mentality, whose echo you've
made yourself, are the caterers of hell. In one way or another,
they have repeatedly fed hell to the human race. How can you fail
to be ashamed of yourself? When I listen to you, it is as if I am
inhaling the stench of the dirtiest of dungeons." [52]

Throughout the drama, both the men of the Resistance and
the collaborators seem to be acting from a sincere consciousness
of their responsibilities. The temptation to judge each side as
categorically evil is great and both sides succumb to this temptation with vengeance. Yet ironically, great deeds and evil deeds

[52] *Ibid.*, pp. 71-72.

are performed on both sides. Clement is liberated by a prisoner who survives him and unknowingly hastens him to an early grave. As for Roland, did he kill himself in a cowardly fashion? Or was he too proud to submit to the grilling of the narrow partisans? Did his mother dispatch herself to be with Roland, or was she dragged down into his despair? Noémie returns from prison, a hate-breathing communist, convinced that Sylvia betrayed her. Sylvia herself is not so sure she did not betray her friend and she has a guilty conscience over the lie of ill health she advanced as the excuse for leaving the Resistance. Why did she refuse to meet Noémie on the latter's return from prison? This flight seems to prove the bad faith within which she has trapped herself. Roger, the atheist, is disillusioned with the Resistance and embittered at the rejection of his suit by Sylvia. He is tortured with a hunger for truth, but can get no further than the cry, "Yes, if only there were truth..." [53] Antoine is neither sure of the purity of his motives nor of the genuinity of his patriotism. If only the men of the Resistance and the collaborators could have understood each other, had more faith in each other. But the poignant tragedy is that sometimes, despite the best will in the world, men cannot help causing each other's misunderstandings and sorrows. The fundamental existential situation is always ambiguous and sometimes hopelessly complicated. When Sylvia asks Antoine if he has, at last, liberated himself from his mental agony, Antoine answers: "Yes and no, Sylvia, this is the only answer when we ourselves are concerned: we believe and we do not believe, we love and we do not love, we are and we are not. But if this is so, it is because we are heading toward a goal which we see and do not see at the same time." [54]

Perhaps Sylvia's response to her mother contains the truth that would have saved them all: "It may be that the important thing is not to be alive, but only to be...reconciled." [55] In the last analysis, Antoine's faith indicates the road to transcendent salvation, to the time and place of unchanging reconciliation:

[53] *Ibid.*, p. 110.
[54] *Ibid.*, p. 108.
[55] *Ibid.*, p. 89.

"There is one thing I have discovered since my parents' death: what we call being a survivor is in reality to live not so much *after* as *under*: those we have never ceased to love with whatever is best in us becoming something like a living, invisible arch which we sense and even brush against, on the strength of which we are able to go on even as our powers diminish, wrenched from ourselves, toward the moment when everything will be caught up in love." [56]

Le Signe de la Croix (The Sign of the Cross), (1938-1951, a play in three acts)

The time is 1938, the place Paris. Madame Lena Lilienthal is a Jewish refugee recently driven from Vienna and now living with her niece Pauline Bernauer and Pauline's husband Simon, an accomplished musician whose life is wrapt up in music. The Bernauers have four school-aged children, three sons—David, Jean-Paul and Henri—and one daughter, Odette. Simon Bernauer is eminently endowed with qualities that have distinguished outstanding Jews throughout this people's long and glorious history. He is sensitively conscious of the universal brotherhood of man, has an incomparably compassionate disposition, suffers an acute nostalgia for the Absolute and ardently rejects all irrationally narrowing categories. Yet, such is the ambiguity of his personality, Simon is also a regular reader of *L'Action Française*, going along for the most part with Maurras and Daudet's call to patriotism, but not with their vilification of the Jews. When David, his oldest, brilliant, high-spirited collegiate son, upbraids Simon for not gnashing his teeth while reading *L'Action's* attacks, Simon flies into a rage:

> So, I am condemned to think and feel like a Jew? Do you presume to wall me into a set way of thinking? Into a kind of mental ghetto? Don't you understand that the worst nonsense, the vilest imprisonment arises precisely from racism? Why, it is through such racism that you arm our very enemies. You justify in advance their most shocking and dangerous accusations. Oh! I have often thought that

[56] *Ibid.*, p. 109.

the Jews themselves have launched the idea of racism into the world. [57]

Simon refuses to club together with fellow Israelites in a segment of society that stands aside from the French citizenry. It is the practice of such unreasonable Semitism that spawns an equally unreasonable anti-Semitism. He complains that the Jews so stick together that one of their number no sooner arrives at a superior social and economic echelon than he turns and pulls the others up with himself. This is not evil in itself, but the tragedy of his people consists in their refusal to take root within the national fraternity that furthers their fortunes. In France they crave equality with all Frenchmen, yet simultaneously live as if they were members of a French Freemasonry. Simon seeks fraternity far more than equality; the former is an intersubjective presence of love, the latter is a hostile competition over things. Thus Simon excludes himself from any treasonable parasitic segment of society —the we-a-different-and-superior-people—for such a collectivity only divides the body politic.

Pauline, on the other hand, exudes the repulsive assurance that wealth bestows. She is fiercely clannish and hopes to hold her family together more by ethnic than ethical bonds. On learning that the brilliant Jewish contestants for high medical posts were all rejected on racial grounds, she exclaims: "If France reject us, she is no longer our fatherland." But Simon is irritated by his wife's bigoted behavior. They argue bitterly. Pauline resents Simon's designation of his confreres as "a tribe." "We are a community," she cries, "and the more we are persecuted, the more we are bound to sense and affirm this community." [58] Simon vehemently attempts to insert reason into their argument: "But you don't see, indeed, the vicious circle you are in. How tragic! How infernal! It is precisely because you are obstinate in keeping yourselves apart, in marching ceaselessly shoulder to shoulder that you advance your enemies and arm your persecutors." [59]

[57] G. MARCEL, "Le Signe de la croix" in *Vers un autre royaume*, p. 161.
[58] *Ibid.*, pp. 170-171.
[59] *Ibid.*, p. 172.

Jean-Paul, the second son, unable any longer to sustain a life committed to nothing, converts to Protestantism, with the tolerance of his father and against the bitter opposition of his mother. Meanwhile, in the collateral relationships, another tragedy is being enacted. Léon, Pauline's brother, is married to highly anti-Semitic Odette. Rejected in French medical circles, Léon is invited to practice in the United States. He would willingly accept, if only his beloved Odette would come back to him. But Odette has wandered into the arms of Xavier Reveillac and is seeking a divorce so as to marry him. Xavier is anti-Semitic not so much from hatred of the Jews but because an historical imperative calls for this posture at the present time. He predicts the war, the German victory and the inevitable extermination of the Jews. Once the fall and occupation of France is established, the arrest and deportation of the Jews begins. Simon, Pauline, Aunt Lena and the small children flee to the South of France. David and Jean-Paul remain in Paris. In a brazen show of racial pride and love of liberty, David attends the Bach concert at the home of the Colonnes, wearing the Jewish star for all to see. It was a rash disobedience against a specific order of the occupation forces. David is violently overpowered and disappears in the hands of the Nazi torturers, never to be heard from again. Jean-Paul escapes south to relate the tragedy to his family and friends.

Meanwhile, in the South a magnanimous priest, the Abbé Scheweigsam, offers to hide Aunt Lena from the Nazi dragnet which is slowly closing over the whole of France. Monsignor de Romière's refuge is opened only to Jews of French citizenship, thereby excluding Aunt Lena who is not yet a naturalized citizen. But the Abbé offers his home as a place of refuge for her, suggesting she become a member of his family. Aunt Lena, with delicate finesse and warm sensibility refuses, saying that she could not exploit for her own profit a religion to which she has never belonged. Instead, she consigns herself in faith to the transcendent Being and willingly accepts her approaching death by torture. "I belong more and more to another king-dom." [60]

As the German dragnet moves southward, Odette and Xavier offer to facilitate the escape of the Bernauers to America. Simon decides to remain with Aunt Lena, preferring to share the perils and dark destiny of his Jewish confreres than to escape to the comfort of America. Pauline, unwilling and unable to understand the profound commitment in Simon's soul, condemns him as a husband who is harsh and derelict in his duty towards his family. She escapes with the children. As for Simon, his refusal to flee transforms him into a new man. The closer tragedy approaches his people, the more intensely he wills to participate in their sufferings. Persecution has created a new and stronger bond, a more than ordinary human bond, between Simon and all people, especially between him and the downtrodden. He now speaks of a "sacramental bond" which has sprung up between himself and his fellow Jews. And thus Simon remains in a spirit of self-oblation, convinced that to flee his suffering confreres would be an act of perfidious treason.

In an epilogue written in 1948, Marcel presents the survivors to us. A letter from a prisoner who has escaped the death camp shared with Simon is read by the Abbé to the Bernauer family. It relates that Aunt Lena was liquidated on arrival at the camp. Simon lingered on for a while, softened and sanctified by the suffering and example of Aunt Lena, in whose presence he moved. But his health failed rapidly and he died attended in his last

[60] *Ibid.*, p. 199. It should be stressed that Marcel fully realized that diverse resonances would be awakened by his treatment of the delicate subject of Semitism. He is willing to accept this fact and the enlightened criticisms that will arise therefrom. But he opposes the interdiction of this subject from rational discussion, for no good can come from refusing to discuss the errors and illusions to which so many well-intentioned Israelites have succumbed since the end of the Second World War. Precisely on this point Marcel has written in the Postscript to the play:

"No one can question the fact that the problem of Israel has regained dramatic intensity. Today, as I am informed, conversions are growing among the Jews, but, on the other hand, a laicized and enraged Judaism is threatening to degenerate into a new form of nazism as indefensible as the former breed. Between these two extremes, there are many Jews of genuine faith and good will. This play is written for their reflection." *Ibid.*, p. 233.

moments by a Protestant minister. Odette is present at the reading; Léon and Pauline refuse her forgiveness. In an effort to bring them around, the Abbé reveals that Simon, before he died, forgave and prayed for Odette and Xavier who had saved his family. As for Xavier, he was later apprehended and executed by the Resistance. While in prison he had attempted suicide, but failed; he repented and returned to the faith of his childhood before his execution. Perhaps the prayers of Simon had saved him. Could not Pauline imitate her deceased husband's magnanimity? Bitter to the end, Pauline and Léon refuse to admit grace or miracles as possible, much less to accept them as facts.

And so the tragedy closes on an agonizing paradox. Simon and Aunt Lena cannot become Christians for fear of failing to identify themselves with their persecuted brethren. Yet they live and die in a faith and love that undoubtedly places them within the communion of the saints. The fire of persecution expanded the constricting mentality of the "we-a-special-and-superior-people" into the transcendent activity of compassionate communion. For the sign of the cross can always conquer superficial conformism and odious pharisaism whenever this symbol of suffering is embraced as a means of communion. Persecution can purify from clannishness; persecution orients man from the posture of the "we-who-stand-apart," to the "we-who-are-thine." The sign of the cross is meant to hold people and things together in him whom it shatters for the sake of the cosmos and the community. If this sign is freely accepted, it is a means of reconciliation. If it is rejected, it is the occasion for alienation and disintegration.

When we complete even a quick journey through Marcel's dramatic world, we come away imbued with the spirit of reverence toward the human individual that pervades every scene. The human person is seen as the all-important center of experience— the center of this spinning earth, of planetary revolutions, of an exploding universe, of an on-rushing history, all of which are trifling when contrasted with the rise and fall of this demi-god. Persons, each unique and irreplaceable, are constantly being discovered in an atmosphere of admiration, compassion, alienation.

The plays are orchestrations of intersubjectivity with harmony and disharmony resounding from the clash of personalities. Even when the characters apparently succumb to despair and suicide, the spectator is left with a ray of hope that, perhaps beyond the invisible threshold, the inner conflict has been healed and the protagonists lifted to a realm of transfiguring transcendence. In any case, the individual tragedies always seem to promise hope for human existence itself by inviting the spectator to go beyond particular failures or successes to what is essentially and universally valid in human life—"the sense and reality of communion which is to exist as little as possible for oneself." [61] Drama is for Marcel the way of wisdom, the way to arouse man to the spirit of gratitude for being alive and to invoke him to become fully committed to the human calling to communion. The dramas are certainly "psychological" in technique, dramas of thought, of the soul, yet they are concerned not merely with the destiny of the individual characters, but with the destiny of human, spiritual survival which is necessarily interlocked with the transcendent view of human existence. In the words of Kenneth Gallagher, "Unless the spectator who beholds the action on stage is moved to say, not 'so it is with them,' but 'so it is with me,' the play remains relatively trivial." [62] But all Marcel's plays move men of maturity to say, "so it is with us." For Marcel's drama rejects the decadent, emasculated and tepid humanity that has lost faith in the individual person and that opts for isolated, self-centered or collectivized existence—the Sartrean society. His theatre is rather addressed to men of flesh and blood who, though immersed in a tragic milieu, nevertheless, are dedicated to a human way of life that knows how to fructify the marriage between the visible and invisible, between the temporal and eternal into ascending degrees of participation in being— into the communion of saints.

[61] G. MARCEL, *The Existential Background of Human Dignity*, p. 125.
[62] K. GALLAGHER, *The Philosophy of Gabriel Marcel*, p. 114.

CHAPTER VIII

The Dialectic of Communion
and Community

In the preceding chapters, we have approached the person through a phenomenological reflection on lived experience. As a result of this investigation, it has been seen that the human existent is not static; he is not a *tabula rasa* or a kind of wax tablet which receives sensations and impressions from the outside. [1] Rather, the person is characterized by a dialectical movement which is capable of various degrees of participation in being. Here we may use a spatial image: on the vertical plane, man reaches from the atom below to the Absolute above; on the horizontal plane, which is that of social communion, the person is capable of expanding or contracting his presence to others. He may bury his talent and seek to isolate himself like a cell divorced from the rest of the social body, or he may reach towards a commonwealth whose consummation is found in a divine society.

In any case, the dynamics of life make it difficult for a man to remain in total isolation. The thrust towards communication, communion and community represents a necessary facet of the interpersonal dialectic of the human situation. Even though man seems initially immersed in matter, the person in him is impelled by his hunger for being to expand and to mount. Not only is he impelled from within, but the outer world is not neutral. It radiates the presence of that which is beyond; it appeals to the

---

[1] Emmanuel MOUNIER, *Existentialist Philosophies*, trans. Eric Blow (Bristol: Rankin Bros., 1951), p. 9.

176

ASCENT TO BEING

incarnate spirit to rise above sensation and emotion towards reflection and volition, and finally towards that dedication and self-
donation that opens the door to the full community of love. One
is, of course, free to reject this appeal; but the consequence will
be an eternal loss. The one who chooses himself necessarily
rejects the possibility of transcendence and moves towards self-
destruction and the "community" of hate. Those who find a
paradox in the *"esse est co-esse"* usually represent it as a static
situation. The universe of persons is fluid. To be alive and
conscious is to be involved in events with their threat or promise of
a richer or diminished future.

Marcel will never let us forget that, whether we like it or not,
we are embarked and engaged from the first moment of our
conscious existence. We are not free not to be, or not to be involved. Our only choice lies in the goal which we set for ourselves.
The "man of abstention" can always justify his refusal to take a
stand on the basis of prudence. But such rationalization is
already a kind of infidelity, even when colored with romantic
illusions about the future. The evasion of personal responsibility
is often clothed in a show of omniscience; but there is no substitute
for "the courage to be." The refusal to commit oneself to life
deprives the abstainer from the most intense and concrete way of
knowing; for authentic knowledge only comes through dedicated
action where there is a degree of insecurity and personal risk.
There are times when action is the only way of winning the truth. [2]

Even so, we are all subject to the temptation of supposing
that we can win security without a struggle. Positivism offers an
excellent example of this kind of philosophical detachment. It
has no place for the unpredictable in man, and it characterizes as
"fanaticism" every instance of spontaneous fervor or zest for
living. The ideal, of course, would be to petrify man, then take
him apart like a well-mounted machine, so that each part is
ticketed. It would be easy then, when the machine was put back
together, to predict every act and destroy every semblance of
freedom. This would result in the contrived and controlled man.

[2] Emmanuel MOUNIER, *Personalism*, trans. Philip Mairet (New
York: Grove, 1952), p. 93.

Such a robot would be safe; he would never be the occasion of uncertainties, nor give rise to anxieties about the future. Least of all would he take the initiative as an *agent provocateur* who might instigate political change. All that is needed to bring about peace in a Utopian universe is planning. And here the Positivist would, of course, do the planning and contrive the kind of man he needed to execute his plans.

But such a universe would be one in which men would be empty shells, without inwardness. It might have some advantages in a world of technocracy—man would become a machine operating machines—but it is questionable whether this could be called life, least of all human life. Indeed, if there is one sure way to madness, it is to promise man the tranquility of the machine.

But true inner tranquility cannot, in Marcel's view, be founded on anything less than the dialectic of conversion and reverential communion. Not that lived experience minimizes the tragic appeal of human existence. On the contrary, it is forever demonstrating that lasting values are born in conflict and that the good society is the reward of a struggle. But before one can realize the outward life of communion, there must be a *sanatio in radice*. The first conquest must be of one's own inner life through meditation. Without this cultivation of inwardness, involvement in outer events diminishes one's being with its *effusio ad exteriora*. The product here is not even the shadow of a man of communion, but the socialite or the man of calculation and connivance, both of whom are parasites on society.

It is stated at times that the quest for inwardness is a flight from society, an unconcern for the other that is caused by a preoccupation with the self. Yet timely seclusion can be the first thrust toward communion; inward communion can give an awareness of the state of the community without. Prophets and reformers have emerged from deserts of prayer and study with remedies that have saved or lost whole societies. It is a paradox, too, that the man of inwardness is often the man most exposed to tragedy or triumph in the social struggle. His self-donation may be the occasion for the rise or fall of his own fortunes.

But the dialectic of communion can be frustrated by the absence of a dialectic of communication. Matter demands a certain primacy. Without it, man stagnates and dies; with it, he fills certain basic needs and can move on to his full personality. Marx, then, is right in stressing the importance of economics. He is wrong in making economic values unique and superior to everything else. Disorder in the dialectics of economics produces a most menacing disorder in the dialect of communion as the Communist colossus is historically proving.

The dialectic of communication is appreciated once we understand the unity in man upon which it is founded. The strange thing about the human person is that he is related to, though never identified with, moving matter. If I ask the question, "Where is John?," the reply coming back is, "There he is." That moving body over there is pointed out to me as being John. And it is true. But a body is not a person, nor does vital or non-vital motion necessarily make it one. Yet the person of John is somewhere in that moving body, not as if in a space, yet certainly not beyond the space that that living body occupies. Human persons have so much to do with their living bodies that Marcel can say: "I am my body."

Nevertheless, despite the body which is material and divisible, every human person is one in a most emphatic and indivisible way. Spiritually and personally each person is unique, incapable of being divided, nor substituted for. Whatever may be the pathological splittings that may psychologically affect a person, the fact is that the person cannot be split in ontological principle; his oneness is absolutely simple in the line of personality. Even the abstract division of man's powers does not represent the person as he exists *in concrete*. So-called faculties of sensation, appetition, intellection and volition are not distinct and separate powers in man; they are rather different manifestations of the one person in vital activity; they are not functions that are distinct and separated from one another; the person performs all these functions totally.

Marcel warns us never to "reify" a person. This diminishes his mysterious fulness. A person is infinitely more than all that goes into his make-up, than all the characteristics that attempt to list him. Human personality escapes human comprehension. Though the person lives an emotional, intellectual and volitional life all in one, he infinitely transcends these activities.

Man's unity is such that he can in his transient life perform actions that achieve things outside of himself. This power to project his life into creative works distinct from himself reveals his openness to the transcendent. Because his curiosity brings him out of himself, because he becomes involved in the other, man becomes a doer and a maker. This projection into transcendence reveals man's relationship to the higher, to the Absolute itself. The unity in man propels him onto the interpersonal sphere, where he performs a variety of acts of communication and communion. These very acts beget in man a profounder consciousness of his own uniqueness, of the indivisibility and cohesion of his personality.

The dialectical process of interpersonal communication proceeds by degrees and different types of outward thrust. To illustrate these degrees and types of thrust into communication and communion, we would like to use examples analyzed and discussed by B. V. Schwarz. [3]

Let us suppose that I am expressing my admiration for some public figure. My person sets out on a sortie of communal conquest in one specific intentional direction. But if the person I am openly admiring is completely unaware of my admiration, there does not yet exist between us an interpersonal act. True, I have related myself to that other person. Nevertheless, the I of this act of admiring has not yet become a presence to the object of this act of admiration. Nor has the object of this sentiment as yet become a concrete presence or thou for the I. There is no mutuality of presences, not even any mutuality of communication and, *a fortiori*, no mutuality of communion. *Actio in distans numquam fiat communio.* Communication and com-

---

[3] From a course entitled "Philosophy of Community," given in the Graduate School of Philosophy at Fordham University, Spring, 1961, in which the interpersonal sphere—contact, relation, communion, basic forms of community, the role of community in human life—were phenomenologically explored. The examples used enter in depth into this sphere which constitutes the heart of Marcel's philosophy.

munion can never be built on the foundation of isolated sentiments, however ardent and pure these may be. The dialectical motion of intimacy is absent because the thou, who is meant to share with the I—in a simultaneously centrifugal and centripetal action—the movement towards an *Intimius intimo meo*, [4] is as yet non-existent as a concrete presence. He has as yet not entered the dialectic of another person.

To take another example, suppose that I am in the act of giving information to another person. He is on the receiving end of my activity; actual contact is going on and my act is registered in the other person. In return, the person with whom I am communicating responds and his response is registered with me. This type of action is called a social action of communication. They are social because these actions are registered within the communicating parties. I can never make a promise to someone who never becomes aware of my offer, so too with a contract; the contract must be something mutually heard, seen, written, registered, understood and answered. Communication is achieved when the parties to the proposition take note of the content of the oscillatory action going on between them and when they stabilize and resolve this action with either the "yes" of their approval or the "no" of their disapproval.

Why are social acts of communication merely social transactions and not acts of communion? The reason is that in such activity we are not directing our notice to the other person in such a way as to make the other person the primary content of this activity. Some third thing is the center of our preoccupation. We may be contracting about some property, for instance, and we notice one another, courteously of course, primarily because of this property. In addressing ourselves to each other, we are not appealing to the person of the other, but to the other either as property-owner or as property-seeker. We are making use of one another's capacities only in so far as they are needed for this transaction, for this communication. Neither the "I" nor the "thou," nor the I-thou presences, are topics of our confrontation.

[4] Emmanuel MOUNIER, *Existentialist Philosophies*, p. 80.

We are not nearly that deeply interested nor concerned about one another. We may be manipulating and maneuvering one another, even perhaps, using one another, for social acts of communication merely skim over the surfaces of the persons involved. We exchange civility, justice, things, but not our persons. We may even become partners, associates, but we stop short of becoming full presences and persons to one another.

Let us proceed to still another example. Imagine that I am suddenly face to face with my enemy. I promptly emit an intensely felt: "I hate you!" Or stand at the other extreme of the scale of confrontation. I am in the presence of the beloved and every sign between us sings the song of the Psalmist: "I to my beloved and my beloved to me." Are these confrontations situations of mutual information? Hardly. Here faces are much more than fields of information; they are stages of inner exposition, of awesome realization and participation in the emotional response of person to person. Acts of love and hate transcend by far the noisy arena of social functions and communications. We no longer have the situation of social links nor of peripheral contacts; we are summoned to the summit of confrontation and the wrestling is one of intense love or intense hatred. The persons in this kind of confrontation are directly involved; they are the topics for communion or rejection; they are completely exposed and must receive something, in one way or another; in the examples given above, it can be said that the other is upon me and I am upon the other. We have broken through our social defenses and stand in the sanctuaries of one another's souls as friends or foes. I have to receive the "thou" in one role or another and the "thou" must receive the "I" in one role or another. We must, we are forced to enter into communion with one another. We must, again we are forced to give some sort of personal reply either to a tremendous offer of love or to a horrendous attack of hatred. It is impossible for the persons involved to fail to take note of each other; they cannot even temporize by diverting each other to a third posited in the inbetween stage of communication. There is no third between us. We are both naked to each other as enemy or friend. The very attempt to ignore, to snub the other would be the act of personal rejection. In such a situation, there is only the "I" and the "thou," spiritually naked to each other and thoroughly involved in a state of communion that is promising with the delights of intimacy or fraught with the hazards of alienation, enjoyed as the experience of final and total acceptance or suffered as the cross of total and irrevocable rejection.

Just as we cannot understand the true value, beauty and grandeur of the person without understanding the transcendent beauty of the I-thou relationship, so too we will never truly appreciate the sublime grandeur of the community until we realize that the person and the community are ontologically linked and that the I-thou relationship of communion is the act of love that creates the community.

We know historically that men have been enamored of the beauty and power of the individual person, even unto rendering it an idolatrous service. Individualism is the idolatry practiced toward the single person. But the community too has attracted, and even holds today, its own sect of adorers. And whatever the form these sects may take—Nationalism, Fascism, Nazism, Communism—their own brand of idolatry is no less severe a political and social sickness, since it inflicts men with a universal blindness to the real value of both the person and the community.

The basic elements of all communion are also the basic elements of all communities—I-thou and we. "Wherever we two does not succeed in materializing," says Mounier, "there can be no we people." [5] Thus when we speak of a community we are referring to a real entity. Unlike the Positivists who deny the existence of communities in their true sense and who say that man is merely describing persons in their empirical relations when he uses the word community, we say the community is a *corpus*, a "moral" substance, that it is an integral, wholly serious and permanent being. Hegel makes the community the fuller and the primary reality, while man, the person, is the dimmer, partial and secondary reality. He succumbs to a sort of community mysticism. For us, the person is the real, existential substance; there is some-

[5] *Ibid.*, p. 89.

thing mysterious about the community, for after all it is made up of mysterious persons. But the deeper mystery is the independent and priorly existing person.

Can the community be reduced to a mere unity, a family, a nation, a State? Communities are too variegated to be merely restricted to these few forms, although it is true to say that a nation enjoys a cultural unity and the State is a political and governmental unity.

In the first chapter of this book we warned against viewing the community too rigidly after the analogy of a *corpus*, that is, a whole organism with integral parts. In a certain sense the community is a whole and persons go to constitute its being and unity. But persons always remain ontologically independent of this whole, and, since they are prior in existence to the community, they can never be absorbed into the whole community the way inferior parts and organs are absorbed in the physical body. Ontologically, persons infinitely outrank the communities they freely constitute. [6]

Of course, there are different types of communities. There are formal, material and formal-material communities. Formal communities are those which are established with a predominantly juridical structure. Material communities lack this juridical structure and come together more naturally, somewhat like a circle of friends. Formal-material community is a combination in which the community established is both formal and material, but via complete organic interpenetration.

Exclusively formal communities do not touch our entire persons with the same warmth and intimacy as material communities. The latter have a deeper meaning for us and bestow an inner and fuller plenitude of being upon us. To be sure, both types of communities are perfective of the human person and

[6] Mounier, *Personalism*, pp. 116-117: "The transcendence of the person means that the person belongs to nobody else but to himself: the child is a subject; it is not a *RES societatis*, nor a *RES familiae*, nor a *RES ecclesiae*. Not that it is purely subjective nor an isolated subject. Inserted into various collectivities, the child is educated by them and within them; if they are not all-powerful in its eyes, they are its natural formative environments—the family and the nation and (the Christian adds) the Church are all avenues that open up towards a wider humanity."

attain intersubjective communion. The metaphysical bureaucrat eschews the material community, being content to burrow in the formal community. The metaphysical bohemian would not be caught dead or alive in a formal community. He is constitutionally incapable of being hemmed in by the laws of society. Yet we must appreciate and do justice to both these types of communities. Moreover, we may never foist communal forms on social realities that have no aptitude for these forms. It would be a great mistake to attempt to formalize a circle of friends into a juridical community. It would, in fact, be the spiritual suffocation of that material community.

Communities can also be classified into duo-personal and pluro-personal. Marriage, which can only take place between two persons, is an example of a duo-personal community. The State is an example of a pluro-personal community.

Can we be members of a community without knowing that we are members, that is, without realizing that we are the center of a whole host of affective and disciplinary ministrations? Certainly it is impossible to awaken and find oneself a member of a married community. As adults we never become members of communities—the Nation or State, for instance—without realizing we are members. With respect to the collectivity of the human race, we become members of the human family at birth. Only gradually do we awaken to a consciousness of ourselves and to the consciousness of belonging to the whole human family. But the dialectic of this communal awakening begins in what Marcel calls "the mystery of the family," when he treats the one's immediate community of blood relatives.

The primitive idea of the family evokes a certain pattern or constellation. The child, of course, is the sun of this social solar system. He is the center of solicitous glances, of overwhelming embraces, of an infinity of anxious ministrations. The child receives everything. Not a shadow of a movement escapes him, for everything seems aimed at him personally. Then there are the voices. Their inflections pass from softness to sharpness, from gentleness to severity, from persuasion to threats. Little by little the child discerns the relationships which bind these beings to each other and to him. His own relationship to them emerges slowly. The child will eventually come to see that each one around him has his own life, his own inviolable relationships to all others. For some of them, the child learns he is the cause of preoccupation; for all of them he is the subject of conversation when out of sight. The child thus knows only partially how he affects these others and what their thoughts and feelings are towards him. He sees one side of them publicly and that side more or less is the same. Yet he learns that everything is truly complicated in these new relationships of intersubjective activity between him and them. [7]

The family, then, is the first dialectical social cell of society arising from the consummation of the marriage community. The child *is*, without having originally suspected or willed its existence. The child *incarnates* the *reply* to the reciprocal appeal which two lovers made to each other. The child is the incarnated transcendence of their appeal, of their communion, of their persons, of their presences. The child is the extension of the spousal communion and community by his radiant presence with new human life. [8] This new reply, this transcendent word of love, at first unformed and inarticulate, gradually comes to learn that he is both the living expression and judgment of his parents who have called him into being and of the incomprehensible Power whose loving approval endowed him with life.

With these persons, divine and human, the child forms new and infinite relationships of the mind, of the heart, and of the whole spiritual center of his being. This growth is equally true of the parents whose beings are now radiant with a participation in the perfection of that paternity whose source is God. The grandeur of the community of the family consists precisely in this spiritual dialectic of development—this permanent establishment of these relationships of love within all the members of the family community, but especially within the awakening and innocent child.

The importance of the dialectics of union and communion within the community of the family cannot be overstressed, for

[7] *HV*, p. 70.
[8] *Ibid.*, p. 71.

the spiritual vitality of the family, its internal tensions and reten-
sions communicate themselves to the larger societies and communities of which it is a cell: to the Nation, to the State, indeed, to the
international communities of an ever-shrinking world.

It is Marcel's conviction that in our days we are beset with
the crisis of the broken world precisely because the family is
succumbing to the process of spiritual atomization:

> I would say that we are living in a world in which the prepo-
> sition "with"—and I might also mention Whitehead's noun,
> "togetherness"—seems more and more to be losing its
> meaning; one might put the same idea in another way by
> saying that the very idea of a close human relationship of
> large families, of old friends, of old neighbors is becoming
> increasingly hard to put into practice, and is even being
> rather disparaged. [9]

Marcel concludes that perhaps the greatest cause of family
disaster is the loss of that reverence for existence that so characterized the Christian West formerly. This was a reverence for
oneself, for the world outside, for the mysteries surrounding us—
the mystery of birth, death, presence, the poetry itself which the
created world breathed into us. This sense of reverence, which
has always been the spiritual bond of community life, has given
way to the pressure of pride and the temptation to despair.
Instead of preserving the dialectic of communal maturation, whole
nations have succumbed to the dialectic of social dissolution.

The community of the family, which can prosper only on
the condition that it is reverently apprehended both as a value and
a living presence, has been experimented with as objectively as
the solar society of the atom. Whereas the rupture of the latter
produces vast material destruction, divorce in the social unit of
society produces far greater spiritual destruction. One cause for
the upheaval of the family-community is the "loss of a home of
our own." [10] A stable place, where the members of the family can
be protected from the hostility of the world outside, is especially

---

[9] *MB* (I), p. 34.
[10] *HV*, p. 77.

necessary for growing children. But the privileged *us* of the family has been uprooted, with incalculable harm to the children. Wars and the needs of industrialized areas have displaced hundreds of millions from stable homes on the soil and reduced them to nomadic existences in tenements and furnished rooms in city jungles. The dissolution of the ancestral home, the evaporation of family traditions have rendered the family incoherent, undermined its ritual foundations and brought about a deterioration of its spiritual fiber. With local customs, folklore, festivals gone and forgotten, families have become monotonously standardized. The religious rhythm of the family community has changed to the tempo of getting and spending, with a loss of the most precious values of communal life. Without time for contemplation on eternal values, the family gradually loses consciousness of its own soul. It is Marcel's conviction that cities, with all their artificiality, hardness, maddening pace, are serious threats to the survival of the family.

There is an unutterable sadness emanating from great and overcrowded cities. This sadness afflicts everything with spiritual devitalization. The sadness feeds on the self-betrayal of life and is bound up in a most intimate fashion with the decay of the family. Sterility is the name by which this sadness is recognized. For it is a disavowal arising from the heart that attacks the very conditions of life. [11]

The town with its amusements and distractions has gradually contaminated the family man. What is the explanation for the fact that so many members of so many families have become insatiable diversion-seekers? It seems to be an incontrovertible fact that the excessive need for amusements is bound up, as Marcel says, "with a certain ebbing of life's tide." [12] And the tragic aspect of this plunge into a variegeted assortment of *divertissements* is that the human beings frantically pursuing them imagine that they are regaining life "by seizing every occasion of experiencing violent sensations of no matter what order." [13] Yet these so-

[11] *Ibid.*, p. 81.
[12] *Ibid.*, p. 83.
[13] *Ibid.*

called stimulants towards a fuller life are but another demonstration of the profound truth in the Gospel warning: "He who would
keep his life, shall lose it," a truth which holds both for natural
and for supernatural levels of existence.   To identify life with
escape from the boredom of a disintegrating family community is
to identify life with escape from the ego.   Marcel is pitiless in his
analysis of this spiritual malady within the body of the family community:

> The *ego* is without doubt faced with a dilemma: to fulfill
> itself or to escape.   Where it does not attain fulfilment, it is
> only conscious of itself as of an unendurable gaping void from
> which it must seek protection at any price.   Anyone who is
> absorbed does not know this void; he is, as it were, caught up
> in plenitude, life envelops him and protects him.   "One is
> borne along only by one's responsibilities," Gabriel Seailles
> said most excellently. [14]

Although the community of the family presupposes the
community of marriage, nevertheless, the essential act which
constitutes marriage is obviously not the pure and simple mating
which is only a human act, common alike to men and animals.   It
is not the momentary union that constitutes the marriage
community, but the communion that is *to endure* as something
rather permanently established.   The community of the family is
founded, erected like a cathedral which serves man in his most
sacred forms of self-expression, self-fulfilment and self-donation.
Hence its "hewn stone is neither the satisfaction of an instinct, nor
the yielding to an impulse, nor the indulgence of a caprice." [15]   It
becomes a matter of life and death for the family community that
the rock upon which its sacred domicile is to be built—the marriage
partners—be immovable.   Mutual fidelity to and absorption in
common marital responsibilities is a solid foundation for a stable
family.   Christians add the fortifications of grace and the sacraments.   Without these cohesive forces, one can scarcely be sur-
prised to see millions of families, built on capricious sentimentality,
end in divorce.

[14] *Ibid.*, p. 84.
[15] *Ibid.*, p. 85.

In a society where divorce is both accepted and regarded as a normal contingency, a time will surely come when this leaven of irresponsibility, widespread among heedless unbelievers, will then be communicated from one to another until it infects even those who by tradition, human respect or some remnant of religious faith, still feel impelled to take and keep the vow of marital fidelity in the presence of God.   Once spiritually infected, the fallen believer will discover that he is trapped in such a way that his only route of escape entails the scandalous renunciation of his faith and a life of dishonorable subterfuge. [16]

To equate the marriage bond with a contract is to drain the marriage community of its mystery.   The bond of marriage is much deeper than a mere juridical contract.   In fact, the more it is seen merely as a simple contract, the more the married partners come to think they may renounce this juridical agreement by common accord.   This pernicious abstraction of the marriage community is a logical movement towards the consideration of the possibility of divorce.   A process of rationalization, claiming that divorce in this "special" case would actually benefit society at large, is all too easily agreed upon.   Marcel's condemnation of divorce is founded on the community aspect of marriage and the family.

Those suffering most under divorce accept but one condemnation of divorce as justified—that pronounced in the name of their own will.   In principle the marital union finds its sanction and completion in the arrival of the child in whom both husband and wife are fulfilled and transcend themselves.   This being so, it is certainly absurd to consider it natural for a married couple to go their separate ways, free again, simply because the sentiments that prevailed at their union have changed for some reason or other. Too much has happened to be canceled out by common consent. Their reciprocal act of conjugal union has been ratified and metaphysically corroborated by an even stronger bond, the existence of a new being for whom they are morally responsible and who has rights and ontological claims upon them.   The parents may not simply shrug off these claims.   And it is sheer cynicism to ration-

[16] *Ibid.*

alize divorce with the argument that animals lose all interest in their offspring, once the offspring no longer need their progenitors. [17]

But this latter plea for the plausibility of divorce is merely the violent swing from the extreme of abstract formalism to the extreme of abstract animalism. Both extremes ignore the essential unity and community of marriage and the family, apart from which the mystery of the family community cannot be appreciated. In both extreme cases of metaphysical and moral aberration, casual progenitors beget broods; they do not found families; such progenitors are even more irresponsible toward their offspring than irrational animals are to their broods.

And what of the marriage of convenience, of the mere association of mutual interests? Is this truly a community? Marcel thinks not, unless the mutual interests include in their planning a regulation and a preparation for possible offspring. Otherwise, it would seem that this duet adds up to a form of social communication and not to social communion.

Concerning the question as to whether a marriage, concluded simply with a view to procreation, is a true spiritual community, Marcel warns that the danger of degeneration is present if this marriage does not settle onto a firmer spiritual basis. The operation of the flesh is always in danger of being degraded, and the spiritual powers of the soul, if permanently starved, will eventually take a terrible revenge upon the married partners and the children, once the procreative forces, whose overemphasis stifled the soul, are diminished by the passage of time.

Is it true to say that procreation is the end of the marriage community? Marcel thinks that this statement is not true by itself and he opts rather for both the operation of the flesh and the operation of the spirit as complementary phases of each man's creative activity in the attainment of his communal destiny. The creative operation here designates the free active contributions of each soul to the universal work of his social vocation which is accomplished not only here but also hereafter. Marcel insists that the operation of the flesh loses its dignity and degenerates if it is

[17] *Ibid.,* p. 86.

not simultaneously an act of thanksgiving and of creative testimony. [18] When it is also and primarily the latter, such moral crimes against the family community as divorce, the use of contraceptives, the practice of abortion and birth control do not pervert the operation of the flesh under the guise of bringing to the married partners a so-called emancipation from a too-constricting and antiquarian morality. What is actually atrophy of the family community is passed off as a social blossoming by ideologues who imagine that they are disentangling the family person when all the while they are spiritually destroying him.

The family community, being the matrix of the person, is really the meeting place for the marriage between natural life and spiritual life. The marriage community is the human prism through which the "divine fatherhood" is accommodated and defracted into human capacities so that men will be able to share and participate in the infinitely creative power of God.

This essential dependence of the family community on the divine source, reveals why, of themselves, good family relations afford no guarantee of communal consistency nor of human solidarity. Only when referred back to and securely anchored in its superhuman source, does the community of marriage and of the family effect a society of a truly sacred character, a society that will radiate into the larger political, economic, educational and international families that spiritual tranquility of order which is the peace that only a Divine Person can bestow on all levels of community life. If, as St. Paul says, "a woman is saved by childbearing," this is essentially and especially true of the woman who is living in the spiritually sound community of the family anchored in God, because in such a family what Marcel calls "the creative vow" is generously accepted and lived-up to by parents who, in the days of a socially disintegrating world, remain the great spiritual adventurers who would uplift the falling world of communities.

What Marcel says of fatherhood in the following passages can be equally applied to responsible motherhood and to all mature parenthood even of the adoptive nature.

[18] *Ibid.*, p. 88.

Fatherhood cannot, by any means, be restricted to mere procreation. Procreation as such and humanly speaking can hardly be considered an act. Fatherhood essentially consists in carrying out a responsibility that is willingly shouldered and perseveringly sustained. Marcel himself has had experience of this truth. His marriage was childless, but he adopted a son and raised him to mature, responsible manhood. And he knows that fatherhood, like all things human, is capable of vitiation. It degenerates as soon as it is subordinated as a means to some special end, for example, the satisfaction of a parent's ambition through the medium of his children. Fatherhood utterly denies its nature when it is reduced to blind generation by persons incapable of providing for their offspring or of directing their spiritual advancement. The progenitor who refuses to realize or fulfill his obligations towards his children has never been a father to them. [19]

In attempting to explain the mysterious spirit of the creative vow, Marcel has this to say:

> The best formula for the *voeu* would then be to offer it as a prayer: "I beg you to reveal yourself to me, to make your presence real for me, so that it will be possible for me to consecrate myself with a full understanding—since in my present state I can only see you through the clouds of uncertainty which encircle me. Moreover, I do not claim that you should attach any value on your own account to this consecration which can add nothing to what you are; but if you love me, if you consider me as your son, it seems to me that, not for your own sake, of course, but for mine, you must want me to know and serve you, since, if it is not given to me to know and serve you, I am doomed to perdition." [20]

The creative vow is thus a *fiat* by which the parents decide to put all their energies at the service of the members of the family community; it is a total engagement to the temporary and transcendent degrees of human existence and being in the family of the community.

[19] *Ibid.*, p. 116.
[20] *Ibid.*, pp. 117-118.

The initial attitude of humility is that parents realize that they can no more give existence to another being than they can give existence to themselves. Having first organized their own lives with the clear knowledge that they are not their own, they now, by a dedication to the creative vow, organize the lives of their children with the clear knowledge that their children no more belong to them than they do to themselves. This signifies that these children, like their parents, will be brought up destined to render special service to others, to the divine author of their beings, to their parents, to all their fellowmen. Moreover, they will be brought up to share in the work of their own vocations and in that of others. These children, like their parents, will be imbued with personal humility, with an unshaken confidence in life, conceived as divine in principle and given as a gift or talent to be worked in a responsible manner toward an infinite increase of spiritual participation in the thou of others and in the Absolute Thou. So much for the dialectic of communion in the community of the family.

CHAPTER IX

Christian Plenitude
of Marcellian Communion

Every era is called upon to collaborate in the perfection of the human being and the human condition. This call is often concretized as a dramatic challenge to survive a present crisis and to emerge with transfigured vigor to a more exalted state of personal and communal living. There seems to be no doubt that mankind is presently in a particularly grave state of crisis in which a struggle has been raging between false utopias and authentic incarnations of truly humane and human community-institutions. The issue as to which type of community—the ideologically abstract or the concrete and authentically valid one—will possess and rule mankind has not yet been settled. But that the struggle grows fiercer is quite evident.

It is quite possible that the deterioration of the human species and his existential cultures are taking place before our very eyes today. Someone endorsing the optimism of the Enlightenment would disagree. But when one analyzes in depth what is happening today, he will be startled to realize that Marx is the legitimate heir of the Enlightenment. For Marx accepts, as a principle, the surety that the movement of history is inevitably towards social and economic fulfilment. Such a principle, divorced from every religious reference, has actually worked for the reestablishment of slavery on a colossal scale. Now if this reality of social progress were founded on religious grounds, the reintroduction of slavery need never have taken place. Perhaps rationalistic deists can predict God's plans for the future. Secularistic scientists are sure of the beneficial consequences that progress in science will bring mankind, if man will only profit by his past mistakes and crimes. But that is the very point at issue. We have no guarantee that disaster suffered in the past produces wiser men in the mass for the present or future. Recent ghastly experiences leave no room for optimism on this point. Perhaps the survivors of the next war may draw some elementary lesson from disaster? Even if they do, will this insure a spiritual quality to their incipient learning? History seems to demonstrate the opposite as more likely. The alternative lies between conversion and non-conversion; man's ultimate task is to elucidate the meaning of this much-needed conversion. [1]

And Marcel has unerringly identified and exposed the major contestants in this struggle to the death:

> But recently I have quite often had occasion to say that here we have what does seem to me a real possibility of choice for man: *between the termite colony and the Mystical Body:* and the gravest danger anybody could commit would be to confuse the one with the other. [2]

Mankind, then, does seem to be moving rapidly toward a frightening decision, a decision that gets harder to postpone or evade as the war between the Mystical Body and the termite colony erupts everywhere and involves more and more people in a test of fidelity. Shall it be conversion and incorporation into the *communitatem Dei* or aversion and insertion into the *communitatem Diaboli*? Whence has man come to this showdown? Why is he forced to choose either to keep company with the believers or to join the iconoclasts of belief? And how, indeed, is it possible for mankind to commit "the gravest error anybody could commit," i.e., "to confuse one with the other" when it is a question of joining such antithetical societies?

We have already seen that in his efforts to organize social life, man has the ambiguous ability of modeling the world for himself, with God as his absolute, or of modeling the world

---

[1] *MB* (II), pp. 205-206.
[2] *MMS*, p. 140.

for himself, on himself, as his own absolute. When the Greeks did the former, they came up with two malformed communities because they had organized their world from a schematization that suffered from an inadequate and even false knowledge about the ontological nature of both man and God. Yet the ancient philosophers, denied the gift of Revelation, are to be excused for these inadequate communities. It would seem that Plato and Aristotle, at heart, were all-unknowingly hungering for something like the Mystical Body when their heads were planning their absolutist ideocracy and democracy. Flaws in their philosophy led to all the restaints that exist in a community based on a self-enclosed naturalism. How could they know that the good man is a good citizen—and much, much more? Even so the Greek politeia was vastly superior to Oriental despotisms which sacrificed individuals and communities to divine potentates for whom they lived, labored and died.

It has been reserved for modern man to attempt to organize his world for himself without God. How can we explain the fact that modern man is oblivious of his divine origin, unenthused about his divine resemblance and even resentful of his divine destiny?

Henri de Lubac gives a lengthy and excellent explanation. Misunderstandings, distortions, multiple mutilations, infidelities arising from blinding pride and arrogant impatience have brought man to his present disoriented state of crisis. Numerous and complex are the historical causes that have contributed to this sense of drifting. But the solid, simple fact remains. Church Fathers, medieval scholars, saints had all exalted man by setting forth the brilliance of his relationship to God. "In this is man's greatness, in this is man's worth, in this he excels every creature." But man ceased to be impressed or moved by his divine connections. On the contrary, he concluded that unless he broke with the Church and with Transcendent Being, he would never be able to develop his freedom or self-esteem. Dependence seemed to be the original sin. The first steps towards independence were an ardent return to paganism. From there the urge to be free grew in momentum and scope in the eighteenth and nineteenth centuries. It reached its climax, daring and destructive, in modern atheism and, above all, in anti-theism.

Absolute humanism is its creed and dogma, a humanism that has rejected Christianity as absurd and deified the natural man. But in dismissing God in order to regain human greatness, man was no longer able to control the absolute power he had usurped. God and Church were kicked over as obstacles to learning and freedom. The new tyrant was absolute man, absolutely free man.

Thus, the new humanism, in its very modernity, is seen to be built upon resentment. It begins with a choice which is at once a violent rejection and a dedication to the naked power of force. Anti-theism is the new humanism. It first conquered in the social field where it struck at the doctrine of a Divine Providence. This was a superstition. Anti-theism refused to be resigned to the "economic contradictions" productive of penury on a massive scale. It accused economists and property owners of entering into a conscious conspiracy, using religion as an ally, to hold down the pauperized masses. God was not so much to blame as a certain form of recourse to His authority. Thus philosophized Proudhon.

Anti-theism, as conceived by the new humanists, was something more radical than mere atheism. Its refusal is complete; its resentment total. At its maximum point of concentration, it is the supreme crisis of our times. Its violent course seeks disorder, begets tyrannies, perpetuates collective crimes and finds its expression in fanaticism, power and blood. [3]

In this struggle between believers and unbelievers Gabriel Marcel can in all truth be called a mediator. He has always been conscious of writing for unbelievers.

> ... when I recapitulate what I have written since my conversion in 1929, I must admit that I have always addressed myself to unbelievers. And I do not mean by

[3] Henri DE LUBAC, S. J., *The Drama of Atheist Humanism*, trans. Edith M. Riley (New York: Sheed, 1950), pp. 6-7.

this only to them and only on their behalf, but I have also and above all placed myself as much as possible in their position so that I could understand them and lead them beyond their refusal to the approaches to the faith. [4]

Because he is constantly addressing himself to what has not yet been evangelized both in himself and in others, Marcel has opened himself up to a serious objection from unbelievers. Has whatever has not yet been evangelized lost its value? Is the natural and humanly perfect invalid because it is raised gratuitously and elevated into divine transfiguration? If it is, then Christianity must bear the brunt of the world's resentment for having destroyed the naturally good and beautiful by totally absorbing it. Marcel elects to face and answer this objection on the plane of philosophy.

There is a particularly serious objection to Marcel's philosophy. The whole of his philosophy implies an unformulated reference to the data of Christianity. His philosophy of communion can only be understood in the light of these data. Presence is understood if one thinks of the Eucharist; creative fidelity is embodied in the Church. Is this a philosophy with any value? Perhaps it has value for Christians alone. But what of a-Christians or of those who ignore and reject Christianity? Marcel admits that it is quite possible that Christian data may be necessary *in fact* to prepare the human mind to conceive and ruminate on some of the concrete notions in his philosophy of communion. But the notions themselves do not depend on the data of Christianity, nor do they even presuppose Christianity.

But, the objector continues, as a philosopher you must strike out anything which is not from universal data of thinking as such. This demand, says Marcel, is exaggerated and in the last analysis illusory. Why? Because the philosopher is always thinking in a given historical milieu from which he cannot abstract himself completely, nor ought he try. It is the height of self-deception for the philosopher to think he can create a complete

[4] M. M. DAVY, *Un philosophe itinérant: Gabriel Marcel*, p. 51.

void within and around himself, out of which he can spin his philosophy.

Today's historical situation proclaims the presence of the Christian fact as one of its essential data. Whether one accepts or rejects the Christian religion as true or false, the Christian religion is an incontrovertible reality of history. A philosopher cannot reason today as though there were not behind him centuries of Christianity. Even so, in the domain of theoretical knowledge, scholars cannot pretend that there have not been already centuries of positive science. In both examples, the existence of Christianity and of much previous positive science plays the role of fertilizing principles for today's philosophers and scientists. Both favor the development of ideas which we might never have conceived without them. Marcel admits that he himself experienced the influence of Christianity on his thought twenty years before he had "the remotest thought of becoming a Catholic." [5]

Ever since Christianity appeared upon the scene of human history, then, she has played what Marcel calls the "role of a fertilizing principle" in all aspects and avenues of human living. Catholicism certainly favored the development to rich levels of human understanding, of certain ontological mysteries like person, presence, communion and many others, throwing upon these natural mysteries the infinitely superior light of supernatural mysteries. The downward dialectic of Revelation has revealed to reason something of the deeper reality hidden in these natural philosophical truths. We know, of course, that the philosophers of antiquity absorbed their fellowmen into the city and family, making both subservient to the blind destiny prepared by the Fates. Slavery was a normal condition for people in certain strata of life, as Plato and Aristotle taught. Impersonal thoughts— Ideas—were of the highest value both in the order of nature and ideas. As for the concrete particular, this was a blemish in and on reality. The individual was being punished for some primordial crime, in exile here below far from the beatifying

[5] *PE*, pp. 29-30.

Ideas.   Some sort of salvation was possible, so claimed Socrates and Plato, somewhere beyond the grave; but it was vague and not very alluring.   Aristotle grounded Plato's ideas in the individuals, the only real existents for him.   But his God was quite impersonal, finite, frozen, incapable of personal freedom. Plotinus saw the plight of guilty individuals as desperate, unless they got back to the peaceful anonymity of the One and the Timeless.

The light of Christianity was able to dispel the error in some of these doctrines and to expand the partial truths they contained to their fulness, aiding reason in its quest for more of the mysteries hinted at in its first philosophic forays into being and its activities.   Of course, the shock of being scandalized that the Greeks experienced at the Christian philosopher's development of the natural mysteries of being can be imagined.   The "evil" of multiplicity, which perennially plagued the Greek mentality for an adequate solution, was presented by the Christians as the great paradox of the *creatio ex nihilo*—a repugnant idea to the philosophers of antiquity.   Their supreme impersonal being, who was to draw up all particular beings into the unity of Ideal Good, the Christians identified as the Supreme Personal Being of Love who multiplies individuals as evidence of His desire to share and interchange the underived love of His own Being with an indefinite number of other personal loves.

We have here no tyranny of a destiny that must come to pass; no heaven of pure ideas, no impersonal thought indifferent to individual destinies, that reigns over all men with an iron rule.   But we have a Personal—eminently tri-personal—God who gives Himself to take on and transfigure the conditions of mankind, to fill up each person and the human community into a participant in the Divine Being and Community.

> For as the body is one and has many members, and all the members of the body, many as they are, form one body, so also it is with Christ. [6]

[6] I Cor. 12:1.

Mankind's quest for community, seen under the light of Revelation, takes on a meaning of higher transcendence. Jews or Gentiles, slaves or free men are not called to be members of natural communities only; they are also called to be "member for member" in the community of Christ. Immortality and salvation for each person and for the community of men consists in the free, communal cooperation of both with Christ at the head of his own historical community. The community of the Trinity itself, emerging from two centuries of controversy, stands forth as a society of Three Persons which is both a dialogue of Truth itself and a dialectic of Love itself, whose essence is the negation of nothingness, necessity and solitude. *Ab aeterno et in aeternum,* they are the exemplary community of truth and love.

While admitting the beneficent influence of Christianity on the discipline of philosophy, Marcel, nevertheless, issues a timely warning to philosopher and theologian.

The distinction between the natural and supernatural is valid and must be rigorously maintained. Does the word "mystery," as Marcel uses it in philosophy, confuse the issue? Really there is no reason to confuse those mysteries which are revealed—such as the Incarnation or Redemption—for no effort of thought on our part can bring us even to the suspicion of their existence, much less to their attainment. Whereas the natural mysteries of presence, communion, freedom, evil, participation are experienced in everyday life.

Why use the same word, then, for two such vastly different and distinct notions? Marcel's answer is that revelation itself is inconceivable except to beings involved, committed, already participating in the non-problematical dimensions of reality. For it is upon these latter mysteries that revelation is founded and thrives in the souls of men. Natural mysteries prepare men to become docile subjects for the supernatural mysteries. Supernatural life must and does take hold in the natural, not as a flowering of the natural, but as a new and gratuitous endowment from Transcendence itself who permeates human subjects with unimagined and unimaginable degrees of presence and communion. A study of created nature, therefore, leads Marcel to this conclusion: "There is in the depth of Nature, as of reason which is governed by it, a fundamental principle of inadequacy to itself which is, as it were, a restless anticipation of a different order." [7]

Henri de Lubac, attempting to account for this "fundamental principle of inadequacy to itself in created Nature," and for "its restless anticipation of a different order," enters into an exploration of the metaphysics of this paradoxical position. He observes, first, that paradox is the reverse view of a reality which, if properly perceived, would shine forth as a synthesis. But *homo viator* cannot capture the totally proper view of anything. Much as man contributes by his own existence, "to the weaving of the wonderful tapestry" of being, he will never possess, within the range of his personally lived experience, the perfectly completed panorama of the drama of being.

For the proper view of reality is constantly eluding our grasp. Our experiences and the reflective processes of each human thinker contribute to the "weaving of the wonderful tapestry" of a reality that is always becoming more unified into an harmonious synthesis. But the full picture will never be painted within our temporal range of vision and perception. Even in the field of facts, just as in the realm of the spirit, synthesis is always our quest for the plenitude of being. *Quamdiu vivimus necesse habemus semper quaerere.* As long as we live we must ever be seeking. Paradox is thus seen as the provisional expression of an incomplete view which is ever striving for fulness. [8]

We have seen that Marcel's whole philosophy proceeds by ever-deepening explorations into lived experience. Marcel is the first to admit that, although his philosophy only shows his own provisional depicting of reality, although it is ever incomplete, nevertheless, because of his ever-recurring explorations, this same philosophy does advance closer to fulness—at which point it will never arrive as long as Marcel is still an itinerant philosopher.

[7] *PE*, pp. 30-31.
[8] Henri DE LUBAC, S. J., *Further Paradoxes* (Westminster, Md.: Newman, 1958), p. ix.

Paradox, as a metaphysical challenge, will always be with us; it will always be opening up, to the contemplative dialectician, new aspects of being. Along this line of analysis, paradox may be seen as the expectant aspiration of being for synthesis in the fulfilment of order. Dialectics appears as the chase toward the summit of communion. Paradox seems to stand forth as the enigmatic feminine principle of fruitfulness in being, which allures and is fertilized by the virility of dialectics.

Paradox presents itself as charming, realistic, modest, relaxed and unhurried; whereas dialectics is tense, impatient, virile and on-the-run for the fulness of truth. Of course, the dialectician is never at rest; this is so because the paradoxical aspects of what he already knows only remind him that there are still uncharted oceans of truth that beckon to infinite progress. The dialectician is always going "from beginnings to beginnings."

The higher life rises, the richer it grows in transcendence, the more interior and reflective it becomes, the more paradox opens up the infinite horizons of truth. Even in a merely human life, paradox opens up, as its specialty, the realm of the spirit. Its ultimate triumph is to usher the man of wisdom into the realm of mystery at the heart of mystical life. [9]

But the fecundation of paradox by the principle of dialectics, although it reveals an ever-expanding universe of mystery to the mind of man, nevertheless, will only depict a family of beings that remains within the bounds of the merely natural and spiritually human. Left to themselves and their own resources, the principles of dialectics and paradox, in their advance to the fulness of being and truth, can never transcend the sovereignty of the humanly perfect alone.

But have these principles of natural growth been left to themselves? The historical situation of this universe and of everything created within it is such that nothing has been left to itself in its merely natural state. Revelation informs us that an entirely new dialectics and, above all, an entirely superior and undreamed-of paradox have entered the human condition and

[9] *Ibid.*, p. x.

have encountered the merely human attempts at development towards transcendence. The paradox of redemption is a gratuitously new outpouring of the divine community. It consists in divine missions to the human community. The important movement in this new dialectic of love is the downward leap of the divine Logos, a new Incarnation that establishes the most mysterious paradox in all creation—the paradox of the God-Man. This Incarnation surpasses in every way the incarnation of man; this Incarnation assumes the human family beyond its natural completion to a supernatural deification.

The Christian community alone claims to fulfill the need for transcendence that is discovered in created Nature's "fundamental principle of inadequacy" and in its "restless anticipation of a different order." She is that fulfilment. *Eritis ut dii* is a prophecy that is realized by man within the Christian community in such a manner that to the truth, "man is made for God," must now be added its paradoxical complement, "for us men and for our salvation" God is made man. And yet the hunger of man's nature is not a desire for a God who is "our size." Rather it is the aspiration whereby man, while remaining man, somehow might be made to His measure. And this human aspiration is realized in that paradoxical fusion whereby a divine person, while remaining a divine person, somehow becomes human and raises the human in each individual person and in every human family to the throne of the divine. An undreamt of commingling and communion in a community which is now the meeting place of all mysteries, ontological and theological.

Marcel gives an excellent summary of his position on the assumption of the natural into the supernatural. For him the recognition of the ontological mystery that lies at the heart of all reality is made possible only through a sort of radiation that emanates from revelation itself. This radiation can affect all souls, even strangers to any religion. The reason is that the historical atmosphere of all peoples is imbued with the breath of Christianity. Now this recognition of the ontological mystery in no way forces nor involves men in an adherence to any given religion. But for those who do adhere, say to Christianity, there is vouchsafed the further ability to see, through the light coming from the ontological mystery, the possibility of a supernatural message in a way which is not open to those who have freely enclosed themselves within the borders of the problematical. These latter have never even reached the position from which the mystery of being can be recognized and asserted. Whereas for the former, their philosophy of communion is carried forward by an irresistible attraction towards the light that beckons them from afar and "for which they are suffering the secret attraction," the hunger for being and for plenitude. [10]

The secret attraction of Marcel's philosophy of communion is that it disposes the reflective thinker to see in lived reality, in the making of history all around him, the actual working out, in a rather full degree, of the mysteries contained in the scriptural words, "Now in Jesus Christ all things are made new."

On the plane of natural and inanimate being we can distinguish three levels of transformation and of fulfilment. The first transformation is accomplished when the disparate togetherness of beings that are inanimate moves up to the vital togetherness of beings that are alive whether in the vegetable or animal world of existence. The second transition or transcendence is when the elementally vital becomes spiritually alive through union and incorporation into the human person. This transition to the spiritual is already a prefigurement of that highest transformation which is the glorious ascendence of the spiritual into the supernatural. Of course, this latter admits of infinite degrees of ascending participation, from the initial degree in the darkness of the first act of faith to the unveiled splendor of the beatific vision. Yet even here, in this valley of shadows, in the very act of this third transformation, things that are natural become supernatural through a sacramental togetherness of service performed in the community of Christians. Can there be any higher transcendence for bread than to become His Body, or for wine than to become His Blood? Can there be any higher transfiguration for natural elements than to become the matter

[10] *PE*, p. 31.

for sacraments and sacramentals, or for natural speech than to become the supernatural forms that give, restore and increase divine life in human persons? Here are intersubjective experiences and degrees of incarnation and of transcendence that move men to marvel at their mysteriousness.

On the plane of natural human experience, the degrees of transcendence are varied and capable of different degrees of intensity. Incarnation moves upward through sensation, primary reflection, secondary reflection, presence, contact, communication, self-donation, commitment, consecration to communion within an authentic community. But when the Christian community assumes man and his society, new life is infused into the whole human milieu through seven channels of divine and human intersubjective activity. Membership in the Christian community involves man in a dialectic of faith, hope and love of a superior order with the aim of inserting the whole of humanity by its own cooperation into the community of the Absolute.

A struggle for the renewed sense of community and the organic feeling of participation within the Christian community has taken the approach that appeals so much to Gabriel Marcel and which he uses in his quest for a concrete philosophy of communion. The liturgical approach is the immersion of oneself into some concrete experience of the daily life of the Christian community. Involvement in her prayer, sacrificial, teaching, ministerial life makes members of this community present to each other because they are present to Christ. Their engagement is constituted by the faith, hope, love and service they render each other and the community of man. Weak and strong share this lived experience. Commenting on this existential approach for a revival of the sense of community among Christians, Walter Lypgens uses the work of Romano Guardini as an example.

He finds that the freshness and inspiration in Guardini's books lies in their break-away from the deductive, systematic, abstractionist emphasis in the study of theology. The keynote of this fresh method into Christian experience is the constant consideration of the concrete circumstances of the Christian life. These are described as accurately as possible in order to display their full significance and essential forms in the light of revelation. This is phenomenology transported to the realm of the Christian experience in communion. It concerns itself primarily with the active participation of sons and daughters of God in the mysteries of God's community. [11]

While praising the blessing that an intersubjective religious living bestows on man and his institutions, we must beware of strengthening the illusion that the Christian community is established to guarantee earthly happiness. A handle has been made of this illusion to accuse the Christian community of failing to have brought all men together in perfect happiness. Jean Daniélou ably rebuts this accusation.

Christianity was not founded to create a perfect world. No organization can do this, for no such reality is possible. Tragedy, pain, sorrow will always be the heritage of this world. They are part and parcel of our present condition. They are not man's essential lot as Sartre would have it. They are his present lot by bad choice and just sanction. Yet our sorrows can be alleviated to some degree. Christ cured and fed multitudes. The question is: Is our faith in God and the Church still relevant to this human task? [12]

The existential understanding of the Christian mystery of Communion is grasped in an action which transpires before the eyes of the people who are consciously involved. We need to recall that the liturgical meal of the Christians used to be taken in the homes of the faithful. It was somewhere around Renaissance times that a silent and dumb devotion to a mystic rite afflicted Christian spectators at this repast. Today the much richer conception of the Christian community has been revived. We read in Koenker:

[11] Ernest B. KOENKER, *The Liturgical Renaissance in the Roman Catholic Church* (Chicago: The University of Chicago Press, 1954), pp. v-vi.

[12] Jean DANIÉLOU, S. J., *The Lord of History* (London: Green, 1958), p. 92.

Even Father Jungmann ... gives a remarkable description from a letter he received from a young priest-brother of his order, who was killed at Stalingrad. He says this experience might be multiplied a thousand times:
I once had the opportunity to celebrate the Holy Eucharist among them—with all (about 13) banded together about the table of offering—and I could administer Holy Communion to them. Here it becomes clear experientially that the Holy Offering is consummated in the form of a meal. Here one is led back to the origin of the symbolism. We all sat around the table engaged in agreeable conversation and ate our evening meal, and in the morning the same table was adorned for the holy celebration, and the brethren stood around the table. Just as, e.g., in existential philosophy the original meaning of many words has been revealed, so that the word suddenly flashes forth as though newly-born, correspondingly I experienced this celebration of the Holy Mass, only far more existentially. [13]

The Christian community bestows the most transcendent form of communion between God and men and among men themselves. It is, as Marcel asserts, no mere continuation nor completion of the communities of men. Transubstantiation is the symbol of what happens when this community's appeal is accepted and lived; every public act of transubstantiation transmutes something natural into something divine and binds the participants in this act and the whole Christian community more intimately to the divine community.

The Christian community calls human society back from the community-myths that promise transcendent paradises here in time. Marcel sees this question of man's goal as essential in the struggle between the collectivist and the Christian embodiments of the human race. The collectivist camp identifies the Christian community as deceiving men with the hoax of a paradise hereafter. In return collectivists offer humanity utopias that will make men citizens of culture, progress, science, plenty, knowledge and leisure. The Christian community accepts these noble goals, but states they are not nearly good enough

---

[13] E. KOENKER, op. cit., pp. 116-117.

for human society. Thus, while fostering all of these achieve-
ments, the Christian community is also engaged in lifting them
all to higher transcendence in the community of the Absolute.
Marcel indicates the irreconciliability that must exist between
self-inclosed humanisms and the community of Christians.

Christianity and humanism have tended to part and go
their separate ways through a series of misunderstandings. The
more one reflects concretely on the structure and condition of
man, the more one sees that modern humanism, seeking its
fulfilment in a progressive naturalism, has divorced itself from
the trans-human dimension of reality. Man will never regain
a human world until he regains afresh his transcendent God. It
is impossible for the humanist to rediscover the marvelous and
awesome, which are rooted below the banal and immanent. The
reason is that the humanist is continually fascinated with platitudes
and with the cultured veneer of superficial critics and mere
observers of the passing scene. Only the slow recovery of the
real, indeed of concrete being, will work mysteriously to bring
man to his fulness in adherence to Catholicism. [14]

Marcel calls upon Christians to reject the spirit of
excommunication and to adopt the universality of "the will for
non-exclusion." This attitude of spiritual welcoming can
dissolve the ostracisms that derive from the spirit of abstraction.
Christians are informed that they must regain the joyful
consciousness of the presence of God within their community,
if they hope to satisfy the world's severe nostalgia for communion
in community. The loss of consciousness of His presence has
led to the disruption of society.

Once the presence of God is no longer felt nor recognized,
then everything is questionable. Man models himself on Lucifer.
And constant questioning degenerates into the negative will to
resentment. Can the Lucifer-man be parted from his errors?
Only through conversion. But no creature is the author of
conversions. The domain of grace grants these gifts; the domain
of intersubjectivity wins conversions also, but not through the

[14] R. TROISFONTAINES, *De l'existence* ..., II, p. 371.

chain of cause and effet. We have here Kierkegaard's paradoxical situation in the presence of God. It is a position of distress, of agony, even of frustration. Yet anguish is not the last word. The last word is joy and love. And the intelligible aspects of faith assure and satisfy us of this impregnable truth. [15]

So the terms of the worldwide nostalgia for communion in community seem clear; men must decide whether they want to be collectivized or Christianized. The Christian community, through a resurgence of its intersubjective liturgical action, unites every diversity within itself, elevating, yet preserving individuals. Itself an incarnation, it effects what God effects among men. Diverse nationalities, customs, traditions are inserted harmoniously into its community-life. Scholars, philosophers, members of all professions together with the rude and rustic are all incorporated into it. Yet such communion does not confuse their hierarchical excellence. And the whole is oriented toward a city hereafter.

Marcel assures us that we become aware of being "literally arched over by a living reality." This transcendent being is infinitely more alive than we are. It possesses us to the extent we release ourselves to it. It possesses us to the extent we extricate ourselves from the meshes of schematization and abstraction. The sublime service philosophy can render is to increase our awareness constantly, even in time, of this overarching reality which surrounds us on all sides. Paul could say of this Absolute Thou that "in Him we live and move and find our being." Moreover, philosophy must also constantly remind us that, thanks to our condition of freedom, we must perseveringly say "No" to "the awful power to withhold ourselves" from the Absolute Thou. [16]

At this turning point in history Marcel tells us that it is not so much a question of saving political and social orders that are incurably dying, but of gathering together the seeds of the Christian community and sowing them in newly-discovered

[15] *MB* (II), p. 198.
[16] *Ibid.*, p. 209.

ground, and, above all, in lands that have been renewed by the terrible agonies that have ploughed through them.   Perhaps the greatest role the Christian philosopher can play is to become engaged in the struggle to save society.

And Marcel suggests both the meaning of social salvation and the means the philosopher can take to attain it.   In a sense, his salvation is indistinguishable from peace.   This is a living peace, not a spiritual trance that congeals the spirit in some far-off and fixed star.   Not the peace of stupor or suspended animation, the sleep of hypnosis.   The living peace Marcel speaks of is a progress in love and truth; it is the consolidation of the intelligible city, the city of souls *par excellence*.   And how shall the philosopher attain this peace?   Marcel answers that from this point of view, "it is perhaps on the Christian idea of the Mystical Body that the philosopher may be called to concentrate his attention." [17]

[17] *Ibid.*, p. 205.

BIBLIOGRAPHY

PRIMARY SOURCES

Philosophical Works

MARCEL, Gabriel, *Being and Having*, trans. Katherine Farrer (Westminster: Dacre Press, 1949).
— *Le déclin de la sagesse* (Paris: Plon, 1954).
— *The Decline of Wisdom*, trans. Manya Harari (London: Harvill Press, 1954).
— *Être et Avoir* (Paris: Éditions Montaigne, 1935).
— *L'homme problématique* (Paris: Éditions Montaigne, 1955).
— *Les hommes contre l'humain* (Paris: La Colombe, 1951).
— *Homo Viator* (Paris: Éditions Montaigne, 1945).
— *Homo Viator*, trans. Emma Craufurd (Chicago: Regnery, 1951).
— *Journal métaphysique* (Paris: Gallimard, 1927).
— *Man Against Mass Society*, trans. G. S. Fraser (Chicago: Regnery, 1952).
— *Men Against Humanity*, trans. G. S. Fraser (London: Harvill Press, 1952).
— *La métaphysique de Royce* (Paris: Aubier, 1945).
— *Metaphysical Journal* containing the essay *Existence and Objectivity*, trans. Bernard Wall (Chicago: Regnery, 1952).
— *Le mystère de l'être*, 2 Vols. (Paris: Aubier, 1951).
— *The Mystery of Being*, 2 Vols. (Chicago: Regnery, 1951).
   Vol. I: *Reflection and Mystery*, trans. G. S. Fraser.
   Vol. II: *Faith and Reality*, trans. Rene Hague.
— *The Philosophy of Existence*, trans. Manya Harari (New York: Philosophical Library, 1949).
— *Position et approches concrètes du mystère ontologique*, Introduction by Marcel de Corte (Paris: Vrin, 1949).
— *Présence et immortalité* (Paris: Flammarion, 1959).
— *Du refus à l'invocation* (Paris: Gallimard, 1940).
— *Royce's Metaphysics*, trans. Virginia and Gordon Ringer (Chicago: Regnery, 1956).

Plays

MARCEL, Gabriel, *Le cœur des autres* (Paris: Grasset, 1921).
— *Le dard* (Paris: Plon, 1938).
— *L'horizon* (Paris: Éditions aux Étudiants de France, 1945).
— *Un homme de dieu* (Paris: Grasset, 1925).
— *L'iconoclaste* (Paris: Delamain, Boutelleau et Cie, 1923).
— *Le quatuor en fa dièse* (Paris: Plon, 1925).

— *La soif,* précédée de *Théâtre et mystère* par Gaston Fessard (Paris: Desclée de Brouwer, 1938).
— *Three Plays: A Man of God, Ariadne, The Funeral Pyre,* the first trans. Marjorie Gabain; the last two Rosalind Heywood (New York: Hilland Wang, 1958).
— *Trois pièces: Le regard neuf, Le mort de demain, La chapelle ardente* (Paris: Plon, 1931).
— *Vers un autre royaume,* containing the two dramas: *L'émissaire* and *Le signe de la croix* (Paris: Plon, 1949).

SECONDARY SOURCES

A. Books and Articles on Marcel

BERNARD, Michel, *La philosophie religieuse de Gabriel Marcel,* appendix by Marcel (Paris: Les Cahiers du Nouvel Humanisme, 1952).

CAIN, Seymour, *Gabriel Marcel* (New York: Hillary House, 1963).

CHENU, Joseph, *Le théâtre de Gabriel Marcel et sa signification métaphysique* (Paris: Aubier, 1948).

COLIN, Pierre, "Existentialisme chrétien," *Existentialisme chrétien* (q.v under Étienne Gilson).

COLLINS, James, "Gabriel Marcel and the Mystery of Being," *Thought,* XVIII, 71 (December, 1943), pp. 665-693.

DAVY, M. M. *Un philosophe itinérant: Gabriel Marcel* (Paris: Flammarion, 1959).

DE CORTE, Marcel, *La philosophie de Gabriel Marcel* (Paris: Pierre Tequi, n.d.).

DELHOMME, Jeanne, "Témoignage et dialectique," *Existentialisme chrétien* (q.v. under Étienne Gilson).

DUBOIS-DUMÉE, J. P., "Solitude et communion dans le théâtre de Gabriel Marcel," *Existentialisme chrétien* (q.v. under Étienne Gilson).

FESSARD, Gaston, "Théâtre et mystère," essay published as an introduction to *La Soif* (Paris: Desclée de Brouwer, 1938), pp. 7-116.

GALLAGHER, Kenneth T., "The Philosophical Method of Gabriel Marcel" (New York: Fordham University Doctoral Dissertation, 1958).

— *The Philosophy of Gabriel Marcel,* Foreword by Gabriel Marcel (New York: Fordham University Press, 1962).

GILSON, Étienne, "Un exemple," *Existentialisme chrétien: Gabriel Marcel,* presentation of Étienne Gilson (Paris: Plon, 1947); texts of Jeanne Delhomme, Roger Troisfontaines, Pierre Colin, J. P. Dubois-Dumée, Gabriel Marcel.

OSTERMANN, Robert, "Gabriel Marcel: The Discovery of Being," *Modern Schoolman,* XXXI (January, 1954), pp. 99-116.

— "Gabriel Marcel: The Recovery of Being," *Modern Schoolman,* XXXI (May, 1954), pp. 289-305.

— "Gabriel Marcel: Existence and the Idea of Being," *Modern Schoolman,* XXXII (November, 1954), pp. 19-38.

PRINI, Pietro, *Gabriel Marcel et la méthodologie de l'invérifiable*, letter-preface of Marcel (Paris: Desclée de Brouwer, 1953).

RICŒUR, Paul, *Gabriel Marcel et Karl Jaspers: Philosophie du mystère et philosophie du paradoxe* (Paris: Éditions du Temps Présent, 1947).

TROISFONTAINES, Roger, S. J., *De l'existence à l'être*, 2 Vols., letter-preface of Marcel (Paris: Vrin, 1953).

— "La notion de présence chez Gabriel Marcel," *Existentialisme chrétien* (q.v. under Gilson).

— "What is Existentialism?" *Thought*, XXXII, 127 (Winter 1957-1958), pp. 516-532.

WAHL, Jean, *Vers le concret: Études d'historie de la philosophie contemporaine* (Paris: Vrin, 1932), pp. 223-269 are devoted to Marcel.

B. Books on Existentialism

ALLEN, E. L., *Existentialism from Within* (New York: Macmillan, 1953).

BLACKHAM, H. J., *Six Existentialist Thinkers* (London: Routledge & Kegan Paul, 1951).

BOBBIO, Norberto, *The Philosophy of Decadentism, a Study in Existentialism*, trans. David Moore (Oxford: Blackwell, 1948).

BRUNNER, Auguste, S. J., *La personne incarnée* (Paris: Beauchesne, 1947),

BUBER, Martin, *I and Thou*, trans. Ronald Smith (Edinburgh: Clark. 1937).

COLLINS, James, *The Existentialists* (Chicago: Regnery, 1952).

COPLESTON, F. C., S. J., *Contemporary Philosophy, Studies of Logical Positivism and Existentialism* (Westminster: Newman, 1956).

FOULQUIÉ, Paul, *Existentialism*, trans. Kathleen Raine (New York: Roy, 1950).

GRENE, Marjorie, *Dreadful Freedom* (Chicago: University of Chicago Press, 1948).

HARPER, Ralph, *Existentialism, A Theory of Man* (Cambridge, Mass.: Harvard University Press, 1948).

HEINEMANN, F. H., *Existentialism and the Modern Predicament* (New York: Harper, 1953).

JEANSON, Francis, *Le problème moral et la pensée de Sartre*, letter-preface of Jean-Paul Sartre (Paris: Éditions du Myrte, 1947).

KUHN, Helmut, *Encounter with Nothingness* (Hinsdale, Ill.: Regnery, 1949).

MOUNIER, Emmanuel, *Existentialist Philosophies* (New York: Bristol, Rankin Bros., 1951).

ROBERTS, David E., *Existentialism and Religious Belief* (New York: Oxford University Press, 1957).

REINHARDT, Kurt F., *The Existentialist Revolt* (Milwaukee: Bruce, 1952).

TROISFONTAINES, Roger, S. J., *Existentialisme et pensée chrétienne* (Paris: Vrin, 1948).

— *Existentialism and Christian Thought*, trans. Martin Jarrett-Kerr, C.R. (London: Adam & Charles Black, 1949).

USSHER, Arland, *Journey Through Dread* (New York: The Devin-Adair Company, 1955).

WILD, John, *The Challenge of Existentialism* (Bloomington, Ind.: Indiana University Press, 1955).

C. Background and Cognate Readings

ARISTOTLE, *Politics and Poetics*, trans. B. Jowett (New York: Viking, 1959).

BERDYAEV, Nicolas, *The Beginning and the End*, trans. R. M. French (New York: Harper, 1952).

— *The Meaning of the Creative Act*, trans. Donald A. Lowrie (New York: Harper, 1955).

— *The Divine and the Human*, trans. R. M. French (London: Geoffrey Bles, 1949).

— *Solitude and Society*, trans. George Reavey (London: Geoffrey Bles, 1947).

— *Spirit and Reality*, trans. George Reavey (London: Geoffrey Bles, 1946).

BRADLEY, F. H., *Appearance and Reality*, second edition revised (New York: Macmillan, 1902).

BUBER, Martin, *Between Man and Man*, trans. Ronald Smith (London: Kegan Paul, 1947).

CAMUS, Albert, *The Plague*, trans. Stuart Gilbert (New York: Knopf, 1948).

— *The Stranger*, trans. Stuart Gilbert (New York: Knopf, 1948).

COCHRANE, Charles N., *Christianity and Classical Culture* (New York: Oxford University Press, A Galaxy Book, 1957).

CORTES, Donoso, *Ensayo Sobre el Catolicismo, el Liberalismo y el Socialismo* (Buenos Aires: Editorial Americales, 1943).

COSTANZO, Joseph F., S. J., "The Graeco-Roman Politeia—The City of Men," *Fordham Law Review*, XX, 2 (June, 1951), pp. 119-155.

DANIÉLOU, Jean, S. J., *The Lord of History*, trans. Nigel Abercrombie (London: Longmans, Green, 1958).

D'ARCY, M. C., S. J., *The Mind and Heart of Love* (New York: Meridian Books, 1956).

— *The Meaning and Matter of History* (New York: Farrar, Straus and Cudahy, 1959).

DAWSON, Christopher, *Religion and the Modern State* (New York: Sheed, 1935).

DE LUBAC, Henri, S. J., *Catholicism, A Study of Dogma in Relation to the Corporate Destiny of Mankind*, trans. Lancelot C. Sheppard (London: Burns, 1950).

— *The Drama of Atheist Humanism*, trans. Edith M. Riley (New York: Sheed, 1950).

— *Further Paradoxes*, trans. Ernest Beaumont (Westminster, Md.: Newman, 1958).

FRIEDMAN, Maurice S., *Martin Buber, The Life of Dialogue* (Chicago: The University of Chicago Press, 1955).

HARPER, Ralph, *The Sleeping Beauty* (New York: Harper, n.d.).

HEIDEGGER, Martin, *Existence and Being*, trans. and intro. by Werner Brock (Chicago: Regnery, 1949).

HUSSERL, Edmund, "Philosophy as a Strict Science," trans. Quentin Lauer, S. J., *Cross Currents*, VI (Summer, 1956), pp. 227-246, and VI (Fall, 1956), pp. 325-344.

JASPERS, Karl, *Man in the Modern Age*, trans. Eden and Cedar Paul (New York: Henry Holt, 1933).

— *The Perennial Scope of Philosophy*, trans. Ralph Manheim (New York: Philosophical Library, 1949).

JOLIVET, Regis, *Introduction to Kierkegaard*, trans. W. H. Barber (London: Frederick Muller, 1950).

KAUFMANN, Walter, *Existentialism from Dostoevsky to Sartre* (New York: Meridian Books, 1956).

KAFKA, Franz, *The Trial*, trans. Willa and Edwin Muir (New York: Knopf, 1948).

KIERKEGAARD, Søren, *Either/Or*, 2 Vols., trans. Walter Lowrie (Princeton: Princeton University Press, 1946).

— *Fear and Trembling and The Sickness unto Death*, trans. Walter Lowrie (Garden City, N.Y.: Doubleday Anchor Books, 1954).

KOENKER, Ernest B., *The Liturgical Renaissance in the Roman Catholic Church* (Chicago: The University of Chicago Press, 1954).

LAVELLE, Louis, *La présence totale* (Paris: Aubier, 1934).

MARITAIN, Jacques, *Existence and the Existent*, trans. Lewis Galantiere and Gerald B. Phelan (New York: Pantheon, 1948).

MOUNIER, Emmanuel, *Personalism*, trans. Philip Mairet (New York: Grove, 1952).

OWENS, Thomas J., S. J., "The Problem of Interpersonal Relationships as Posed in Contemporary Thought" (New York: Fordham University Doctoral Dissertation, 1952).

PLATO, *The Republic*, trans. B. Jowett (New York: Random, Modern Library Paperback, 1960).

ROYCE, Josiah, *The Philosophy of Loyalty* (New York: Macmillan, 1916).

SARTRE, Jean-Paul, *Being and Nothingness*, trans. Hazel E. Barnes (New York: Philosophical Library, 1956).

— *L'existentialisme est un humanisme* (Paris: Collections Pensées Nagel, 1946).

— *Nausea*, trans. Lloyd Alexander (Norfolk, Conn., New Directions Paperback, 1959).

— *No Exit, and Three Other Plays* (New York : Vintage Paperback, 1963).
    a) *No Exit* (Huis Clos) trans. Stuart Gilbert.
    b) *The Flies* (Les Mouches) trans. Stuart Gilbert.
    c) *Dirty Hands* (Les Mains sales) trans. Lionel Abel.
    d) *The Respectful Prostitute* (La Putain respectueuse) trans. Lionel Abel.

— *The Devil and the Good Lord, and TwoO ther Plays*, trans. Kitty Black (New York: Knopf, 1960).

— *The Words*, trans. Bernard Frechtman (New York: George Braziller, 1964).

SCHWARZ, Balduin V., *The Human Person and the World of Values*, A tribute to Dietrich Von Hildebrand by His Friends in Philosophy, edited by Balduin V. Schwarz (Essays by Balduin V. Schwarz, Alice Jourdain, Jacques Maritain, John V. Walsh, Bruno de Solages, Aurel Kolnai, Gabriel Marcel, Michele Frederico Sciacca, Henri de Lubac, S. J., Robert W. Gleason, S. J., Jacques Albert Cuttat) (New York: Fordham University Press, 1960).

SPANN, Othmar, *The History of Economics*, trans. Eden and Cedar Paul (New York: Norton, 1930).

VON HILDEBRAND, Dietrich, *Christian Ethics* (New York: McKay, 1953).

— *True Morality and its Counterfeits* (New York: McKay, 1955).

— *Graven Images: Substitutes for True Morality* (New York: McKay, 1957).

N. Y. 29. — Printed in Belgium by DESCLÉE & Cie, ÉDITEURS, S. A., Tournai — 10.790